THE PHILOSOPI

J.R Concept on the poor provides a
useful way of looking at the
relationship between social workers
and poor peoples. This paper will
attempt to build on that and discuss.

On work with migrants are concer...
about dismantling oppression
Think for them. But it is time
to listen and learn from them.
Analyse the oppression, be part of anti-racist
movement but now

JACQUES RANCIÈRE

The Philosopher and His Poor

Edited and with an Introduction by Andrew Parker

Translated by John Drury, Corinne Oster, and Andrew Parker

DUKE UNIVERSITY PRESS :: DURHAM & LONDON 2003

Le Philosophe et ses pauvres by Jacques Rancière, © 1983 Librairie Arthème Fayard. English translation by Andrew Parker © 2004 Duke University Press. All rights reserved. Printed in the United States of America on acid-free paper ∞ Designed by Rebecca M. Giménez. Typeset in Quadraat by Keystone Typesetting, Inc. Library of Congress Cataloging-in-Publication Data appear on the last printed page of this book. Third printing, 2007

Contents

Editor's Preface vii

Editor's Introduction: Mimesis
and the Division of Labor ix

A Personal Itinerary. xxv

I. PLATO'S LIE

1. The Order of the City 3

2. The Order of Discourse 30

II. MARX'S LABOR

3. The Shoemaker and the Knight 57

4. The Production of the Proletarian. . .70

5. The Revolution Conjured Away. 90

6. The Risk of Art 105

III. THE PHILOSOPHER AND
THE SOCIOLOGIST

7. The Marxist Horizon. 127

8. The Philosopher's Wall. 136

9. The Sociologist King. 165

For Those Who Want More 203

Afterword to the English-Language
Edition (2002). 219

Notes 229

THE ENGLISH TRANSLATION of Jacques Rancière's *Le Philosophe et ses pauvres* has had, already, a curious history. In the mid-1990s *Books in Print* announced that it was available from Temple University Press in a translation by John Drury, who earlier had translated Rancière's first book for that press, *The Nights of Labor*. When, after making repeated inquiries, I found it impossible to obtain the new book, Temple admitted that it had never gone into production and subsequently voided the contract—though as of today it retains a Temple ISBN and is listed as available for purchase on Amazon.com. (A strange way for a book to be ahead of its time.) No one seemed to know, moreover, whether a copy of Drury's manuscript existed and, if so, where it could be located. At Rancière's suggestion I contacted Donald Reid, the University of North Carolina historian who had written the introduction to *The Nights of Labor*; he discovered in his files what was, perhaps, the only extant copy of Drury's work—an initial draft, with some of Rancière's emendations, of the first two-thirds of the book. That early partial version was then corrected by Corinne Oster, a graduate student in comparative literature at the University of Massachusetts at Amherst, who also drafted the book's remaining chapters. Encouraged that the manuscript finally was nearing completion, I revised it in its entirety with the goal of making Rancière's highly allusive prose sound as English as possible.

Though perhaps not *too* English. If, as Jonathan Rée has suggested, "thinking only becomes philosophical when familiar words grow strange," then "serious philosophical writing" can be recognized by its propensity to read "like a translation already."[1] One mark of this seriousness may be the ways such writing exploits as a resource its non-self-identity, a possibility embraced by *Le Philosophe et ses pauvres* in the scrupulousness with which it measures not only the distance between its own French and Plato's Greek or Marx's German, but also that between "its own French" and itself. Rancière often presses hard on a number of terms whose polyvalency will be lost or neutralized by any single

English equivalent. Thus *partage* is "division" *and* "sharing," and both of these antithetical senses must be kept in mind even when, depending on context, we opt in the translation for one or the other.[2] Similarly, a *savant* can be an expert, a scholar, or a scientist; though we limit ourselves in each chapter to using only one of the three, the different nuances between them resonate in the original. *Fin* is translated generally as "end," though on occasion it will also appear as "aim," "goal," "purpose," or "conclusion." The neutral "actor" and the more pejorative "comedian" are both renderings of *comédien*; Rancière plays systematically with this tension which, again, is unavailable in the English cognates. These are only a few of the many problems that we simply record in our translation rather than resolve. However inelegant it may be to insert a number of bracketed French phrases in our text, we do so to remind our English-language readers of what they are missing.

We employ whenever possible published English translations of the texts Rancière discusses, though on occasion these have been altered tacitly to conform to the terms of his usage. Parenthetical interpolations are always by Rancière, while those placed between square brackets—whether in the text proper or the notes—are by the translators.

This project was underwritten in part by an Amherst College Faculty Research Grant. Many individuals also provided indispensable aid: I am happy to acknowledge various debts to Derek Attridge, Judith Butler, John Drury, Maud Ellmann, Robert Gooding-Williams, Rick Griffiths, Margaret Groesbeck, Nat Herold, Fredric Jameson, Michael Kasper, Nancy Kuhl, Meredith McGill, Corinne Oster, Catherine Portuges, Lisa Raskin, Donald Reid, Bruce Robbins, Robert Schwartzwald, Anita Sokolsky, and Abby Zanger. My greatest debt of course is to Jacques Rancière, who was never stinting in his kindness, enthusiasm, or patience. Despite so much excellent assistance, this translation remains, perforce, imperfect. Its flaws are mine alone.

Mimesis and the Division of Labor

Are they my poor?

RALPH WALDO EMERSON,
"Self-Reliance"

WHAT HAS PHILOSOPHY to do with the poor? If, as has often been supposed, the poor have no time for philosophy, then why have philosophers always made time for them? Why is the history of philosophy—from Plato and Marx to Sartre and Pierre Bourdieu—the history of so many figures of the poor: plebes, men of iron, the *demos*, artisans, common people, proletarians, *lumpen*, series, groups in fusion, masses? Why have philosophers made the shoemaker (of all workers) a remarkably ubiquitous presence in this history? Does philosophy constitute itself in thinking of the poor? If so, can it ever refrain from thinking *for* them?

Jacques Rancière's *The Philosopher and His Poor* meditates on these questions in its close readings of major texts of Western thought in which the poor have played a leading role—sometimes as the objects of philosophical analysis, sometimes as illustrations of philosophical argument. Published in France in 1983 and made available here for the first time in English, the book is a consummate earlier study by a figure increasingly known today in the Anglophone world for his pathbreaking writings on the nature of equality.[1] *The Philosopher and His Poor* initiates an exploration of themes and questions to which Rancière will return over the course of what continues to be a singular intellectual and political itinerary. But the book's significance is not merely historical. A series of linked essays assessing the consequences for Marx, Sartre, and Bourdieu of Plato's admonition that workers should do "nothing else" than their own work, it offers innovative readings of these figures in turn as each struggles to elaborate a philosophy of the poor. The long chapter on Bourdieu should prove today to be of special interest given the extraordinary attention his work has received since his death in 2002. Presenting a left critique of Bourdieu the terms of which are largely unknown to an English-language readership, *The Philosopher and His Poor* remains remarkably timely twenty years after its initial publication.

Rancière was in his early forties when the book appeared in France, and he alludes in his foreword to the twenty years' worth of "detours" that interrupted his progress: "a seminar on *Capital* called to an unexpected notoriety; a thesis on Feuerbach interrupted by the din of the street; some time spent circulating between university halls and factory doors; ten years of research in worker archives" (xxv). Rancière had been a student in Louis Althusser's famous seminar on structural Marxism whose work led in 1965 to *Reading Capital*, the group project to which Rancière contributed an important essay not included in the original English translation.[2] After the events of May '68 ("the din of the street"), Rancière turned decisively away from this work, publishing in 1969 an essay highly critical of Althusser's teaching that he expanded into book-length form in 1974. Charging that Althusserianism secured its élite status by distinguishing between science (its own) and ideology, he later called this critique "a first clearing of the terrain for a longer-term reflection on the philosophical and historical relations between knowledge and the masses."[3] An active participant at this time in Maoist student-worker organizations that kept him "circulating between university halls and factory doors," Rancière helped to found in 1975 the journal *Révoltes logiques*, whose approach to the social history of labor was predicated on the hard-won acknowledgment that what professional intellectuals said about workers and what workers said about themselves were often different things.[4] What followed for Rancière was a decade-long immersion in neglected nineteenth-century labor archives in an effort "to establish what working-class tradition was, and to study how Marxism interpreted and distorted it. For many years I took no more interest in philosophy. More specifically, I turned my back on what might be called political theories, and read nothing but archive material. I posited the existence of a specifically working-class discourse."[5] This assumption that the working class indeed had a voice of its own—a voice that found authentic expression in an "indigenous" form of artisanal socialism—led to the publication in 1976 of *La Parole ouvrière*, a wide-ranging collection of nineteenth-century worker texts that Rancière edited with Alain Faure.[6]

It was, however, just this assumption that Rancière began to challenge next in a series of essays dating from the late 1970s and early '80s. Where he had expected the archives to disclose an image of the working class behaving for the most part "like itself" (that is, autonomously), he discovered instead "a working class which was more mobile, less attached to its tools and less sunk in its own poverty and drunkenness than the various traditions usually represent it" —a class, in short, that had no "itself" to which it could conform.[7] Rancière found, for example, that the value of "pride in work" was far from a universal working-class norm; indeed, the most militant tradesmen were those, like the shoemakers, who desired most to escape from the monotony of their jobs—those whose work allowed them to imagine doing something else than that to which they seemingly were fated. Now criticizing *La Parole ouvrière* for having given "excessive credit to the idea of a workers' discourse collectively addressed to the bourgeoisie," Rancière concluded from his new research that "we look too much at worker culture and not enough at its encounters with other cultures."[8] Such engagements between classes in public and semi-public spaces furnished nineteenth-century workers not only with relief from the drudgery of their tasks but also, in a remarkable number of instances, opportunities to try their hand at imitating the discourses, genres, and tastes of the bourgeoisie. Violating class-specific rules of decorum in expressing a voice *not* their own, these imitations harbored, for Rancière, a politically explosive potential unremarked by Marxist theorists and labor historians alike in their common anticipation of a working-class essence:

> For it is possible that any disruption of the prevailing system came less from a specific working-class culture than from these singular apprenticeships in a common culture; it was less a question of an uncivilized culture than of an uncivilized relationship with culture, or, to put it another way, of a culture in disorder (where the prevailing system was in the process of disruption). A worker who had never learned how to write and yet tried to compose verses to suit the taste of his times was perhaps more of a danger to the prevailing ideological order than a worker who performed revolutionary songs.[9]

Challenging received boundaries between the domains of head and hand, arrogating to themselves the leisure to think and write

to which workers were not entitled, the nineteenth-century figures to whom Rancière was drawn conducted experiments in
the politics of *mélange*—what a current idiom calls hybridity. He
warned that unless we can learn to be surprised by what the
archive offers—working-class writing structured not by an expected homogeneity but by a constitutive iterability, an imitative
incorporation of discursive norms foreign to itself—"we thus run
the risk of reconfirming the old philosophical adage that workers
not concern themselves with anything beside their work."[10]

This old adage is expressly disconfirmed both in *The Philosopher
and His Poor* and in the volume that preceded it by two years and
is in many ways its companion, *The Nights of Labor*.[11] "Readers
should not look for any metaphors in my title" (vii), Rancière
explained: *The Nights of Labor* recounts what occupied the evenings
of a great many mid-nineteenth-century French workers—*writing*.
Following hundreds of worker-intellectuals who found themselves "doubly and irremediably excluded for living as workers did
and speaking as bourgeois people did" (ix), the book relates in
loving detail the experiences of those who—like the philosopher–
floor layer Gabriel Gauny, and like other workers who wrote poetry, debated the Christian socialism of the newspaper *L'Atelier*,
engaged in dialogue with Saint-Simonians and Fourierists, or projected Icarian communities abroad—undermined "the ancestral
hierarchy subordinating those dedicated to manual labor to those
who have been given the privilege of thinking" (viii).[12] An experiment in anti-positivist social history, the book refrains formally
from taking the writings it surveys as the ingredients of documen-
tary. Indeed, it discounts the project of recovering authentic
worker voices since these workers relinquished all claims to authenticity in their very act of writing: they were "not men and
women bearing the word of the masses, but bearing simply the
word."[13] What gave this writing its political efficacy was not that it
reflected or embodied a specific class identity but that it disrupted
such identities in miming the norms of a culture foreign to its
writers' origins. The "equality" to which these workers aspired
thus would be less simply a theme that they addressed in their texts
than a speech event, the very condition of their performance as
writers. In his later work Rancière will define equality not as a goal
to be achieved over time but as a founding axiom, and we see
already the nucleus of this view in his demonstration in *The Nights
of Labor* that the mere fact of writing, for its worker-intellectuals,

was radically democratizing, since it verified in practice that they were capable of producing not just noise but reasoned discourse.[14] Interestingly, some readers judged the book itself to be insufficiently reasoned, one reviewer admitting perplexity over its "a-conceptualism," another complaining that it skimped on explanation: "*The Nights of Labor* is more a work of philosophical meditation than conventional historical analysis. Rancière makes little effort to set his writers in context, compare them systematically, or even make explicit his own working assumptions or line of argument."[15] But this reticence would be the point, for the book's anti-positivism entails that the historian can be no more self-identical than the writers he takes as his model. If we are unable here to differentiate systematically Rancière's "working assumptions" from Gauny's—if we fail to disentangle "objective" narration from free indirect discourse—this reflects the book's commitment to an equality legible even in the form of its *Darstellung*.[16] Deconstructing the split between thinker and worker in its subject and in its structure, *The Nights of Labor* is as much (or as little) a work of literature as it is history or philosophy.[17]

The Philosopher and His Poor, by contrast, looks like a traditional work of philosophy: though more "literary" than many such works in its highly allusive prose, the texts it considers are nonetheless familiarly canonical where its predecessor's were obscurely archival. And where it proved difficult in The Nights of Labor to differentiate Rancière's voice from that of his worker subjects, The Philosopher and His Poor seems instead to respect philosophical protocol: its readers will likely find it easier to tell its author apart from the figures he reads—and this will be the case especially whenever Rancière's argument turns critical, as in the chapter on Bourdieu. In revisiting classic philosophical topoi from Plato's three metals to Sartre's wall, Rancière canvasses what amounts to a history of Western philosophy from the ancient Greeks through the twentieth century. But in telling that history *as* the history of formal thinking about the poor, the book no longer qualifies unequivocally as philosophy but as a reflection on its closure. Rancière argues that in Bourdieu as much as Plato, the poor comprise in their very exclusion from the vocation of philosopher the condition of philosophical possibility. Present as objects rather than subjects of knowledge, appearing only in the guise of philosophy's *exempla*, the poor enable the philosopher to constitute himself—as other than the poor. To pursue this argument, however, is immediately to force the question of whether *The Philoso-pher and His Poor* is, or ever could be, a work of philosophy. Can Rancière speak *as* a philosopher while exposing the exclusions that constitute philosophy? If philosophy depends for its exis-tence on its foreclosure of the poor, from what space could the book situate the limits of philosophy without already having com-promised that space and those limits? No wonder this book is so fond of the Cretan Liar's Paradox![18] At once philosophical and necessarily other than that, closer in its heterogeneity to *The Night of Labor* than it first may appear, *The Philosopher and His Poor* em-braces in its objects and discourses the hybridity that philosophy seeks to expunge or reduce in going about "its own business."

While Rancière shares with other recent French thinkers this preoccupation with the heterogeneous, he is unique in discerning the steady pressure of "the poor" behind philosophy's attempts to secure its autonomy.[19] Though the names given to the poor have changed over time, their essential function—to play the ersatz of philosophy—remains constant: "An ersatz that philosophy cannot do without since, in order to preserve its role in the legislation of legitimate thoughts, it is itself obliged to produce a discourse on non-philosophy, on illegitimate modes of thinking" (131). In Plato's *Republic*, the ersatz is first and foremost the artisan "who can do only one thing at a time" since he has been given the time to do only one thing—his trade and nothing else (4). Plato takes extraordinary pains to keep the artisan occupied exclusively with "his own business" so as to preclude his pursuit of the different business on which the philosopher enjoys a monopoly. Though Plato occasionally enlists the artisan to furnish homespun mod-els for the practice of philosophy, the artisan threatens philoso-phy more often since he is preeminently a technician who lodges within himself the capacity for an unrestrained polytechnics. The sophist Hippias, hybridity personified, merely exacerbates this potential; doing many more things than one, he is "the philoso-pher's living counterfeit—the artisan of lies, the intellectual jack-of-all-trades [*bricoleur*] whom the mob confusedly equates with the philosopher: the sophist" (31). But only the philosopher has the right to lie, and that lie is a whopper since it "explains" a division of labor in which the philosopher's "own position cannot figure at all" (33): the myth of the three metals barring artisan pretenders from following philosophy's path. Rancière suggests that this mythical account of social hierarchy is not simply "a 'pro-slavery' discourse designed to justify an inegalitarian social order or to shut men up in the 'totalitarianism' of its idea"; philosophy's concern "is less to lock others up than to protect itself from them," to defend its own sanctuary against interlopers from below (52). Yet despite these prophylactic measures, the artisan remains a problem that philosophy cannot master in its own terms:

> He is not a free man sharing in the virtue of the city, but neither is he a slave whose virtues derive from the diligent administration of the domestic economy. A false free man and part-time slave, the artisan belongs neither to his trade nor to the one who assigns him work. He cannot derive virtue from his own sphere or from a relationship of dependence. But one who has no virtue has no nature. The artisan is not simply a lowly being to be kept away from the government of the city. Properly speaking, he is an impossible being, an unthinkable nature. The free worker of the market economy is a denatured being, an accident of history. Neither included nor excluded, this hybridity is an unpardonable disturbance for the city. (24)

The artisan is no more thinkable for Marx, for whom "the poor" is not the working class but its disappropriation as the proletariat, the non-class that has its "own work" to do: revolution (70). Drawn to contradiction instead of mélange, Marx follows Plato in resisting the double, the bastard, the polytechnic. While in a celebrated passage Marx imagines that with the advent of communism man will be able to do many things each day, the occupations he lists are discrete and contiguous rather than hybridized, and if "neither industrial fabrication nor artistic imitation" is included among them, this is "certainly the most radical way of not mixing the two together" (67). Though he opposes praxis "to productions of technique, what Aristotle called 'poietics'" (209), Marx nonetheless experiences a world in which technē remains irreducible, the worker insufficiently proletarianized, the scientist too much like his conjuring adversary, the historical irremediably theatrical. Casting the lumpen in the role of scapegoat, Marx discovers ultimately that the hybridity he seeks to purge not only afflicts all classes but lies even closer to home with the Straubinger bohemians—the Cretan Liars of communism (82–89). Sartre, similarly, dreams of a world in which "a worker and a philosopher no longer will be technicians but virtually, already, subjects of the group"—a world where matter could work "by itself before the prestidigitations of technique can begin" (162, 164). Even so, as Rancière indicates, "the universe of *ordinary* technique remains what it always was for Plato: the universe of splintered rationality belonging to those bastard beings— 'amphibians,' Sartre calls them—who are artisans. A world of undecidable ends, of fabrications that become imitations of themselves, of partial socialities—short-circuits in which is lost the explosive force of the Nothing that engenders the All" (155). There is, for Sartre, less time than ever (and even more fatigue to overcome) for workers to be able to do two things at once—which means that his "poor," too, can only ever do what they do already, and nothing else: "In the realm of vulgar fatigue there is no place for vulgar freedom, the sort that is earned or lost or regained, that goes astray or loses itself in the intervals of exploitation—the freedom of male and female workers who decide that *they have the leisure* to think of something else while working; the time after work to learn; the possibility of writing literate prose or verse; the choice of having the children they *cannot* have or of not having the children they *should* have; the obligation of organizing worker societies that they do not *have the right* to create or *the time* to run: in short, the luxury that they *cannot treat themselves to*" (146–47). That this luxury is exclusively the philosopher's constitutes the limit of a philosophy of freedom—of "the only true freedom, that of the philosopher, which is conceivable and operative only as the exact opposite of the impotence of serialized individuals" (147).

For Pierre Bourdieu as well, "the poor" can do only one thing at a time—and this even though he is widely known as a critic of class privilege. Though Bourdieu's sociology is hostile to Plato and to philosophy's masking of social distinction, Rancière argues that this sociological reversal of Platonism is "only the confirmation, indeed the radicalization, of its interdictions" (204). As explained in the Afterword, *The Philosopher and His Poor* mounted its lively critique of Bourdieu at the moment when the new Socialist government of the early '80s, committed to reducing inequality in education, took Bourdieu's *The Inheritors, Reproduction* and *Distinction* as its program. As these books are more influential today than ever, Rancière's critique retains its point. Perpetuating the hierarchy it purports to reduce, Boudieu's sociology assumes an inequality even more obdurate than Plato's since, for Rancière, its logic is now necessary rather than arbitrary—and this is a logic only the sociologist can read (204). Even while condemning philosophy for its naturalization of class distinctions, the sociologist-king presupposes that the poor can only ever do their own business, for such homogeneity is what Bourdieu's notion of habitus entails (178). The hybrid writer-intellectuals of *The Nights of Labor* would be inconceivable on this model since "the denunciation of the *scholē* also denounces the parvenu who arrogates to himself the leisure to study that he does not have" (175). If no one ever strays here from his or her habitus, this is only because sociological analysis demands "the suppression of intermediaries, of points of meeting and exchange between people of reproduction and the elite of distinction": "Everything happens as if the science of the sociologist-king had the same requirement as the city of the philosopher-king. There must be no mixing, no imitation" (189). Nowhere, then, is there the slightest chance that "the popular *gestus* could, by accident or fraud, meet up with the bourgeois *gestus*" (191). Impervious to the poor's "aesthetic and militant passion for reappropriation," Bourdieu resists making room for "an allodoxia that is the only way to heterodoxia" (200). It is rather Kant and Schiller who can make such room in offering, Rancière concludes, "a fiction of the possible responding to the fiction of the impossible, a utopia opening again the space bolted shut by the myth of the three metals" (199).[20]

Where Gaston Bachelard proclaimed that "there is no science but the science of the hidden," Rancière responds by saying that distinctions between mere appearance and concealed truth reflect only the needs of those who profit from maintaining these distinctions: does mystification exist anywhere but in the words of the demystifier? (170, 173). For this very reason *The Philosopher and His Poor* is best regarded as neither an "ideology critique" nor a "symptomatic reading" of Platonism and its political legacies: "nothing in fact is concealed" by Plato, who indeed "has no propensity for dissimulating inequality" (18, 206). Though Rancière puts great weight on the question of language—recall that he defines equality as a speech event—his project, so different from Habermas's or from Foucault's, takes its measured distance from philosophy's "linguistic turn."[21] Rancière obviously shares with Derrida a fascination with an other that is not philosophy's own, and the notion of the *demos* as supplement that Rancière develops in his later work clearly owes something to deconstruction. But Rancière's differences from Derrida are as significant as their similarities—differences that are discernible in their respective glosses on the myth of writing's origins that Plato recounts in the *Phaedrus*.[22] Unlike Derrida, who sees in Plato's condemnation of writing a constitutive ambivalence that philosophy cannot govern, Rancière reads this rejection immediately in political terms as an allegory concerning "the poor":

> This mute discourse, which knows neither its audience nor their needs, can transmit anything anywhere. It does not know to whom it is speaking, to whom it should speak, who can and cannot be admitted to a sharing [*partage*] of the *logos*. The living *logos* of the philosopher, the science of truth and lying, is also a science of speech and silence. It knows the right time for keeping quiet. Written discourse, on the other hand, is as incapable of keeping quiet as it is of speaking. Mute in the face of philosophers' questions, it cannot restrain itself from speaking to the uninitiated. The uncontrolled democracy of this discourse-at-liberty makes philosophy's fine titles and beautiful appearances sparkle before the eyes of our too-clever artisans. Its infirmity is bastardy. It puts the *logos* at the disposal of men whose work has damaged their bodies and mutilated their souls. (40)

Forgetting "to signal for which habitus it is suitable and for which it is not" (186), writing in the *Phaedrus* is thus the image of democracy in making itself "equally available both to those entitled to use it and those who are not."[23] Rancière later terms this structural capacity of writing "literarity" [*littérarité*]; in *The Philosopher and His Poor* it goes by the name "theatrocracy," the rule of the audience disdained by Plato as "the mother of democracy" (45).[24] No wonder Plato rejected theatrical mimesis and democracy in a single gesture: "The tragic illusion itself belonged to the democratic reign of appearance and flattery, in which the arbitrariness of the orator and that of the *demos* reflected each other interminably."[25] One of Rancière's achievements in this book is his way of regarding philosophical attempts to regulate mimesis *as* attempts to ground the division of labor—and vice versa. Plato, he shows, even tried to argue that "human nature is 'minted in such small coinage' that one can imitate only one thing at a time. Unfortunately, the new machines of the theater are there to belie his nice optimism. On the stage, before a public that is no longer one of warriors but of artisans, these machines tear to pieces his fine principle of the functionality of the division of labor in producing the whole of creation" (10–11). Marx and Nietzsche, too, will discover in their different ways that "there is no escaping from the theater" (62–63, 121). In all such instances, what makes theater "dangerous" is just what enables the poor to do more than one thing at a time—the iterative miming of roles not one's own. Which is why authorities are as interested in keeping audiences from mingling as they are in censoring what takes place on stage.[26]

And the shoemaker? He is, surprisingly, *everywhere* in the history this book surveys. He is introduced in the *Republic* "whenever it becomes necessary to think about the division of labor" (4); he becomes "the generic name for the man who is not where he ought to be if the order of estates is to get on with the order of discourse" (48); he leads the way in the nineteenth century in the battle against the "glory" of work (59). Wagner's Hans Sachs, of course, was a shoemaker. Karl Marx was once called a shoemaker, though he considered the shoemaker-poet a figure of Bad History (61, 68–69). "Ashaverus, the Wandering Jew, was a shoemaker."[27] While omnipresent, the shoemaker is always where one least expects to find him. A random example—here is Gérard Genette dismissing in an extended huff "the ponderous tradition Schopenhauer calls 'the metaphysics of the beautiful' ":

> In this tradition, stretching from Novalis to Heidegger or Adorno, and, consequently, a bit beyond, I generally find nothing but unverifiable affirmations, rather heavily laced with the ideology of antimodernism, together with celebrations of art's revolutionary subversiveness or exalted glorifications of its power to make ontological revelations. One can, perhaps, do art no greater disservice than to overestimate its role by counterposing it, in a way smacking of obscurantism, to that of science or technology, and by unwarrantedly assimilating its message to philosophy's—even if the complementary and inverse complaints (which derive, negatively, from the same expectation, once it has been disappointed) about art's inability to "make" anything at all "happen," put right Auschwitz and Hiroshima, or make up for the death of a child seem to me a little naive and, all things considered, out of place—*as if a cobbler were to apologize for being unable to bring about a solar eclipse.*[28]

As if the cobbler were not the very principle of being out of place. As if his invocation as the sign of the ridiculous were not the oldest philosophical trick. As if a shoemaker and the heavens could have nothing to do with each other. As if a defense of art's autonomy must unwittingly recall what Plato said about his "poor": "A work of art is an object . . . which draws us into, or invites us to have, an aesthetic experience—*and nothing else.*"[29]

The Philosopher and His Poor

Dirk Rembrantsz was a Dutch peasant, a native of the village of Nierop in the northernmost part of Holland bordering on Frisia. Practicing the shoemaker's trade in his birthplace barely provided him with the necessities of life. But he found a way to vanquish fate through his exceptional knowledge of mathematics, which he could not refrain from cultivating though often at the expense of his livelihood. The great name of M. Descartes, along with the meager satisfaction he gleaned from mathematics books that he read in the vernacular language, prompted him to leave his village and set off to consult the philosopher. Renown had pictured the latter to him as the most easily approachable person in the world, and the notion he had of a philosopher in seclusion hardly suggested that access would have to be under Swiss guard. But Rembrantsz was rebuffed as an impudent peasant by M. Descartes's attendants, who so informed the master of the house after they had sent him away. Two or three months later, Rembrantsz returned in the very same suit of clothes and asked to speak to M. Descartes with the air of someone determined to confer with him about important matters. His appearance did not help him win a better reception than the first time. When the attendants brought word to M. Descartes, they portrayed him as an importunate beggar who, in search of a handout, asked to speak to M. Descartes about philosophy and astrology. Not wishing to pursue the matter further, M. Descartes went along with the view of his attendants; he sent money out to Rembrantsz and had it explained that this would excuse Rembrantsz from the trouble of having to speak to him. But poverty had not diminished Rembrantsz's dignity and he refused the liberality of our philosopher, saying that since his moment had not yet arrived he would go away for a time, but that he hoped a third visit would prove more expedient. This reply was reported to M. Descartes, who now regretted not having seen the peasant and ordered his people to inform him if the man returned.

A few months later, Rembrantsz came back for the third time. Making it known that he was the peasant whose eagerness to see M. Descartes had cost him already two fruitless trips, he finally received the satisfaction he had been seeking with such earnestness and perseverance. M. Descartes recognized his competence and merit on the spot, and wanted to repay him with interest for all his troubles. He was not satisfied in instructing him in all manner of difficult subjects and in imparting his Method to rectify reasoning. He also counted him as one of his friends: despite the lowliness of Rembrantsz's estate, M. Descartes did not regard him as beneath those of the first rank, and he assured Rembrantsz that his home and heart would be open to him at all hours.

Rembrantsz lived only five or six leagues from Egmont. From that time on he paid frequent visits to M. Descartes and became, thanks to him, one of the foremost astronomers of his century.

ADRIEN BAILLET, *Vie de Monsieur Descartes* (1691)

A PERSONAL ITINERARY

I MIGHT AS WELL say it straightaway: this book forms part of an inquiry that will not end with its final period. Proceeding, by way of Marx's suspended revolution, from the Platonic philosopher-king to what reigns today as the sociological conception of the world, I will try to indicate here some of the milestones and retrace some of the paths I pursued in asking two or three questions that are, at once, very simple and very complicated. How are we to conceive of the relation between the order of thought and the social order—as harmony or as rupture? How do individuals get some idea in their heads that makes them either satisfied with their position or indignant about it? How are representations of self and other—which sustain hierarchy, consensus, or conflict—formed and transformed? For twenty years I have had occasion to pursue these questions in various sites and circumstances: a seminar on *Capital* called to an unexpected notoriety; a thesis on Feuerbach interrupted by the din of the street; some time spent circulating between university halls and factory doors; ten years of research in worker archives.

That certainly makes for a number of detours. And several times word got back to me that intentions so pure in principle and labors so laudable in their execution should be, nevertheless, in a bit more of a hurry to display the straight lines of their method and the *terra firma* of their results.

I must acknowledge that with respect to the questions I posed, I have been fortunate to encounter teachers of the highest repute, some rightly so. Unfortunately, a certain irresoluteness of character, fed by an excessive attention to minute discrepancies in detail, always kept me from finding the most promising theories confirmed in the examples that life or study offered me. To which undoubtedly was added a certain Christian sentimentality that made me judge as a bit simplistic and rather disdainful the way in which learned discourses assumed that the common run of mortals forged their vision of the world. To say nothing of the naïveté with which the defenders and historiographers of the people praise the sober simplicity of the ideas they ascribe to them.

And so I had to set out without a guide—without a thread, one master of the art said to me—on the territory of the historian. There the study of a single case, it seemed to me, would help to advance my research: the years 1830 to 1850 witnessed the flowering of utopian socialism and, at the same time, a wide range of working-class expression from ethereal poetry to combative pamphlets and doctrinal newspapers. I tried to learn if these two developments met up with each other, whether we could know what proletarian intellectuals gathered from this utopian flowering, what they were able to oppose to it from their own reserves, and what in this whole process affected thinking in such a way as to modify the order of things.[1] In the course of this research, my interest shifted. Behind the "positivist" question—what could a person think at such a moment in the history of discourses and in such a position within the order of society? —I had to recognize the more fundamental question: how can those whose business is not thinking assume the authority to think and thereby constitute themselves as thinking subjects? The tableau that offered itself to me in response was exemplary in this respect, for when proletarians, in granting themselves permission to think, invaded the territory of the literati, the literati answered evasively by celebrating work as the true culture of the poor and the future of the world, and by warning the representatives of that world of the dangers of developing a split personality.

That scene was to remind me of some earlier readings as well as more recent experiences. I had read previously without particular interest the texts in which Plato borrowed from artisans the paradigms of philosophy, and those in which he ordered these same artisans not to think about anything beyond their jobs. I was born in a century when homage to labor, proletarian consciousness, and the spirit of the people brought to unheard-of perfection the forms of authority and the discourses of servitude. Where I lived, to be sure, the former were more civil and the latter more modest. But I was familiar enough with such efforts to restore to a class its consciousness, and to the people its culture, to sense in them also the trope that can be counted among the master logics of modernity: exclusion by homage. (As I indicated, I had personal reasons for being sensitive to the issue.) Finally, Bourdieu's *Distinction* struck me with its insistence on opposing proletarian *amor fati* to bourgeois culture games—on opposing, if you will, the undershirts that cling tightly to the bodies of workers to the too-large ideas on which workers drift away when answering the questions of the experts [des savants].² And that book's criticism of philosophers as "deniers" of the social seemed to be in curious continuity with the exclusions of the philosophical tradition.

Between the ancient ruses of philosophy and the modern ruses of anti-philosophy, it appeared possible for me to trace a straight line. I would start from the logic used by Plato to make the philosopher a weaver, the better to consign shoemakers to the hell of non-philosophy, and I would arrive eventually at the reverence for popular virtues and the denunciation of ideological vanities that sustain equivocally the modern discourse of experts and leaders. Along the way, I would have to show only how Marx, in destroying the Platonic realm of the Ideas, may perhaps have prolonged what he said he was overturning, giving proletarians truth so as to exclude them more surely from the learned science reserved for experts. The task did not seem to be beyond my abilities.

I forgot that I had never known how to draw a straight line. And both Plato and Marx had more than one trick in store to ensure my failure once again. Plato forced me to notice that the sorry fate he reserved for artisans was also, precisely, the price to be paid for pursuing insistently a question that still has some importance for us: how can justice be established beyond all questions of technique and the hygiene of individual and social preservation? From the opposite angle, Marx's brutality toward the old moons of the philosophical firmament was purchased at the price of ever-recurring lacerations and paradoxes. I had to ask myself why Marx laid the blame not on Don Quixote the chimerical lover of justice, but on Sancho the realist; why his proletariat was so inconsistent and his bourgeoisie so quick to swoon; and whether his work had been made interminable simply by reasons of his own health or by a more fundamental question regarding the distance between revolutionary justice and social health.

A few added twists and turns, then, so that what began as a rather dispassionate inquiry into the image of the worker in scholarly discourse came to transform itself as it reopened all the venerable conflicts between philosophy and rhetoric, justice and health. The contemporary blindness of policies that take one of these for the other, and that identify sociology's framing of the question (and responses to it) with the advance of democracy, undoubtedly contributed to that change. The final section of this book may well have ended up, as a result, more lively than I had anticipated. But I realized that if we show too much respect for others' arguments, we do them the worst injury, which is to make them insipid.

A closely related thought accounts for two presuppositions of my reading. I have never been able to subscribe fully to the golden rule that prevailed during the era of my schooling, which is not to ask an author any questions except for those that he had asked himself. I have always suspected a little presumption in that modesty. And experience seemed to teach me that the power of a mode of thinking has to do above all with its capacity to be displaced, just as the power of a piece of music may derive from its capacity to be played on different instruments. I need hardly point out that to argue the contrary has some relation to the doctrine urging everyone to mind his or her own business.

For similar reasons I have not bowed to the propriety that distinguishes between the recognized and disavowed works of a given author, or makes allowances for such circumstances as youth and maturity. Precautions and retractions may attest to an author's courage or prudence. The fact remains that any mode of thinking that is the least bit singular reveals itself in always saying basically the same thing, which it cannot but hazard every time in the colorful prism of circumstances. Contrary to what interested parties may say, only imbeciles ever truly change, since they alone are free enough regarding all thought to feel at home in any particular mode of thinking. I personally have always tried to follow a simple rule of morality: not to take for imbeciles those about whom I was talking, whether they happen to be floor layers or university professors.[3]

1 :: PLATO'S LIE

"But," added Critias, "it will be necessary for you to abstain from speaking of those shoemakers, and carpenters, and smiths; indeed, I think
that they must now be worn out,
from being so often in your mouth."

"I must therefore," said Socrates,
"abstain from the illustrations that I
attach to the mention of those
people, illustrations on justice, piety,
and other such subjects."

XENOPHON, *Memorabilia* I, 2:37,
trans. J. S. Watson (1896)

1 :: The Order of the City

IN THE BEGINNING there would be four persons. Maybe five. Just about as many as the needs of the body. A farmer for food, a mason for housing, a weaver for clothing. To these let us add a shoemaker and some other worker to provide for material necessities.

That is how Plato's republic presents itself. Without a deity or founding legend. With individuals, needs, and the means to satisfy them. A masterpiece of economy: with its four or five workers Plato founds not only a city but a future science, sociology. Our nineteenth century will be grateful to him.

His own century had a different judgment of it. His disciple and critic Aristotle put it succinctly: a city is not simply a concentration of needs and a division of the means of production. Right from the start something else is needed—justice, the power of what is better over what is less good. There are greater or less noble tasks, jobs that are more or less degrading, natures appropriate for one group or for another, and all these must be distinguished. Even in a republic of four or five citizens, there must be someone to represent and ensure respect for the common good that defines the aim [la fin] of the city above and beyond the satisfaction of needs. How else could justice ever come about from simply gathering together equally indispensable workers?[1]

There must be a misunderstanding somewhere. Or a trick. For justice is, precisely, the subject of Plato's dialogue, and in order to define it he constructs his society as a magnifying glass. So justice must be there already in his egalitarian gathering of workers, or else it will never turn up at all. It is up to us to look for it.

THE FIFTH MAN

A first clue might be a slight fluctuation concerning the number of equals. Four or five, we do not know exactly. But whether the number is even or odd ought to have some consequence for a philosopher infatuated with mathematics. Later on he will subject even the couplings of his warriors to the golden number, but for the moment he seems indifferent to the details of his inventory. In the city of necessity he leaves open the possibility that there is one person too many.

That may be a first reply to our question and to Aristotle's objection. No one among the equals is superior, but one of them could be less indispensable than the others. Could it be the fifth man, whose essential function is not spelled out any further? Or could it be the shoemaker? Is a specialist in footwear really needed when a single worker suffices to handle all aspects of building houses? It is no big deal to provide Attic peasants with footwear, and Plato himself tells us later on that they will carry on their work in summer "for the most part unclad and unshod."[2] If so, should one-fourth of this primitive labor force be assigned to that office? Or should we assume, rather, that the shoemaker is also there for *something else*? The fact is that at every strategic point in the dialogue—whenever it becomes necessary to think about the division of labor, to establish difference in natures and aptitudes, or to define justice itself—the shoemaker will be there in the front line of the argument. As if he were doing double duty behind the scenes. As if this worker who is not to judge anything but footwear retained some usefulness for the philosopher that goes far beyond the products of his trade: the marginal and at first glance paradoxical function of allowing a doubt to hover about the actual utility of useful workers.

And yet our shoemaker and his fellow tradesmen are there to teach us a fundamental principle: a person can do only one thing at a time. It would be inconvenient for the farmer to stop his labor in the fields and devote three-fourths of his time to repairing his roof, making his clothes, and cutting out his shoe leather. The division of labor will take care of that problem. It will assign a specialist exclusively to each activity, and all will be for the best: "More things are produced, and better and more easily, when one man performs only one task according to his nature, at the right moment, and is excused from all other occupations."[3]

Many things in such few words. First, a question: it is true that more will be produced under this system, but why is it necessary to produce so much? Apparently these people are already living within a market economy, even if this market is quite limited. And one need not have read Adam Smith to realize that such a division of labor will quickly produce unexchangeable surpluses. Starting with shoes, of course. With such a limited population and such limited needs, the division of labor is an absurdity. It may not be "more convenient" for the shoemaker to cultivate a plot of ground, but it is certainly a safer bet for him to do so.

So argues the economy of Adam Smith. Plato's economy differs in that the needs of the first members of his society are not restricted—indeed, at the beginning they are infinite. He tells us at the start that these men need many things. Later he will tell us that these workers need many tools. From the very outset it is necessary to make *more*, and for that, time is lacking. It is not that the worker must work all the time, but he must always be available to do his work at the right moment, and that is why he must have only one job. An observation then occurs to Socrates just in the nick of time: experience shows that nature provided for this necessity by distributing diverse aptitudes to different individuals. These aptitudes will be suited in turn to various occupations and everything will run smoothly.

Though not very clearly. The argument about time is itself already not so simple. If it is true that the job does not wait for the worker, the converse is not true as well. Nature may have given the farmer exactly the right dispositions for working in the fields, but it has also given vegetables their growing cycles. And it has made the seasons, which put unequal demands on the exercise of these agricultural dispositions. Is the farmer really supposed to spend the whole off-season and bad-weather days waiting for the right moment to turn over the soil? Isn't there a right moment for him to cultivate his field and another moment, just as right, for him to make his clothes and those of others? That is what many farmers still will think in the very midst of the Industrial Revolution, without agriculture or industry having anything to complain about—except wages. But that is a different matter.

Would a philosopher so expert at describing for purposes of comparison the operations of artisans be so ignorant of the conditions surrounding their exercise? That is highly unlikely. If he pretends not to know whether nature leaves the farmer and the mason with sufficient leisure, and whether society does the same for their fellow workers, it is because he has decided that they should not have all the time that circumstances, sometimes too generously, have given them. The very principle of a *social nature* shaping temperaments to functions could be the price of this omission. Behind the apparent paradoxes of this economy another game is being played, slightly askew, as four terms arrange themselves into a pattern: countless needs, time in short supply, workers who are more or less indispensable, and aptitudes among which we do not know how to distinguish. For while we readily admit that nature gives individuals different aptitudes and tastes, and that it forms some bodies better suited to work in the open air and others to the workshop's shade, how are we ever to differentiate a weaver-nature from a shoemaker-nature except through that absence of time which, combined with the urgency of the tasks at hand, never allows the one worker to be found in the other's place?

And so the argument moves ahead on its two lame legs. The difference in natures comes to rescue the poorly demonstrated impossibility of performing two separate functions. And that impossibility, in turn, evades the questions posed by the same enigmatic difference that would shape in advance the division of labor. If this economically improbable division can be expressed in the natural evidence of social utility, the reason is that this is where the arbitrariness of nature and the conventionality of the social order exchange their powers. The agent of this exchange is a notion too trivial to engage much attention: time.

QUESTIONS OF TIME

Time, Feuerbach will tell us, is the privileged category of the dialectician because it excludes and subordinates where space tolerates and coordinates. Again we must be precise. The time of which Plato is speaking here is not that of physical necessity, the time of generation, growth, and death. It is that more ambiguous entity—half philosophical and half popular, half natural and half social—which determines one's availability for a task or the right moment for supply to meet demand. It is not the time needed to accomplish a task (ergon) but the time that permits or prohibits a pastime (parergon)—i.e., the fact of being beside the necessity of work. It is not the time measured by water clocks but the time that compels some people to its measure and exempts others from it. It is leisure (scholē) or its absence (ascholia).

The factor of exclusion is the absence of time, or absence of leisure, ascholia. The notion is not peculiar to Plato; it is a commonplace in discussions about the relationship of the order of labor to the political order. But if the place is common, the paths leading up to it are anything but: from Plato to Xenophon, or from Xenophon to Aristotle, the absence of leisure lends itself to the most contradictory and disconcerting lines of argument. For Xenophon, it is impossible for artisans to participate in the political life of the city. They are always working in shadows, seated by a corner of the fire. Theirs is an indoor life, an effeminate life that leaves them no leisure to concern themselves with anything but work and family. Farmers, on the other hand, out in the open air and bright sunshine, are the best defenders of the city because they have—a strange way of putting it—not the most leisure but the least *absence of leisure*.[4]

In Aristotle the same criterion produces the same alternative, but his argument is exactly the reverse. Artisans are effectively the ruin of democracy, but the reason is that they have too much leisure. They spend all their time loitering in the streets or the agora, which means they can attend all the assemblies and meddle in everything indiscriminately. The democracy of farmers, on the other hand, will be the best—or rather, the least bad. Farmers are confined to their fields, and the assembly is too far away; they will not have the leisure time to go to town and exercise their power, so things can only run better. Because if they did go to town, they would behave like men who do not possess the only leisure that counts, the leisure of thinking. Farmers make the least bad sort of democracies, those in which the democrats do not have the time to exercise their power. But for the very same reason, in a well-governed state they will not have their place.[5]

Thus leisure and its absence zigzag in these cases to produce the same result: the artisan cannot be a good citizen. The originality of Plato's *Republic*, however, lies in its *not* posing this question as such. Aristotle, Xenophon, and Plato himself in the *Laws* frame the question in its alternate form: can one be a citizen while engaging in a trade? Which occupations qualify or disqualify people, provide the time to participate in political life or take it away? In the *Republic*, on the other hand, citizenship is neither a trade nor a status but simply a matter of fact. One belongs to the *community*, and this community knows only different *occupations*. Where Aristotle, for example, distinguishes between four types of manual labors, Socrates can raise in passing the case of people whose bodies are sturdy but whose minds are rather slow, all of whom will be admitted into the community nevertheless—they will be the common laborers, the unskilled wage earners. There are different natures but apparently no *differences in nature*. The jobs themselves are all equivalent. There are no slaves.

So there is only one principle of exclusion. Plato's *Republic* does not decree that one cannot be a shoemaker and a citizen at the same time. It simply establishes that one cannot be a shoemaker and a weaver at the same time. It does not exclude anyone by reason of the baseness of his job, but simply establishes the impossibility of holding more than one job at a time. It knows only one evil, but this is the absolute evil: that two things be in one, two functions in the same place, two qualities in one and the same being. Only one category of people, then, finds itself *de facto* without employment, those whose specific occupation consists in doing two things in one—*the imitators*.

The Order of the Banquet

There is no reason for the imitators to trouble the first city's order. To expand beyond its four or five pioneers, the city needs only three or four supplementary categories: some joiners and smiths to make the tools for work; some wage earners for the heavy labor; and two kinds of tradesmen to handle exchange—small shopkeepers for the local market, and merchants for trade between cities. Since the merchants must have goods to exchange for those that will satisfy the needs of the community, the number of producers will be increased accordingly. And with that we can consider the community complete and perfect. The citizens will live joyously in harmony and piety; crowned with myrtle and reclining on beds of bryony, they will feast fraternally on wine and wheat cakes served on reeds or fresh leaves.

This is not a form of communism but an egalitarian republic of labor, vegetarian and pacifist, adjusting its production to its needs and its birthrate to its resources. An apolitical society of industrious well-being [*la santé travailleuse*], the myth of which will come to life again in the age of anarchism and neo-Malthusianism.

Health, we grant. But what about justice? The regulation of equal and unequal? Socrates and his interlocutor are searching for it, and we have sensed its field of play in this society in the slight inequality to itself of strictly divided labor—i.e., in the abundance of needs, the fluctuation of the number of workers, the regulation of time that is equally lacking to all but could not be lacking to some.

It is at this point that Glaucon intervenes. He is Socrates's interlocutor and Plato's brother, and in his view this republic of workers is fit only for pigs. He wants its banquets to have different forms of pomp and new ornaments: couches and tables, fancy seasonings and dainty tidbits, fragrances and courtesans . . .

Raising the bar is a regulative function of Plato's dialogues, which need to portray someone rejecting the maxims of good sense, the counsels of prudence, the regimens for the hygienic life proposed by Socrates. This role is usually filled by people of quality: the ambitious Callicles or members of Plato's own family—his cousin Critias the tyrant, and his two brothers Adimantus and Glaucon.

To please Glaucon, Socrates will bid a nostalgic farewell to the healthy city and we are ushered into the city of humors and arts of refined living. Glaucon's intervention makes visible the subterranean logic of the preceding moment. Justice exists only through the disordering of health and, as such, was already indirectly at work in the interplay of lacks, excesses, and fluctuations that were upsetting slightly the perfect equilibrium of the healthy city. Justice is the returning of healthy and useful workers to their specific place.

The new city, the one where injustice and justice are possible and thinkable, begins with the seasonings and decorum of the banquet. Should we say that we also have here the origin of politics with the table manners of the ethnologist, the distinction of the sociologist? Perhaps, but the banquet is confusion as much as distinction. At the banquet of the poet Agathon, for example, the intoxication of Alcibiades the pleasure seeker encounters the enthusiasm of the philosopher Socrates. In other instances, the simulacra of discourse conspire with the reality of needs, and democratic aspirations with aristocratic pomp, until they all become, at the very heart of the modern age, one of the symbols of political subversion.

IMITATORS, HUNTERS, AND ARTISANS

The order established by the banquet is the order of mixture. If the city began with the clearcut distribution of useful workers, politics begins with the motley crowd of the unuseful who, coming together into a mass of "workers," cater to a new range of needs—from painters and musicians to tutors and chambermaids; from actors and rhapsodists to hairdressers and cooks; from the makers of luxury articles to swineherds and butchers. But in this mixed crowd of parasites don't we need to acknowledge that some workers really are as useful as those in the original group, so long as they, too, agree to do only one thing at a time? After all, the first workers themselves were obliged to mingle the superfluous with the necessary for the dishes, tables, and trimmings of the banquet.

We can, however, easily discern a division within this group of newcomers, even though the split is not emphasized. The superfluous is itself divided into two types that may overlap but still remain for the most part distinct: the simple production of luxury goods and the production of images. Plato elaborates further on two kinds of arts, those of acquisition and those of imitation. The new workers of the city are split accordingly into two groups, acquisitive men (the hunters who provide for superfluous needs as such) and imitators who introduce into the realm of the superfluous a production of a wholly distinctive sort, one that reproduces and falsifies the image of the necessary.

Now we are in a position to see injustice enter the picture, but not from the quarter we might have expected. Luxury is not what corrupts the city. It is of little import that the joiners embellish banquet couches instead of honing their tools, or that the smith turns himself into a carver. And while it is quite true that the taste for luxury, especially when such goods become scarce, impels people to invasion and war, a life of softness finds in war its antidote. War is a professional trade, so one need train warriors to do one thing, and one thing only; like good guard dogs, they must bite the enemy, but only the enemy. Gymnastics and music will train them to be hard on their adversary and amiable toward the city.

But here is where the imitators come in. They are, indeed, good at music. With the poet's lyre they soften the hearts of the future warriors; with their fables about violent and deceitful gods they introduce immoderation. And behind their invitation to imitate bad actions is the principle of evil itself, the invitation to imitate in general—the power of the double, of representing anything whatsoever or being anyone whosoever. In vain does Socrates attempt to protect himself against it by choosing to see in imitation once again the division of labor: he asserts that human nature is "minted in such small coinage" that one can imitate only one thing at a time.[6] Unfortunately, the new machines of the theater are there to belie his nice optimism. On the stage, before a public that is no longer one of warriors but of artisans, these machines tear to pieces his fine principle of the functionality of the division of labor in producing the whole of creation. It is an excess far more dangerous than that of luxury, since luxury adds new specialties to the division of labor and corrupts only those with the means to afford it. The art of the total imitator, on the other hand, implicates all members of a society by putting in question their very simplicity, i.e. their adherence to their respective functions.

Note the crossplay [*jeu croisé*]: it is in the relationship of the chief hunter to the imitator that the simplicity of the artisan will receive new meanings. As opposed to the imitator, the artisan could be given immediately the positive role of counterexample. The artisan shows what the simple artist must do in order to occupy his place. He is the one who knows how to make useful objects of which the painter produces the inconsistent copy. Smith or saddler, he places himself in the service of the horseman in making the horse's bit and bridle, subordinating his technical knowledge to the warrior science of ends. If he is a joiner, he makes beds, patterning them on an idea of a bed. Not the Idea of the bed, or the real Bed of which God alone is the author. But those who use his services do not demand that much. It suffices that the artisan's know-how be guided by an idea in keeping with the purpose of the object.

The painter knows nothing about all that—nothing about horsemanship, saddlery, or joinery. Of the artisan's technique he retains only what is needed to imitate the appearance of his objects. He will make couches, saddles, and bits without knowing anything about them, and in a burst of inspiration he will leap over the barrier separating the work of art from the work of nature. He will make horses, horsemen, and even—God knows for what use—shoemakers and carpenters. He will imitate God. He will paint plants and animals, earth and sky, Olympus and Hades. And on the theater stage the imitator will mix everything into a cacophony: works of nature and those of artisans; thunder, wind, and hail; axles and pulleys; flutes and trumpets; and dogs, sheep, and birds.[7]

By contrast with this forger, the image of the artisan can be recommended to the warrior for several reasons. The artisan is a man with know-how dedicated to the service of others, but he is also in possession of health, the virtue specific to the first city. He will teach the warrior to dispense with the maladies and medicines of indolence, for in a well-constituted state each has his own specific task that no one else can carry out for him: no one "has leisure to be sick and nurse himself all his days." But in our poorly made city only the artisan offers verification of this principle. Because the carpenter feels "that he has no leisure (scholē) to be sick, and that such a life of preoccupation with his illness and neglect of his work is not worth living," whenever he does become ill he asks "his physician to give him a drug that will operate as an emetic on the disease, or to get rid of it by purging or the use of cautery or the knife."[8] From this virtue of necessity warriors will be able to learn the necessity of virtue, the full employment of their time.

The worker is the master of a virtue he thus is not at liberty to choose. The lesson is far from being lost, and even today it adorns the frontispiece of all our chapels. But artisans also have less constraining virtues to offer the defenders of the city. To train warriors in the art of combat, the model that suggests itself is the apprenticeship that governs the acquisition of a trade, the anticipation of the gestures and disciplines of a craft. That is how the sons of potters learn their trade, and that is how the élite warriors of the future will learn theirs.[9] Candidates for political posts— Alcibiades, for example, or Callicles—would be well advised to do the same.

PROFESSIONAL QUALIFICATION:
DICE PLAYERS AND EXTERMINATORS

But if the warriors are to train in the manner of artisans, it is impossible that artisans could look to the warriors for any model. The shoemaker cannot be a warrior. This point, in a sense, does not need to be proven. If war is a specific occupation, it is a matter for professionals. The shoemaker will not bear arms for the same reasons that keep him from the weaver's shuttle, the farmer's plow, and the tools of the building trade: so that shoemaking will be practiced in keeping with the rules of its art. But time marks a slight inflection, for we no longer are dealing here with the mere virtuality of leisure or the right moment, of scholē or kairos, but much more now with the time devoted to professional training. It is not enough to make lots of shoes; they must also be made well.

And the apprenticeship that perfects the artisan is truly unending, which is why it was necessary to assign only one occupation to each—the one "for which he was fit and suited by nature and at which he was to work all his days to the exclusion of others, not letting slip the right moments for doing the work well." How could the demanding business of shoemaking ever leave time enough for learning the business of arms when "no one could become an expert player of draughts or dice who did not practice the game exclusively from childhood but played it only as a pastime"?[10]

The argument undergoes a change here. If the shoemaker cannot be a good warrior, the reason is, first of all, that he cannot be a good dice player. This is not as offbase as it seems. For the dice player shares with the warrior the same privilege that is denied to both the carpenter and the shoemaker: he is a child of superfluity. He reminds us that the warrior has become necessary only because of the taste for luxury and hunting, and he shows us at the same time the logic of this development. The hunt for the superfluous, the transgression of the principle of sticking only to one's own occupation, was needed to make some occupations in the city more important than others, to make justice possible thereby as a hierarchy of functions and virtues. The dice player's superfluousness corresponds to the equivocal necessity of the fifth man and gives the shoemaker's full employment its meaning. The shoemaker is now above all the man who *cannot* be a warrior. The player's move has turned up the deal [*a retourné la donne*] as the division of labor no longer reflects clearly the relationship of usefulness to professionalism. The egalitarian necessity that each keep to "his own occupation" has discreetly tipped over into a hierarchy that now can be only a hierarchy of *natures*. This is what the draughts player recalls here and in the *Statesman*, that the functional distribution of *aptitudes* is also a distribution of *gifts* of unequal value. How could the masses govern their common affairs when so few champion draughts players come from their ranks?[11]

Through this interplay of time and status, the relationship of justice to nature has come into question, and it is this "conformity to nature" that must be examined. We first ran into it as an enigma: how could one recognize justice? Now we must take things from the opposite end. It is in the realm of the superfluous that one can distinguish among and hierarchize natures, since the order of necessary occupations and adequate skills [techniques] can never, on its own, create separate ranks. In the democratic city of the honest sophist Protagoras, the trades belong to specialists and the virtue of the common good to the assembly of all the citizens. Egalitarian rhetoric will incessantly hammer home the notion that the smith is as indispensable to the warrior as the warrior is to the smith. Moreover, utility lends itself only to ambiguous superiorities. Though the general saves the city, it remains an open question whether the city was in fact worth saving. The conquering soldier may well be like the able-bodied seaman who brought men safely through the storms he would have done better to abandon to the justice of the waves.[12] For the elevation of the warrior another principle is needed, a principle known only to philosophers. One philosopher, the biggest homebody of them all, will say later on that "war has something sublime about it."[13] Is this because pure thought better finds its image in the slashing sword or purifying fire? Hardly. The dialectic method claims to be impervious to the social dignity of its models: "When it makes comparisons . . . it does not regard the art of the general as a more brilliant illustration of the art of hunting than the art of the exterminator. Most of the time it finds the first example simply more inflated."[14] The superiority does not lie in the art of war but in the nature of the warrior, which is homonymous with the nature of the malady: the warrior is the man of temperamental humor, of inflated mood. His primary superiority over the artisan or the exterminator is that of humor over health.

That must be our starting point. The warrior is the man who could do something else, such as bite his friend. He is the man who requires a special education, the judicious dose of gymnastics and music that the educator-magistrate can provide only if he is a philosopher. The warrior's superiority lies not in his occupation but in his nature insofar as the formation of his nature is the specific task, the masterwork, of the philosopher-king. The virtue of the warrior also makes the philosopher necessary.

THE PHILOSOPHER IN THE WORKSHOP

Between the philosopher who trains the warrior and the artisan who offers him models of apprenticeship, another cross-relation establishes itself—a skewed one. The philosopher, too, is a child of luxury. He is at the end of the thread drawn out by Glaucon's intervention, at the peak of the new necessity governed by excess. A new function is needed, that of the rulers, to guard the guardians of the inflamed city. And a new nature is needed to optimize the exercise of that new function, the nature of philosophers.

We are talking about *true* philosophers, of course: breeders of herds, not hunters of livestock or bounty; laborers in truth, not artisans of appearance. To mark themselves off from their imitators—rhetoricians or sophists, false politicians or false experts—philosophers, too, will have to learn from true artists. They will refer themselves constantly to the expert gestures and verifiable results of artisanal practice. For want of a divine shepherd, the weaver-king of the *Statesman* will work to plait into harmony the unequal and diversely colored threads of the temperaments that are to make up the fabric of society. The philosopher-guardian of book IV of the *Republic* will prepare human souls for instruction the way dyers prepare fabrics that are to be given an indelible tint. The dialectician of the *Sophist*, in attempting to define philosophical purification, will not hesitate to dwell on the operations of carders, tanners, and fullers, for "the dialectic art never considers whether the benefit to be derived from the purge is greater or lesser than that to be derived from the sponge, and is not more interested in the one than in the other. It seeks to know what is and what is not kindred in all the arts in order to gain understanding and discernment, and it honors them all alike in that respect."[15]

But the dialectician's familiarity with textile workers has a very specific function, which is to make him recall that in the weaver's trade the woof of the governed is not as important as the warp of the governors. It is no accident that among the basic arts the dialectician chose that of the weaver and his helpmates, for their arts bring together the threads of the social order, even as the art of dyeing gives just the right tint to the soul of the warriors. Even more importantly, these are all arts of distinction, sorting, selection. If the philosopher puts the text of any discourse to the test of the carder's brush or the fuller's tub, he does so to distinguish the purification of thought from all the sorting and scouring of artisan trades. As concerns purification, he cares not at all which name fits it best; it suffices to know how to separate out justice from hygiene, what purifies the soul from what cleanses everything else: "The art of dialectic is in no wise particular about fine words, if it may be only allowed to have a general name for all other purifications, binding them up together and separating them from the purification of the soul or mind. For this is the purification at which it wants to arrive, and this we should understand to be its aim."[16]

So the comparison of practices is intended only to mark the incomparable character of natures. And the test of truth, the touchstone provided by artisanal work, serves that purpose foremost. At first sight the shoemaker and the fuller are the philosopher's helpers in his search for the simulacra of poetic, rhetorical, and sophist discourse. One need only translate their propositions into the idiom of shoemaking to puncture their inflated bombast. Callicles claims that the best and the strongest should have more than others. Does that mean that shoemakers will have more and larger shoes than their inexpert customers? The ridiculousness of the application suffices to show that the words of the rhetorician ("the best," "the strongest," "have more") are nothing but the simulacra of ideas. But Callicles is not wrong in expressing annoyance and demanding that Socrates compare comparable things instead of mixing together shoemaking and philosophy.[17] For the comparison constantly presupposes what it claims to prove, positing the kinship of all the *arts* so that it may better affirm the separation between what depends on the arts and what evades their technique: philosophical breeding. To suit the needs of his case, the philosopher gives the artisan a doubly illusory positivity. In the first place, the proof of truth is always a proof by way of the ridiculous, the stigmatizing of baseness. When Socrates denounces the painter or the sophist, the artisan sinks into the "positivity" of an exterminator. And he does it to show Callicles that his grand aristocratic thinking is at bottom only a philosophy of simple resourcefulness, a shoemaker's kind of thinking. Secondly, when the philosopher denounces imitators, he is denouncing technique in general. The painter's major fault is not making falsely what the artisan makes in truth; it is using an artisanal technique to *counterfeit* the work of the deity, which is always a living work and hence unique. God does not engage in mass production, and neither does the philosopher. Through the ridiculousness of comparisons with the shoemaker, the philosopher denounces the sophist's discourse as a *fabricated* discourse that counterfeits the living discourse of his own science.

In denouncing imitators, the philosopher sends the "good" artisan back to the truth of his specific technique. Left to itself, separated from the science of ends that is exterior to it, all technology is mere counterfeiting. The opposition of the useful demiurge to the imitator is illusory. All technology is ignorance of its own end, and thus—as a counterfeit, a lie—it is the power to do anything whatsoever. The work of the poet, painter, or rhetorician radicalizes this potentiality in the deliberate production of appearances. If it is possible for the artisan to be opposed to them, it is not as a technician of the useful but solely as a monotechnician, the producer of one thing and one thing only.

The specialization of the artisan thus becomes the simple prohibition against doing anything else, though precisely that capacity is lodged within technology as such. This "polytechnic" counterfeiting inherent to technology must be compensated for constantly by a *social* rule: the artisan-fabricator is the man to whom play, lying, and appearance are forbidden. The painter and the sophist are not false artisans; they are artisans who transgress the rule fixing their status.

Here it is no longer a question of lack of time or continuing vocational training. The division of labor could now be expressed in the form of a principle that is wholly indifferent to the contingencies of production: the artisan is the technician who has no right to lie. Plato quotes two verses from Homer to make the point: "If the ruler catches anybody else lying in the city, any of the craftsmen, 'whether a prophet or healer of sickness or joiner of timbers,' he will chastise him for introducing a practice as subversive and destructive of a state as it is of a ship."[18]

THE THREE METALS: NATURE'S LIE

It is not that lying is an evil in itself, any more than luxury or play is; the point is that it must be reserved. In the city where superfluousness has been introduced, hierarchy first appears as knowledge and regulation of the simulacrum. The science of order is a science of the lie. It assumes that the order of the simulacrum is radically separate from the order of technology. The absolute simplicity of artisans, their absolute lack of leisure, and the endless process of perfecting their trade must be postulated to exorcize the Promethean threat: not that workers would become, or seek to become, gods, but that they would set in motion a city of productive work that is at the same time a city of absolute artifice, a city producing its discourses as its tools—in a word, a democracy or, what comes down to the same thing for Plato, a technocracy where the power of the tradesmen and that of the people are equivalent.

The superfluousness of luxury, war, and philosophy guards against this danger as it contains the excess latent in the alleged simplicity of technology. As against the potential complicity of useful work with the untruth of technology, justice presupposes a different alliance, a different alloy of the absolute simplicity of nature and the declared arbitrariness of lying. The philosopher will be a specialist in nature and the lie. To be precise, he will be an engineer of souls.

His function is, first of all, to reply to the enigma of nature, which shifted its place with the arrival of the warrior on the scene. Beyond the division of tasks, the warrior is there to exemplify the difference in nature that values the artisan least. But this difference is established solely by the selection of the philosopher-guardian. In other words, it is selection that determines nature. The difference in nature is not the irrational that thought runs up against, nor is it the "ideology" where the history of social oppression conceals itself. Nothing in fact is concealed. Plato says openly that nature must be an object of decree in order to become an object of education. It is the presupposition laid down by the selecter-breeder of souls to begin the work of forming natures. Nature is *a story* declared to be such. As the only one who knows the relationship between suitable means and desirable ends, the engineer of souls is the only one who has the power and the knowledge to lie—the lie that is an imitation of truth, the good lie; the lie that suffices to establish an order safe from the true lie [*du véritable mensonge*], the technological ignorance of principles and ends.

And so the engineer of souls will inaugurate the necessary and sufficient lie, the axiom or undemonstrable principle that bears a resemblance to the end of his work, nature. Through a counter-technology, he will find a means (*mēchanē*) to make the city believe a noble lie—which is to say, a lie about nobility, a genealogy in the manner of the poets, a "Phoenician" tale that took place elsewhere a long time ago and that need not be justified, only told, need not be believed, only accepted. A tale of men who could be persuaded that the education they had received was merely a dream, that in reality they sprang forth from the earth fully armed and prepared for their respective functions. Such is the myth or lie of the three metals: "While all of you in the city are brothers, we will say in our tale, the deity who fashioned you mixed gold in the makeup of those fit for rule, for which reason they are the most precious. In that of the defenders he mixed silver, and iron and brass in the makeup of the plowman and other craftsmen."[19]

THE TWO MONEYS: COMMUNISM IN POWER

We know that Plato did not invent the theme of the three orders of human beings made up of gold, silver, and brass. What interests us here is the particular details he gives it.

First of all, the myth is not exactly anti-egalitarian. It does not seek to consecrate an immemorial order. The philosopher-molder is egalitarian in his own way. Once the educational machine is in operation, it should handle the necessary declassifying and re-classifying for each generation. Most of the time, the brother citizens in each category will have children like themselves. But it might happen that warriors and educators produce children with souls of iron, and these must be dropped down pitilessly into the class of plowmen and artisans. By the same token, the sons of plowmen or artisans who display some gold or silver in their soul will have to be elevated to the class of warriors or guardians. This is a myth of education more than a myth of hierarchy. A meritoc-racy, then? Its application nevertheless may pose some problems. For it is easy enough to see how the apprentice warrior could reveal the soul of a shoemaker, but not as easy to see where and how the apprentice shoemaker will have the leisure to reveal his warrior-soul or guardian-soul. There is, apparently, no provision for sending the children of the laboring classes to school. The egalitarianism is in danger of operating in one direction only—downward. The main concern seems to be preventing iron and brass from corrupting the city's élite.

So it is an anti-oligarchic rule rather than an anti-populist one. The main thing is to separate the gold of power from the metal of trade. Workers grown newly rich should not be able to convert their capital into power, and the guardians and warriors should not be able to make money from their functions. As always, it is a cross-relation. The guardians are the ones being addressed: they must be preserved from the seductions of wealth; they must be paid in symbolic money of a kind scarce enough to turn them away from hard cash, to persuade them to leave to the men of iron and brass the petty advantages of ownership. In short, the chief aim of the myth is to get magistrates and warriors to accept the principle of the non-ownership of goods, which alone can prevent the corruption of the State: "Gold and silver, we will tell them, they have of the divine sort from the gods always in their souls. They have no need of the metals of men, and it is impious to contaminate their possession of divine gold with the possession of mortal gold."[20]

As a result, they will not even handle gold or silver, or enter a house that harbors these metals, or wear them, or drink from cups made of them. But this prohibition must be understood correctly, for the danger here is not the gilded enervation of luxury but the brass austerity of thrift: "But whenever they acquire land for themselves and houses and coin, they will be householders and farmers instead of guardians. They will become despots and enemies of the rest of the city instead of being their defenders, hating and being hated, plotting and being plotted against."[21]

A complex hierarchy of metals both precious and base, of realities and symbols, of possession and what follows from it. The philosopher does not say here that the occupation of manual workers is too lowly to form the soul of a citizen. He simply says that the possession of exploitable goods is incompatible with the defense of the city. The object of the prohibition is the oligarch, the capitalist, rather than the manual laborer (for example, the smith who also profits from a little joinery enterprise on the side).[22]

But the distinguo is the most malicious of tricks. It gives us to understand that what is specific to souls of iron is the thinking only of money, of hard cash, to the exclusion of all symbolic honors. The oligarch, on the other hand, is no conman: "He is thrifty and hardworking. He satisfies only his necessary needs, wasting no expense on all his other needs and repressing them as vain and unprofitable."[23] The oligarch is the good worker, the model worker for whom the modern age will create the savings bank. And that is why he is contemptible: not because he is an industrious body opposed to the leisures of the soul, but because he is the man of material goods, of commodities, whose function degrades body and soul together. The realm of labor can be only the realm of egotism and the war of all against all. Excluded from leisure and dedicated to the ceaseless fabrication of commodities, the worker is condemned to the shameful privileges of thrift, accumulation, and wealth. He is always a potential capitalist and, for this reason, the philosopher can stigmatize him while reserving to highborn souls the symbolic currency of honor and power associated with the rulers' lack of ownership.

In short, to say that the worker cannot be a guardian or warrior is simply to say that he is unworthy of being a communist. His unworthiness derives from the fact that he always possesses some property. Work, in and of itself, is property, and trade is discord. Communist workers of our own nineteenth century, in seeking to realize the city of equal laborers, would experience more or less naïvely or perversely that communism is a system conceived only for the élite guardians of the city. Work and community are strictly antagonistic. Communism is not the fraternity of the classless society but the discipline of a class domination ideally removed from the logic of work and property. At bottom, the squaring of the philosophical circle can be formulated simply. For the city to be well organized, it is necessary and sufficient that the authority of the dominators over the dominated be the authority of communists over capitalists. The Columbus's Egg of the just city: the workers, soldiers, and philosophers of communism have not yet departed from it.[24]

ANOTHER BANQUET, ANOTHER LIE

Let's not feel too sorry, however, for these workers condemned to labor without leisure. They might well have won the privilege, over their incomparable guardians, of a certain right to idleness. For now one fact must be admitted: some functions are more indispensable, some qualifications more serious than others. Thus the guardians will bear the cost of their elevation, and their lives certainly will be poor in gilded enjoyments. On the other hand, they are slated less than any of the others for an individual happiness that is not the goal of the happy city: "We could clothe the plowmen in robes of state, deck them out in gold, and let them cultivate the soil at their pleasure; and we could let the potters recline on couches, let them feast and pass the cup around before the fire, with their wheel beside them, free to work when they felt like it. . . . But urge us not to do this, since, if we yield, the plowman will no longer be a plowman, the potter a potter, nor will any other of the types that constitute a state keep its form."[25]

The danger is clearly delimited and lies in disguise rather than idleness. The state does not need so many pieces of pottery; it merely needs to know how to recognize potters. And how is one to recognize potters if they are not at their wheel? It may suffice, indeed, for them simply to appear to be at work. The danger is not a drop in production but a lack of identity, for while all forms of production may be equivalent, the same is not true of identities. As we are told almost immediately, the issue is quite serious in the case of the guardians: "For cobblers who deteriorate, are spoiled, and pretend to be the workmen they are not, are no great danger to a state. But guardians of the law and of the city who are not what they pretend to be, who are guardians only in appearance, utterly destroy the entire state, I would have you note."[26]

With this right to idleness the artisan has also rewon a right to lie. But to one lie, and not to any lie whatsoever. Only a lie having to do with the specialty that alone defines his being. The shoemaker truly must be nothing other than a shoemaker, but he is not obliged to be one truly.

We already had suspected a bit of exaggeration. Were so many shoes really needed, and so much time to learn how to make them? Now we know that a true shoemaker is not someone who makes good shoes but someone who *does not pass himself off as anything other than a shoemaker*. Indeed, ignorance of the craft may be even better than expertise in it to guarantee the *monotechnics* that alone constitutes the virtue of the artisan. Idleness and incompetence are the dispositions best suited to ensuring what is singularly important, that the artisan does only one thing, the thing that marks him off and serves to put him in his place. Because a person who is expert at making his shoes could also be expert at weaving his cloak, plaiting his belt, and engraving his ring. And why wouldn't he also turn himself into a manufacturer of discourse and a merchant of wisdom? Such a character actually exists—Hippias the sophist, who was seen arriving in Olympia with nothing on his back that was not the work of his own hands. He also brought with him his poems, epics, tragedies, dithyrambs, and his scientific knowledge relating to the true and the beautiful, music, grammar, and mnemonics. Even before the city, perhaps, the philosopher should be protected from this crafty artist who can carry over to every other matter the shoemaker's ways of doing and thinking.[27]

God preserve the philosopher from these too skillful artisans! In all cases it is necessary to limit the pretensions to perfection of any variety of craft [art de faire]. It is also necessary to place philosophy outside and above every one of these. The *Protagoras* spells out the problem well, for if virtue is taught in the same way as shoemaking, then shoemakers are kings in the city and philosophers are useless. The rights of philosophic virtue depend upon their strict separation from the virtue of shoemaking, and the separation of the latter from the quality of shoes.

That is why the test of artisanal truth can be reversed on occasion. Socrates asks Thrasymachus whether artisans mistake themselves on the subject of their art. No, replies Thrasymachus; they are precisely artisans because of their competence. A shoemaker who does not know how to make shoes proves nothing against the art of shoemaking. He merely proves that he *is not* a shoemaker. Only he who can practice an art merits the name of artisan.

His reply makes good sense, but that is precisely the sort of good sense that must be rejected in order to destroy the pretensions of artisans. A shoemaker is simply a man who is forbidden to engage in any activity other than shoemaking. Starting from that premise, the philosopher can play a double game: he can argue for the competence of the artisan as a specialist, or for an incompetence that verifies the insignificance of all such specialities.

The Virtue of the Artisan

Here again the squaring of the circle is simple: the artisan must have a virtue that is not truly one. Each category must have its own specific virtue so that the city may be constituted and justice in it be defined. The artisan, too, must have his virtue, but it cannot be the virtue of his art. Art and nature are antinomic. An artisan will never be in his place if it is art that defines nature. For him we must find a *specific* virtue that is actually *alien*, a positivity that is a simulacrum.

Once again Aristotle states the problem frankly. He rejects the idea of a purely functional division of tasks. For him the difference between functions and natures is primary; those who have nothing better to offer us than the raw use of their body are condemned by nature to slavery. That spotlights a basic question: how are we to define the virtue of the inferior person in general, and of the artisan in particular? The inequality of virtues establishes the hierarchy, but it also makes its exercise hazardous. For the virtue of command to be implemented, for example, obedience must be a virtue, too, and not merely a relationship of dependence. But the one who executes commands must have just the right amount of virtue to obey his orders; if he had more virtue than was necessary, he might imperil the hierarchy of natures.

How is this balance to be achieved? In the slave's case this is not too difficult since it is up to his master to inculcate in him the modicum of virtue needed to carry out his servile tasks conscientiously. But the "free" artisan poses a very different problem. He is not a free man sharing in the virtue of the city, but neither is he a slave whose virtues derive from the diligent administration of the domestic economy. A false free man and part-time slave, the artisan belongs neither to his trade nor to the one who assigns him work. He cannot derive virtue from his own sphere or from a relationship of dependence.[28] But one who has no virtue has no nature. The artisan is not simply a lowly being to be kept away from the government of the city. Properly speaking, he is an impossible being, an unthinkable nature. The free worker of the market economy is a denatured being, an accident of history. Neither included nor excluded, this hybridity is an unpardonable disturbance for the city. And the unworthiness of chrematistics, i.e. of political economy as such, is linked not only to the traffic in money but also to the promotion of this hybrid-being devoid equally of economic and political virtue.[29]

Plato tries to circumvent this unthinkability of the artisan through the interplay of a simulated nature and a fictitious virtue. Each order must be defined by its own virtue, but only a government of philosopher-guardians can give the first order its own virtue, wisdom (sophia). The warrior's virtue, which is rightly applied courage, is a kind of dyeing, of pedagogically inculcating the right opinion as to what he should and should not fear.[30] The artisan, however, is not made of a material that the philosopher could dress and dye. There is no virtue or education that belongs to the laboring people. Their "own" virtue—moderation, common "wisdom" (sōphrosunē)—must come to them from outside. There is no "self-mastery" that the inferior can claim as its own virtue since, by definition, mastery presupposes a superior. The "wisdom" of the people cannot be either a "good sense" or a "common sense" shared equally by the most educated and the least educated; nor can it be a quality specific to inferiors. It is simply the submission of the lowest part of the state to its noblest part. This wisdom of the artisan, which exists outside him, is simply the order of the state that puts him in his place.

THE PARADOX OF JUSTICE

Each person now has his virtue. Justice should not be very far away. Socrates makes a new observation once more based on experience: we often waste a lot of time looking for something that is right under our nose or within arm's reach. He and his interlocutors have been searching for justice, but this is what they have been telling us from the very beginning—that each person should do his own business (ta heautou prattein) and nothing else (mēden allo). Justice is wisdom governing the state, courage inspiring the warriors, and "moderation" (sōphrosunē) reigning among the body of artisans. Indeed, the latter provide us with the model. The image of justice is the division of labor that already organizes the healthy city: "It is right for the shoemaker by nature to make shoes and occupy himself with nothing else, for the carpenter to practice carpentry, and similarly all others."[31]

"Clearly," replies Glaucon. Strange, though, that the false virtue of the inferior should serve as the model of justice in the perfect city. The virtue of "moderation" means simply that the artisan stays in his place, even if it means cheating on his function. And the justice that should harmonize the virtues proper to each order simply reiterates the supposed functionality of this relation of dependence. The justice of the well-constituted state would be analogous to the health of the state fit for pigs if this latter were not already elevated by an order of dependence that is also an order of fiction.

This fiction, for all that, maintains a rather equivocal relationship with common wisdom. Shouldn't each do his own bit of business and not concern himself with that of the others? Isn't that the healthy morality of Cephalus, the merchant of the Piraeus and oligarch and father of the democrats Polemarchus and Lysias, who welcomes Socrates and his aristocratic companions?

Moreover, it is a definition we have heard elsewhere, in another family circle. Socrates is questioning the young Charmides, Plato's future uncle. He asks the wise adolescent to define wisdom—not sophia but the simple sōphrosunē of decent folk. Prompted by his cousin, the future tyrant Critias, Charmides offers his answer: wisdom means that each man does "his own business." Bizarrely,

Socrates finds this definition inconsistent and even ridiculous, for in that case artisans could not be wise since they do business for others. The sophism is obvious, and Critias easily unmasks it: it is simply a matter of not playing games with the word "do." The shoemaker does *his own business* well when he makes shoes for his customers. And the practice of virtue is not to be confused or equated with the making of shoes. Here Critias is a better Platonist than Socrates.

This is a reversal of roles appropriate to a dialogue that is paradoxical in all respects. Critias, the most discredited of the Thirty Tyrants who oppressed the city under the aegis of Sparta, steps in before Socrates to reflect on the "Know Thyself" of the Delphic Oracle. And he insists on what divides this divine invocation from the counsels of prudence and temperance that common sense and vulgar economy have carved alongside it: "Nothing to Excess" and "Be Temperate."[32]

Socrates, on the other hand, shrinks from no sophism to refute Critias's quasi-Platonic theses. It is as if Plato were trying to contrast two genealogies of Socratic thought, a Socrates responding to the exigencies of Critias's aristocratic distinction, and a Socrates reducing the divine invocation to the recipes of popular wisdom. Where Xenophon tells us that the real Critias would have forbidden Socrates to concern himself at all with carpenters and shoemakers, his double in the *Critias* indicts a caricature of Socrates, the plebeian moralist of Plato's competitors for the Socratic heritage, the cynics.

But the game undergoes a reversal here because this caricature of Socratic thought also serves to mark the difference between Platonic justice and the "wisdom" of the tyrant Critias, who wants to separate philosophic and political virtue from artisanal techniques and forms of popular wisdom. But he cannot ground his distinction, and his inability to do so surfaces clearly when he tries to propose a higher definition of *sōphrosunē*: it is, he says, the science of science and ignorance in all things. Socrates wonders what sort of city government could result from such a science: "Then each action will be done according to the arts or sciences, and no one professing to be a pilot when he is not, no physician or general or anyone else pretending to know matters of which he is ignorant, will deceive or delude us. Our health will be improved; our safety at sea and in battle will be assured; our clothes and shoes, and all other instruments and implements, will be skillfully made, because the workmen will be good and true."[33]

But is this city of science really the city of happiness? Weren't they too hasty in agreeing that it would be good for all if "each does the task he knows and leaves the tasks he does not know to competent people"? It is certainly true that the citizens of this state would live better according to science, but that does not mean they would live *well* and be happy. Missing from this panoply of sciences is the only one that counts in this matter, the science of good and evil.

Two things about Socrates's argument strike us. Why, despite Critias's protests, is he always so eager to reduce his "science" to technical competence alone? And what role does happiness play here? What if the technicians in Critias's city do not possess the science of happiness? But Plato himself does not even risk promising his soldiers and plowmen any happiness other than that of living in a city where everyone remains in his own place. In such a city, can the "science of good and evil" be anything other than the science of ends that is identical with the science of truth and error? So where is the difference between the technocracy of the tyrant Critias and the aristocracy of Plato's justice? Perhaps it may lie in the paradoxical fact that in the Platonic city it is not necessary for the specialists to be competent—or, if you wish, that their competence has *nothing to do* with truth and can even be a lie in order to preserve the only important thing: the "nothing else," the virtue of those to whom the philosophic lie concerning nature has bequeathed iron as their portion. Missing in Critias's science and city is this Platonic *incompetence*, which is the other side of the philosophic lie that anticipates truth and reserves the place of science. The science of good and evil comes by way of the science of truth and lying. The latter must first effect the apportionment [*le partage*], reserving room for the royal science of the idea of the good. Only lying permits a radical separation of the royal science from the division of competences.

WOMEN, BALD MEN, AND SHOEMAKERS

Hence the first definition of the division of labor, the adaptation of natural dispositions to indispensable functions, will appear as a double lie—about nature and function alike.

One who is a shoemaker by *nature* should make shoes and nothing else. But we still do not know by which signs we are to recognize the specific aptitude for shoemaking. Moreover, how are we to conceive the precise relationship between natural aptitudes and social functions when the new order comes to overturn the least disputed model of this relationship, the sexual division of aptitudes and tasks? Nature is there to show the philosopher that female dogs are just as apt as male dogs for hunting and tending flocks. Why should it be different with human beings? Why shouldn't women be trained in the same gymnastics and music that prepare warriors? Aside from coarse jokes about nudity, what arguments do the scoffers have to offer? To remark upon difference in aptitudes is to say nothing precise. One must know what sort of difference is relevant for a given function in defining an aptitude or an inaptitude. It certainly would be ridiculous to bar from shoemaking men who have hair on their heads on the grounds that baldheaded men practice the trade. And it would be equally unreasonable to reserve the profession of arms to one sex and forbid it to the other on the grounds that men beget children whereas women bear them.[34]

Élite women, then, will integrate the corps of warriors and leave us with our uncertainty. Being a man or woman is of no more consequence than being bald or hairy. All that matters are differences "relating to occupations," but what these are remains obscure. How are we ever to recognize the differences between a shoemaker-nature and a carpenter-nature, differences that introduce an exclusivity implied not even in the most natural and incontestable of differences, the difference between the sexes?

All that remains for us to identify the worker is his work alone. Not his production, as we now know, but the fact that he is not to do "anything else" than his trade. And even that is no longer necessary: "Do you think it would greatly injure a state if a carpenter were to undertake to do the work of a shoemaker, or a shoemaker the work of a carpenter, or if they were to exchange their tools and their wages, or if one of them were to get it into his head to do both trades at once, or if all trades were exchanged that way?"[35]

"Not much," replies Glaucon. That the shoemaker remains a shoemaker or the carpenter a carpenter is not the important thing. All considerations of nature and social utility aside, they can exchange their trades, and even indulge in the forbidden activity of doing two things at once, without doing any great harm to the state. Why? Because *these* two things are completely equivalent. The differentiation of useful works and aptitudes is reducible to the equivalence of wage-earning labors. The shoemaker-nature is as interchangeable with the carpenter-nature as commodities are with gold and gold with commodities. It is necessary that their virtue should not lack *anything else* than this universal equivalence that defines the unworthiness of the artisan. The only danger lies in confusing orders. Between artisan and warrior, or between warrior and ruler, there can be no exchange of place and function; neither can two things be done at the same time without bringing doom to the city.

The barrier of orders is the barrier of the lie. Nothing remains of the fine functionality of the division of labor. Each was obliged to do the one task for which nature destined him. But the function is an illusion just as nature is. All that remains is the prohibition. The artisan in his place is someone who, in general, does nothing but accredit, even at the cost of lying, the declared lie that puts him in his place.

2 :: The Order of Discourse

THE PHILOSOPHER'S CITY has only one real enemy, a character held in low regard: the parvenu. That is another reason why the philosopher is the best ruler, for he is the only one for whom the exercise of power is not a promotion. Even in the best of cases, the dyeing of the warriors does not compare with contemplating essences.

Still, it is necessary to preserve the radical purity of philosophy from all forms of corruption and counterfeit, since parvenus prowl around the philosopher, too. Worse still, perversion inheres in duality and the philosopher-guardian is necessarily a double being. The contemplation of essences and the guidance of the human herd do not let themselves be reduced to a single occupation.

One can distinguish, of course, between a time for contemplating the essence of the true and a time for applying it to the government of the city. But the question of application is more complicated since the philosopher cannot seek power. Others must call upon him to exercise it, and their arguments [raisons] are not exactly those of the philosopher. How will they distinguish the philosopher from his imitations? And how will the philosopher himself resist their arguments? How will the educator avoid being educated by those he should lead? How will the ship's pilot counter the oarsman's arguments, whether these be mild or violent?

The mild version concerns the corruption of the people's favorites, which is how one of Socrates's best pupils, the traitor Alcibiades, became lost. The violent concerns the "reeducation of intellectuals," which is how Alcibiades's teacher and alleged corrupter perished.

Like the two of them, the philosopher-guardian, the man who knows truth and lying, is always doubly menaced—from the side of truth, which excludes him from the city of the artisans, and from the side of lying, which includes him in it. In order to repel technological imitation [l'imitation technicienne], the ruling philosopher is obliged to become an imitator himself, and every imitator is a manufacturer, a polytechnician. To evade that destiny and maintain the simplicity of nature in ruling the city, the philosopher must separate the kind of imitation and lie specific to him from all artisanal productions. But this demonstration must always be done *a contrario*. It entails the perpetual refutation of the philosopher's living counterfeit—the artisan of lies, the intellectual jack-of-all-trades [*bricoleur*] whom the mob confusedly equates with the philosopher: the sophist. The sophist is a lie from head to foot because he, like Hippias, is an artisan from head to foot—because he has spent too much time fabricating shoes and speeches to spare a moment to learn the dialectical game of draughts in which the philosopher's superior nature is made manifest.

All the uneasiness aroused by the kinship of truth and lying is exorcized in the antagonistic figure of the sophist. The latter does not know how to lie for the very good reason that he is wholly immersed in lying, in ignorance of the truth. And he is there by reason of nature, by reason of *birth*. For the sophist is not just anyone. He is the parvenu par excellence, the man whose activity encapsulates all the features of counter-nature, the servile worker who inflates himself to the point of claiming the freedom of the born philosopher.

For it is now plainly a question of freedom and slavery, of souls and bodies that bear the marks of the one or the other. The passion of book VI of the *Republic* culminates with the description of a usurpation, a crime violating the dignity of philosophy:

> Some dwarfish people, observing that the place is unoccupied and full of fine titles and beautiful appearances, act like men who escape from their chains and take refuge in temples. They joyfully abandon their trade and plunge into philosophy, those who happen to be the most cunning in their little craft. For in comparison with the other arts, the prestige of philosophy retains a superior dignity even in its present low estate. This is the ambition and aspiration of that multitude of pretenders unfit for it by nature, whose souls are bowed and mutilated by their vulgar occupations even as their bodies are ruined by their manual arts and crafts. . . . Do you see much of a difference between these people and a newly rich tinker, a little bald-headed man who has just been freed from his shackles, has had a bath, is wearing new clothes, has got himself up as a bridegroom, and is to marry the daughter of his master who has fallen into poverty and abandonment?[1]

The subtle Adimantus will certainly not allow himself to see any difference there. And he will not return to a question that had been settled already concerning the capacities or incapacities linked to the presence or absence of hair on one's head. It had been granted that the issue is irrelevant to the craft of shoemaking. But if shoemaking is wide open to those who have hair, it does not at all follow that philosophy is open to bald-headed men. Here, as nowhere earlier, Plato deliberately piles up the physical characteristics of an inferior nature: dwarfishness, baldness, and above all the mutilation of the body and the soul by manual labor. The figure of the parvenu now takes on a new dimension. Earlier he was the highroller, the entrepreneur using his economic and social power to play a role in the city, but now he is the manual laborer as such.

Plato carefully avoided starting out from a social hierarchy of noble or lowly tasks. He expunged the aristocratic imagery of straight or stooped bodies that mark by contrast the analyses of an Aristotle or a Xenophon. But now, when the matter of the philosopher's identity is at issue, that imagery reappears in its full measure. No physical criterion was retained to exclude shoemakers from the warrior class; it sufficed to remark that war was too difficult and demanding an occupation for shoemakers to practice it in their spare moments. But when it concerns philosophy, paradoxically, these physical markings indeed appear.

The reason for this is simple enough. Philosophy cannot justify itself as a post within the division of labor; if it did so, it would fall back into the democracy of trades. Hence it must exacerbate the argument from nature, giving it the shape of a prohibition marked on bodies. It is not a question here of evoking Socrates's plebeian origins or his Silenus face, or of contrasting, as Alcibiades does in the Symposium, the coarse exterior with the precious figure within.[2] There simply are bodies that cannot accommodate philosophy—bodies marked and stigmatized by the servitude of the work *for which* they have been made.

Servitude in the strict sense. Here Plato broadcasts what he does not allow himself to say elsewhere: manual labor is a servile labor. The artisan who presumes to meddle in philosophy is more than a newly rich worker; he is a fugitive slave akin to those who take refuge in the temples. And the smith's baldness is not an accidental difference prey to a malicious sophism, the one inquiring after the number of hairs that determine whether or not one is bald. It is the tonsure of servitude, which knows nothing of the more or less.

Servitude receives here a paradoxical status with regard to all economic or social rationality. Shuttles do not require slaves. The necessity of servitude has nothing to do in this context with the division of labor. Indeed the latter can be argued for only on the grounds of the equality of functions. If servitude is now necessary, it is in order to preserve the dignity of the philosopher, who articulates a division of labor in which his own position cannot figure at all. It is for the sake of the philosopher, not the city, that one must postulate a radical break between the order of leisure and the order of servile labor.

Slavery is a metaphor, of course, but not just any metaphor. What does the philosopher complain about at the end of book VI of the *Republic?* About people attempting to flee the bonds of slavery in the temple of philosophy. But what, then, will be his concern at the start of book VII? To free people chained from birth with their backs to the light. And we know what his complaint will be then— that the inhabitants of the cave do not want to be freed and led to the abode of philosophy.

Do they desire wrongly? Or are they wrong in not desiring to be freed? The reply, of course, will be that it is not the same philosophy that is sought for or rejected in each instance. The fugitive slave is attracted by the glitter of what shines above the low wall in the cave: fine titles, beautiful forms, and new clothes. That, of course, is not the way leading up to the invisible sun of the Idea.

But if philosophy is a road and not a refuge, then the philosopher capably could guide the fugitive who is, after all, in search of different kinds of prestige from those hallowed by the voice of popular opinion. The philosopher certainly gets to go and select from the cave prisoners who ask nothing of him.

There precisely is the difference. The philosopher chooses by hand those he wants to take. The order of philosophy is the order of selection and constraint, not of vocation. The excellence of natures manifests itself here through the *askēsis* of renunciation. Warriors and guardians prove themselves worthy of their hegemony in renouncing the advantages of ownership. And if the city is obliged to give power to the philosopher, this is because he is the only one who does not desire it and exercises it only out of compulsion. The philosopher, in turn—forced to accept this violence to prove his identity—will keep from leading onto the path of philosophy those who most aspire to it. He instead will try to identify men who, in pursuit of other goals, reveal the kind of nature best suited to philosophical constraint.

In this game of "loser takes all," the surest loser is always the man about whom it will be said that he has "nothing to lose but his chains." If he gains only through exchange, it is clear that he can be motivated solely by the love of profit. It would be futile for him to protest his disdain for hard currency. In laying such heavy stress on the earnings of the worker-philosopher Hippias, Plato would have us see that the artisan has no choice about the money in which he is to be paid. He has no right to symbolic pleasures [jouissances]. Destined for the iron of work and the gold of capital, the artisan confirms in his very aspirations for philosophical prestige only the native infirmity of his body and spirit.

Even before the story of the cave shows us the difference between educated and uneducated natures, the counter-story of the fugitive slave already has done the sorting. It has separated those who should be educated from those who should not, those entitled to have access to thinking from those whose access to it necessarily would be a violation. At the very least, their access would be an adultery that can give birth strictly speaking only to bastards—the very offspring that the bald smith has in his power to give the fallen princess. "And so when men unfit for education approach philosophy and consort with her unworthily, what sort of ideas and opinions shall we say they beget? Will they not produce what may in very deed be fairly called sophisms, and nothing that is legitimate or that partakes of authentic thinking?"[3]

BASTARD THINKING

It is definitely no longer a question of labor and classes in the city, but a question of the philosophical legitimacy that defines the right to thinking. Here the discourse about birth is quite singular. In the fiction of the autochthonous city and the three metals, "birth" was avowedly an artifice. And in the story of the birth of Eros, the fraudulent coupling of Penia (poverty) and Poros (wealth) was excused in terms of the right of the indigent reflecting the beggarly nature of love. But the audacity of the smith in love with philosophy cannot be accorded any such right. It represents the absolute outrage, the primal scene of philosophical purity under siege.

The problem, however, is that this purity will never be able to prove itself except through the designation of bastardy. The dignity of philosophy comes at the price of a logic that is as absurd as it is rigorous: there are people who *are not born* for philosophy *because* the manual labor to which this birth defect has condemned them has marked their bodies and souls with an infirmity, the best proof of which is their desire to approach the philosophy of which they are not worthy.

Such is the harsh necessity of the proof *a contrario*, the scandal of a philosophical legitimacy identified with the chance of birth and established by bastardy's testimony against itself. Bastardy alone is the "cause" of the legitimacy, the ignoble cause of the noble. The birth mark indicates what is at stake. It is not simply a matter of opposing the authenticity of the highborn philosopher to sophist artifices. One must also produce a difference of bodies that cannot be reduced by any moral medicine. This bodily difference expresses something completely different from mere aristocratic disdain for the artisan. Marking the distance between justice and health, it supports philosophy's claim to be a discourse irreducible to all technologies of moral hygiene. Philosophy is not a medicine but a second birth.

Starting from this point, we can reconsider the question of the keys to this passage. Commentators have been divided in wondering whether the denunciation was directed at the cynics through the bastardy of Antisthenes (who was born of a Thracian mother) or at the sophists either through the artisanal prowess of Hippias or the woodcutter's trade attributed to Protagoras.

In a sense, there is no need to choose. Amalgamation is one of the techniques of the Platonic dialogue. The parvenu could be just as well the jack-of-all-trades Hippias, who plays at being a philosopher; or the manufacturer and democrat Anytus, the denouncer of Socrates who confuses his genius with the commerce of Hippias; or the misbegotten Antisthenes, who democratizes both Hippias's rhetoric and Socrates's virtue. But the hierarchy of urgencies determines the meaning of the amalgamation. The denunciation of the sophists in itself does not justify the physiological phantasmagoria of the text, but the opposition of bastards and legitimate children takes on its full meaning if what is at issue is a question of heritage—the heritage of Socratic thought in this instance. And here the adversary is definitely Antisthenes, the propagator of a popular Socrates who made dialectical conversation into the means of public instruction and preached everywhere a notion of virtue assimilable by the common people. This would be virtue-*askēsis*, virtue-health appropriate to a state fit only for pigs and acquired through techniques of the soul that resemble a gymnastics without music: all these signifiers are gathered together at the end of book VII. There philosophy is once more forbidden to crippled spirits and bastards who wallow like swine in a morality that rejects science—twisted souls fit for human gymnastics but not for divine music. The congenital defect of these pigs-bastards-cripples, insofar as philosophy is concerned, is always recognizable through the same touchstone: they do not clear the bar of the lie that leads to the *science* of good and evil. Like the sophist Hippias, the bastard Antisthenes reserves his hatred for the *voluntary* lie, the ruse that imitates truth. And he fails to recognize the radical lie, the lie of ignorance. But ignorance is too weak a word here: their *amathia* is a will to know nothing of science.[4]

For all we know of it, such is the Socratism of Antisthenes and the cynics, an ascetic morality cut off from initiation into science. Overturning philosophy's hierarchy of virtues, cynicism claims to give philosophy to everyone. Science must be even more on its guard against this *simplicity* than it is against sophist artifice. True simplicity is a divine privilege, a matter of initiation. Thus the wholesome and democratic simplicity of cynic virtue must be likened to sophist fraud. Or rather, both must be relegated to the vice that is the very basis of the city's perversion, the power of the people.

For this astonishing book VI also tells us that the enemy so tirelessly pursued throughout Plato's dialogues does not really exist. If it is the people who believe in the fable hawked and peddled by the parvenu Anytus—the corruption of Athens's finest young folk by the arguments of the sophists—this belief, however, is totally hypocritical. In fact, there is only one sophist and one corrupter, the people themselves who instruct the sophists when their boos and applause drown out the voice of reason in assemblies, courts, and theaters.[5] The people alone, by turning politics into an art of flattery, corrupted the souls of the tyrant Critias and the traitor Alcibiades, souls that had a gift for philosophy. Like the tyrant, the sophist is a child of democracy. And the democratic man is himself the child of oligarchy, of the kingdom of parvenus who made work and thrift the dominant virtues.

So everything fits together in the kingdom of bastardy. The detractor of wealth, Antisthenes, puts philosophy in the power of the squalling brats who make up the democratic party of the capitalist Anytus. And Anytus, on the pretext of hunting for sophists, makes himself the champion of the common people who are themselves the greatest sophists of all and the corrupters of the philosophers of the aristocracy. It is a perfect circle of antiphilosophy, against which must be drawn the circle protecting and prohibiting philosophical sanctuary.

THE PHILOSOPHER'S SLAVE

As we have already seen, this approach defines an egalitarianism of its own. It denies philosophy to the disguised slaves who actually are free artisans. But once before, already, it looked for an authentic slave belonging to the Thessalian Meno to prove that every soul contains within itself the principles of mathematical truths. By rediscovering "all on his own" the formula for the doubling of the square, Meno's slave proves two things—that science is possible, but not just any sort of science. To awaken that drowsy science, what is needed is the torpedo of dialectical provocation reserved for the elect, not the lessons of the democratic sophist Protagoras or the people's philosopher Antisthenes. The boy-slave (pais) is purely the subject of an experiment, a demonstration of paideia. Taken at this early moment when the power of free knowing is still the pure virtuality of a soul chained to ignorance, he shows how knowledge is released, and how he or anyone else could become learned if he needed to be. Once the experiment is over, he can be returned to his nothingness.[6] If, for a brief and crucial moment, this young worker could play the one chosen by the supreme science, the reason is that he is not a social subject, a personage of the republic. He has no position from which to approve or censure discourses or spectacles. And the power of intellection attributed to him could not possibly be his own. The slave who is not master of himself bears witness to a science that could not be transmitted the way properties are. He helps to hollow out the distance prohibiting any democratic teaching of virtue, any popular Socratism. There is nothing the popular philosophers could transmit to artisans; the loftiest knowledges are already present in the soul of any slave. And no educator can teach the virtue of the free man underlying the prudent action of the private individual or politician. Thus the sophist professors of virtue and Anytus, the partisan of paternal education, all can be dispatched since practical virtue is right opinion, a matter of inspiration rather than learning.

A stroke of genius. In Meno's slave Plato invented one of the most durable and formidably effective figures of our own thinking: the pure proletarian whom one can always, as need demands, oppose to the artisan or slide under his image; the man for whom the *possibility of losing his chains* exists only by philosopher's decree, who thus will never lose them except within the rules; the absolute dispossessed whose infinite possibilities should discourage the mediocre and artisanal aspirations of others; the pure autodidact whose virtual omniscience disqualifies the twaddle of workingmen's *doxa* and bars the road to autodidacticism's jacks-of-all-trades. By now they should know that all their efforts can only take them away from the knowledge that sleeps within them. Wisdom is not achieved by the self-accounting, the moral *askēsis*, that the cynic preaches to artisans. All *askēsis* is conversion, the work of the philosopher who turns the gaze of the elect to the blind spot of his knowledge.

Even before the division of the three orders, the dialogue between the philosopher and the young slave effected a first linking of the philosophical to the social order—a certain connection between the question of freedom and the question of knowledge. For there had been too much play in the knot joining the two, and we know those responsible for this looseness: the popular philosophers who are always hanging around artisans, explaining to them the necessity of being educated in the virtue that liberates. Even a certain Socrates, it is said, despite Critias.

To settle this matter between Socrates and the artisans, it takes both a young slave and Socrates himself, who is called upon to refute formally what public rumor and the competing schools attribute to him—and called upon to settle the question in the most radical way. There is no virtue that can be taught to the people, for the simple reason that virtue cannot be taught. It is a matter of nature or second nature, of gift or of dyeing. That is how the virtues of the first two classes are acquired. For Socrates the virtue of the philosopher is a divine election, an initiation for the one whom the philosopher chooses to release from his chains and whose gaze he chooses to transform. Whereas the virtue of the warriors is divine inspiration in the ordinary city, in the ideal city it is the dyeing of the philosopher—the virtue of right opinion that its possessor can neither comprehend nor transmit.

Thus the question of servitude and freedom is settled at the same time. On the one hand, there are kinds of knowledge that should be *unleashed*. On the other hand, there are the right opinions of practical life that should be *chained down* by science; otherwise, they will run away and escape *like fugitive slaves*. In other words, they will become deceptive *like the works of an artisan*—like the statues Daedalus endowed with the illusion of movement.[7]

There is neither a virtue specific to the artisan folk, nor one that could be taught to its members. There is no education of the multitude, and the artisan is always just another face in the crowd.

And so the divisions of the social order and the division of the order of discourse are brought into harmony. In the city there are three classes and no slaves. In the order of discourse there is freedom or servitude. While one discourse, in seeking freedom from its chains, can only sink down into its servility, another ensures its freedom even as it remains enchained.

Nothing else. A popular philosophy, indeed every democratic utterance, is constrained by that division. It can be only an imitation of a living discourse subjected in its fabrication to the servile technologies of writing—subjected in its reception to the law of the crowd whose suffrage is nothing more than the noise of the Many.

THE BABBLING MUTE

To make this division of discourse understandable, another tale about a philosopher-king is in order. This time it is an Egyptian tale rather than a Phoenician one. The god Theuth, master of techniques, comes to King Thamus to offer his latest invention, writing. He tells Thamus it will make the Egyptians more capable in matters of memory and science.

But the king turns the argument around. Possessing the science of ends, he sees the perversion of the medium. Writing will not improve the memory of the Egyptians; it will make them more forgetful. In place of memory, they will have to rely on external marks, and in place of science they will obtain only appearances. A doxosophy rather than a philosophy; a science of appearances, pretensions, and discords. Those who think they are truly knowledgeable will soon prove themselves "burdensome."[8]

To begin with, writing is mute discourse. Like the pictures of a painter, the "external marks" of written discourse seem to be intelligent until you ask them something. Then they reveal their true nature as simulacra. They do not know how to answer questions. Unlike living discourse, written discourse cannot "defend itself." It is content to say the very same thing over and over.

It seems quite evident that this is not simply opposing the oral to the written, but the living discourse of the dialectic method to the fabricated discourse of rhetoric. The living speech of the dialectician, who uses writing only for amusement or as an aid to memory, if at all, is opposed not only to the written treatises of the sophists, the rhetoricians, or Antisthenes, but also to their spoken discourses. For these latter, too, are made up of mute markings, fabricated discourses incapable of defending themselves when the dialectical game of draughts comes to interrupt their phrases.

But this mute discourse is also too loquacious. The text cannot defend itself but, once unleashed, can drift all over the place: "It can get into the hands not only of those who understand it, but equally of those who have no business with it; it doesn't know how to address the right people and not the wrong people."[9]

This defect seems to be contrary to the one that Plato regularly attributes to rhetoric, that it is a kind of cuisine that cares only about the satisfaction of its customers. Here the issue is more serious. This mute discourse, which knows neither its audience nor their needs, can transmit anything anywhere. It does not know to whom it is speaking, to whom it should speak, who can and cannot be admitted to a sharing [partage] of the logos. The living logos of the philosopher, the science of truth and lying, is also a science of speech and silence. It knows the right time for keeping quiet. Written discourse, on the other hand, is as incapable of keeping quiet as it is of speaking. Mute in the face of philosophers' questions, it cannot restrain itself from speaking to the uninitiated. The uncontrolled democracy of this discourse-at-liberty makes philosophy's fine titles and beautiful appearances sparkle before the eyes of our too-clever artisans. Its infirmity is bastardy. It puts the logos at the disposal of men whose work has damaged their bodies and mutilated their souls.

It would hardly do for artisans to become "burdensome." Even more importantly, one must not efface the lines separating those who are made for the banquet of discourse from those who are not. There must be some legislation on the legitimate and the illegitimate—a legislation concerning appearances that cannot be a simple opposition of the true to the false.

Indeed, it is by beginning with idols that one arrives at the Ideas, by beginning with the play of reflections that the adhesion of *doxa* to the sensible world begins to fail and one sets out on the road to the intelligible One. That is the road which must be protected. The legitimacy of pure thought passes through legislation on everything that divides into two, on everything that copies, repeats, reflects, or simulates. World of doubles, world of imitators. The world of techniques and technicians must be prevented from interfering with the play of appearances that governs the road to the Idea. There isn't a true world and another world of appearances. There are two lives, and everything must be cut into two.

This is a philosophical truth, not a social truth. The philosopher of the *Phaedrus* is not a king. He does not separate classes; he decides between modes of discourse. With respect to the kind of discourse allegedly at risk of wandering away, he shows that in fact this discourse *cannot* wander, that everything not the *askēsis* of philosophy's elect is simply immobile movement upon itself, the play of the Many with itself.

Such is the case with rhetoric, brought in here with reference to a discourse by Lysias, son of Cephalus and spokesman for the shoemakers and democracy. The point is to show that rhetoric only mirrors the relationship of the rhetorician with his public. It is certainly true that the rhetorician does not know to whom he is speaking. He is not a "psychagogue" dialectician familiar with the nature of the souls he is addressing and the means of conducting them where he wishes. But he does not need that kind of knowledge because he does not want to conduct souls. He simply wants to hold his public, and he needs to know only this about it: that it is number, the motley multitude that delights in spicy stew. It suffices to please his public, and for that it suffices merely to reflect back its pleasure. And so the logographer, the man of the written word and the people, will begin his eulogy by writing "It has pleased the people . . ."[10] A tautological discourse, a self-demonstration signed in advance by the only self-demonstration of popular suffrage: the applause that is the law of the Many, the pure beating of number.

This analysis is reassuring, which is another function of Plato's criticism of rhetoric. His argument dissipates anxieties evoked by the sophist's *panourgia* (which is capable of mingling its reflections with those of the Idea), and those evoked by the unforeseeable wanderings of the discourse through which the science of the initiated could reach the uninitiated. The criticism of rhetoric makes it possible to solve the problem by restoring the discourse-at-liberty to its purely instrumental function. Alongside philosophy there can be only this art of persuasion, which is capable of destroying philosophers but incapable of troubling with its technical flourishes the mysteries of philosophy. It would be formidable, indeed, if this art were a technique that could be put at the disposal of technicians. But Socrates shows Phaedrus what he had shown Callicles: that rhetoric is less a technique than merely a routine, a kind of cuisine served not to producers but consumers who always choose the same food.

Thus the discourse-at-liberty is put back in its place as, simply, a discourse that one holds with one's "fellow slaves."[11] It is not really an illusion but only a receipt. It does, in short, *its own business.* It separates rather than mingles. Its tricks are limited to an imitation of *sōphrosunē*, a virtue that gets along quite well on its own imitation.

THE ORDER OF DELIRIUM

There is a touchstone with which to judge this discourse and mark its radical heterogeneity to the freedom of the discourse that remains in chains. It does not know delirium; it does not know being in love. The starting point for the conversation in the *Phaedrus* is a discourse by Lysias on love—a discourse that intends to be paradoxical. Love's favors, he explains, should be reserved not for the lover, who is always unreasonable, but for someone not in love, who will treat you always in a manner conforming to reason.

This is a technical discourse whose ultimate purpose is simply to carry the day. Put another way, it is a discourse fabricated to demonstrate the power of its fabricator, who is capable of saying anything and of producing whatever effect he wants—the discourse of someone who is always master of himself directed at someone who wishes not to be had [*ne veut pas se faire avoir*].

Here we find the division formed in the narrative by the waters of the Illissus. Socrates's genius will prompt him suddenly to recross the river to mark the distance separating love from the practices of *sōphrosunē*. For love is precisely the privilege reserved to those willing to *let themselves be had*, to be possessed. Love is a divine delirium forbidden to shoemakers and their orator *because they forbid it to themselves*. They know nothing of love's delirium but only the successful stroke of technique and the routine of reproduction. The people's orator makes discourses on love the way shoemakers make love, which is in fact the way they make shoes.

Passionate delirium is the touchstone that enables us to assign a proper place to the discourses of the people's orators and, through them, to those of the cynic philosophers who propose a moral hygiene purged of that madness.[12] On the one side we have those possessed by the divine. On the other we have men of common *sōphrosunē*, thrifty men who save and are praised by the people for the praises they lavish on these same virtues of servitude.[13] Socrates told Callicles that there are two kinds of love, the love of the people and the love of philosophy. But the love of the people is merely a hatred of love. Eros divides reproductive men from those possessed by the divinity.

For a second time, then, the way is barred to artisans. With their orators and their philosophers, they are securely shut up in the kingdom of the useful. The law of delirium authorizes the division of discourse by dividing up the world of imitations that bars and guards access to it. There are two types of imitators. On the one hand are the inspired imitators who have been called upon by the deity; they have been allowed to glimpse a reflection of the divine splendor and endeavor to imitate it. That is what is done by the chosen poets. And that is what is done by the dialectician-philosopher who is also the supreme imitator, as we are reminded in the *Laws*: "We are ourselves authors of tragedies, and, insofar as possible, of the best and finest tragedy. For our whole constitution is an imitation of the best and finest life, which we truly consider to be the truest tragedy."[14]

On the other hand, we have the false poet, the "counterfeit" poet (*atēlēs*) who makes use of his art as a "reasonable" (*sōphron*) man.[15] Such is the painter who uses the artisan's techniques to remake creation, or the sophist who can imitate everything the painter can. All such people practice an art of imitation that always comes down in the last instance to recipes like those of the rhetorician.

And so begins to change the apparent symmetry between the

denunciation of the poet and the sophist. It may well happen that a poet is in fact a sophist, but never that a sophist is a poet. The honest sophist Protagoras is not invited to the banquet where the vain Agathon and the malicious Aristophanes receive Diotima's message and join Socrates in celebrating the god, Love. For Protagoras, theoretician of technology and democracy, delights in demystifying poets. And in opposing him, Socrates does not hesitate to come to the defense of the dubious Simonides.[16] As against the sophist illusion that remains the work of an artisan (even of a cook), poetry's illusion takes us from the universe of fabrication to that of reflections and divine transports.

THE NEW BARRIER

We thus can comprehend the eschatology of the *Phaedrus*, which has often been thought eccentric. The souls that fall from the procession of the gods are incarnated in a hierarchy of characters corresponding to the more or less complete vision they have had of intelligible beauty. The first soul mingles with the seed of a man called upon to become a friend of knowledge or beauty, an adept of the Muses or of Love. The second soul mingles with that of a strong and just king. The third with that of a statesman, a businessman, or a trader. The fourth with that of an athlete or doctor. The fifth with that of a seer or priest, and the sixth with that of a poet or any other imitative artist. Then comes the turn of the artisan or farmer, and the only ones even lower are the sophist, the demagogue, and (down at the very bottom) the tyrant.[17]

To be sure, there is no obvious reason for putting the trader before the seer, or the athlete before the poet (indeed, the trader seems to be there simply as a joke). There is, nevertheless, a clear order overall. In a hierarchy that could be modified, categories three to six represent men who are governed alike by a higher law; they are men of right opinion or inspiration. But between the poet and the producer the line is drawn separating daimonic from demiurgic men. The artisan occupies a place from which it is no longer possible to climb back toward the divine. On the road where souls may reascend, he is stopped at the barrier of poetic imitation. In seeking to cross it, he can only fall back lower into the rhetoric of sophists and demagogues.

The crucial thing that Eros introduces is a *hierarchy of imitation*.

In this imagined population one character is missing—the warrior, which is to say, the supreme hunter. He would be misplaced here because the three-handed play of the artisan, the hunter, and the imitator is reversed. The "true" imitators, the philosopher and the inspired poet, are those who now define the superior nature of men possessed by the divinity. On the other side of the bar are the false imitators, who really are nothing but hunters—of gifts, votes, or bodies. In its own way the Sophist tells us the same thing. The thousand instruments of sophist panourgia are nothing more than the attire worn by rich young men for a hunting party that departs from the people's cuisine in its clientele but not in principle.[18] A hunter is only a cook on campaign.

THEATROCRACY

On the subject of the artisan the philosopher has made a clean sweep. Divine delirium has put order into the world of imitation. On the one side is the rhetorical double, which is always reducible to the law of the same and confined to a cuisine of persuasion in which the gods of Heraclitus do not partake. On the other side, the image is only the divine splendor's small change, the signal attracting chosen souls to the askēsis that leads sensible forms back to the intelligible One. In a sense, to say that there are two imitations is to say that there is no imitation. The world of imitations divides itself on the subject of the artisan, leaving to the philosopher the guarding of appearances.

Or, at least, it should divide itself. For there remains a problem, a point of contact between inspiration and technē: the displays of the theater.

As we suspected earlier, the question of the warriors was far from being the toughest. The poets' most perverse accomplishment is not recounting indecent fables about gods to the warriors, but introducing confusion between divine productions and artisanal fabrications, putting at the disposal of the crowd music whose laws serve as models for order and disorder in the city. Theatrocracy [la théâtrocratie] is the mother of democracy. We learn this in the Laws, which reminds us that there was a happy time when the authority to pass judgment on music was left neither to "the catcalls and discordant outcries of the crowd" nor to the clapping of the audience, but to the educated people, men of *paideia* who "made it their rule to hear the performances through in silence, whereas boys, their pedagogues, and the rabble were called to order by the official's rod."[19]

How could the power of the men of *paideia* have passed to the people and their pedagogues? Precisely through the divorce inherent in music. Music is at once the reproduction of the immutable order and the trance mediating between the divine and the human, the One and the Many. The musician does not possess the reason of his possession; he does not know how to judge music. In turning himself into a judge, he will give the common people jurisdiction over his art. The artists' power is the precursor of the power of the people: "Afterwards, over the course of time, authority in the matter of transgressions against music passed to composers, who undoubtedly had a poetic nature but were ignorant of the justice of the Muse and its laws . . . They inculcated in the common people false musical principles and the audacity to consider themselves competent judges. As a result, the theaters, which had been mute, became loquacious; and a fatal theatrocracy succeeded the musical aristocracy . . . Starting with music, there grew the opinion that all are competent in everything, as well as the rejection of laws. And liberty has followed in their train."[20]

Things would be simple if the fight against this anarchic principle came down to regulating spectacles and restoring to the friends of the Muse their power over music. The problem is that the Muse's justice is connected to delirium. The power of the musician, the tragedian, or the rhapsodist is a divine power. Even the stupid rhapsodist Ion has his share of it. He need only be beside himself [*hors de lui*], his eyes filled with tears and his hair standing on end as he relives the misfortunes of Troy, for his public, too, to be beside itself, the crowd of artisans mixing itself up with the inspired chain of chorus members that, by means of rhapsode and poet, leads back once more to the god who conducts souls where it will.

If Ion is truly inspired, the disorder is irremediable. Fortunately, the likelihood is that he is not. A wink in the dialogue allows us to assume this. It is undoubtedly true that Ion is possessed, that he believes in Troy and that tears escape uncontrollably from his eyes. Socrates asks him: Don't you realize you produce the same effect on your audience? Yes, says Ion, I can see the tears in their eyes and their hair standing on end. But he does not take his eyes off them because his interest is at stake: "For if I set them weeping, I myself shall laugh when I get my money, but if they laugh, it is I who have to weep at losing it."[21]

Socrates does not react to this. He departs saluting Ion as a "man divine" but leaves us with the thought that Ion really may be just a cook—or, what amounts to the same thing, that Ion may be a "man divine" for the satisfaction of people who want their money's worth. So the philosopher is reassured that we are still within the circle of rhetoric. Ion, the inspired voice of the shoemakers, can see only through the eyes of his clients. And these "lovers of spectacles" who react in everything as if "they had been paid,"[22] perhaps offer no spectacle other than that of their own mass. The noise of number—the very custom of applauding, imported from Italy—is what has created theatrocracy.[23] Power is not so much in the spectacle itself as in the racket that it authorizes. In its noisy applause the multitude expresses only its own essence. In short, nothing here is imitated.

This theory of "popular aesthetics" is reassuring as a tautology. For if the people are lovers of spectacles, the simple reason is that they, as number, are enemies of the non-sensible unity of the Idea. That is what is laid out in book VI of the *Republic*. The people cannot possibly love the Beautiful in itself but only beautiful things. Thus, for Hippias the sophist, the beautiful is a beautiful girl—an occasion for performance, an instrument of reproduction. The multitude never really admires anything but itself in the motley assortment of beautiful things. It simply reveres the productive and reproductive Many as its own essence. The law of applause expresses its self-satisfaction. The matter again becomes a question of regulating spectacles.

THE CHORUS OF CICADAS

Which is to say that the analysis can be read the other way around—as the other side of a commandment. The tautology of the Many applauding themselves is merely the confirmation of the circle in which philosophy, mingling its cause with that of the city, has confined the artisan. This phenomenology of the spectacle, in which the pleasure of the masses boils down to the beating of number, is the inverse of the theory of work governed by the "nothing else" of specialization. The "sociology" is coupled with an "aesthetics" that puts the One and the Many strictly in their places, reserving to the philosopher the legislation and even the poetry of the double. The shoemaker or carpenter must be merely one of the *polloi* who make up the noisy multitude. As if this were a matter of exorcizing the phantasm of an even more formidable anarchy: suppose the shoemaker or carpenter had forgotten the difference between a useful work and a simulacrum, and decided to occupy himself not with judging theater but—supreme folly—the Beautiful in itself. This would be improbable sociologically, of course, but the "sociology" is merely the division between philosophy and anti-philosophy. Shoemaker is the generic name for the man who is not where he ought to be if the order of estates is to get on with the order of discourse. Given that starting point, anything is possible. There already is a *true* bastard, Antisthenes, who scatters to the four winds what he claims is Socrates's teaching.

The great phantasm of the *Republic*—philosophy invaded by dwarfish interlopers—finds its muted echo in the sylvan revery of the *Phaedrus*. The dialogue pauses in the midst of its criticism of the ridiculous logographers who eagerly write "It has pleased the people . . . ," and we may be tempted to see such pauses as efforts to provide "repose" for readers worn out by the aridity of the reasoning. Yet it is not a question of repose but of leisure. More precisely, it is the very concept of leisure that is in question when Socrates draws Phaedrus's attention to the singing of the cicadas in the midday sun.

The "philologist" Phaedrus was anxious to know which discourses provide *true* pleasures. Not the pleasures of the body or the people, not those that concern the relief of suffering, the filling of a void, or the gratification of some need. He was interested, rather, in the gratuitous pleasures that are wholly opposed to the slavish ones associated with need, fatigue, and pain. The search promises to be a long one, but Socrates says they have the leisure for it.

We must realize that leisure is also a duty. Socrates and Phaedrus are obligated not to rest, not to let themselves be lulled to sleep by the midday sun and the singing of the cicadas. For that is precisely why the cicadas sing. They are the descendants of a race of song lovers who were so intoxicated with divine music that they forgot to eat and drink, and eventually died as a result. Messengers of the Muses, the cicadas sing to identify those lovers of leisure and the Muses who are capable of resisting the hypnotic power of their midday concert. As Socrates reminds Phaedrus: "If they were to see us two behaving like the multitude at midday, not conversing but dozing lazy-minded under their spell, they would rightly laugh at us, taking us for a pair of slaves who had invaded their retreat like sheep, to have their midday sleep beside the spring."[24]

Multitude, slaves, refuge: this sylvan scene transposes a play with which we are already familiar. But here the defense of philosophy also solves the question of the theater. The friends of the Muses are transported by the very same singing that drives the laboring people away. The chorus of cicadas traces the circle that isolates free dialectic from the occupations of those whose vigilance merely follows the curves of fatigue and heat. Phaedrus was quite right in dragging the city-loving philosopher far away from the shoemakers and carpenters with whom Critias would forbid him to associate. His theater of the green world, the inverted image of the people's theater, is also the sanctuary of philosophy. It preserves the privileged relationship, the Two of dialectic and divine friendship, from the familiarity of the Many who produce and reproduce. The fact of being incapable of resisting sleep can be used to detect the presence of servile natures among those who are neither bald nor lame nor bastards. As the *Laws* tell us, it is disgraceful for a master to be awakened by his servant.[25] The philosopher is the master par excellence, the man who should not sleep, someone whose free speech should not be interrupted. That is also what *dialectic* means: an endless conversation with disciple and deity, an activity as unceasing as vocational training and the guardianship of the city. If the philosopher-initiator and the lover of discourse were both to fall asleep, that would be the end of philosophical legitimacy. And who then could forbid artisans from mingling their discordant voices with the chorus of cicadas?

The myth of leisure establishes the *natural* link between the law of labor and that of the theater. Just as the lovers of spectacle were only the Many shouting here and dozing there, the artisan folk must be governed solely by the alteration of work and sleep so that the philosopher-cicada may preserve his sanctuary. And this sanctuary is both the refuge of the wise man outside the motley city of artisans and the temple of the guardians who oversee the ants of divided labor. The cicadas' singing anticipates the justice of Hades separating the heavenly destiny of the "men divine" from the honest recompense promised to temperate men who, having cultivated the virtues of moderation (*sōphrosunē*) and justice (*di-*

kaiosunē), will be reincarnated as some species of political animal: as bees, wasps, or ants.[26]

This separation of music and politics marks perhaps the ultimate contradiction of the philosopher-king. The "man divine" is not a political animal but a musical animal made to be the eulogist (if not the marionette) of god rather than to watch over city censuses and regulations.[27] The population of this city is urged to delight itself incessantly by chanting in unison its immutable principles to rhythms fixed by the ruler.[28] Too much emphasis has been placed on this desire as the dream of the "totalitarian" philosopher. It should be seen, rather, as the pointing up of a contradiction and as a futile effort to solve it, an attempt to give to each person the share of music and divine play of which he is capable. The laws and choirs of the city will never be more than a feeble imitation of the divine music. And if the philosopher devotes himself to that, he does so first of all to protect his retreat. Music will be able to unite the citizens only if it has already isolated him from their choirs.

THE DIVISION OF APPEARANCES

The singing of the cicadas allows the order of delirium to be cut by the barrier of leisure. Socrates's and Phaedrus's visit to the country gives the exclusion of imitators its artful twist of meaning. Haven't these latter been chased out of the productive city so that they might better prepare, outside the walls, the divine retreat, the private banquet where the philosopher gets on well with poets (even the bad ones) and lovers of discourses (even the simple ones) by excluding artisans (especially the cunning ones)?

Poets are needed, and then again they are not. There is no need for poets in that they populate the people's theater with actors whose resonant voices compete with the tragedy of the philosopher-guardian. But poets are needed if the philosopher-guardian is not to remain simply a master swineherd. So their exclusion becomes complicity, a private party or banquet far from the roar of the theater where the philosopher meets with lovers of fine forms and beautiful discourses. The philosopher leads them to realize that the principle of their passion has nothing to do with techniques of fabrication and cuisines of flattery. In return, the equivocal society of these superficial men guarantees for the lover of truth that all pleasures—from the mists of intoxication to the company of courtesans—are divided in two. Pausanias's "rhetorical" discourse thus tells the truth of Diotima's inspired discourse: there are two kinds of love, each of which is double in itself. As Socrates says to Callicles: "Both of us are in love: I with Alcibiades son of Clinias, and philosophy; and you also with two, the Athenian *demos*, and Demos son of Pyrilampes."[29] At the end of the *Symposium*, Alcibiades returns the compliment in describing the arguments of his beloved Socrates as enveloped within discourses of "pack asses, blacksmiths, shoemakers and tanners."[30]

For everything to be cut in two, a final birth myth is needed—one that introduces division into the order of illegitimacy as well. It took only a slave boy to disclose the vanity of all those aspiring to knowledge. Now it takes only one poor little girl, Penia, and one bastard, Eros, to bar the door to illegitimate lovers of the Idea, thereby completing an order in which the sociology of functions finds itself entirely recuperated by the genealogy of values.

As concerns the demiurge, the man of the *people* and *labor*, everything is cut in two. The Delphic oracle says to the philosopher "Know Thyself," and to the artisan "Nothing to Excess." For the one, memory is reminiscence; for the other, mnemotechnics. Discourse is the dead letter of rhetorical imitation or the winged song that imitates the divine. The love of theatrical figures is the beating of tool-wielding hands or of wings in remembrance of beauty. The love of bodies is a pretext for the reproduction of shoemakers or the starting point for the *askēsis* of elect souls. The pathway of the Idea is guarded by these appearances that divide themselves in two, each time throwing off to the wrong side of the process the artisan who would like to do something other than his own business.

At the Foot of the Rampart

It would be quite a boorish trick for philosophy to build itself up through a simple exclusion that makes it impossible for manual laborers to know the truth of the soul. The philosopher is not afraid that men of iron will get hold of the truth; he is afraid that artists will get hold of appearance. To elevate the lover of the true to his proper dignity, the shoemaker must be excluded from the world of appearances. The philosopher locks the door on him twice. First he does it with the division of labor, which excludes imitators and keeps artisans in "their" place; he then does it a second time with the delirium of inspiration that carries out the doubling of appearances. Or, if you will, the philosopher-king invents two sciences: a sociology that dismisses appearances from the universe of useful functions, and an aesthetics that causes the appearances guarding philosophical legitimacy to recoil before the functionaries of the useful. On either side of the artisan, then, two figures are distributed: the sophist whose negativity gathers into himself the effects of illegitimacy specific to the artisan who departs from his role, and the poet, the philosopher-king's companion in delirium or, perhaps better, his buffoon. Once the seriousness of his work as an artisan has disqualified him as a master of wisdom, the philosopher can enlist in his own service this specialist in appearances and genealogies, this accomplice conjurer and denier of any beauty or truth in which shoemakers might claim to have a part.

The provocative power of Plato lies in the extraordinary frankness with which he expresses what future epistemologies and sociologies will try to obscure: that the order of the true can no more be grounded in a science of science than the social order can be grounded in the division of labor. The social relation and the order of discourse depend upon one and the same fiction, the fiction that chases the artisan from the realm of fiction. What is excluded is the lie of art, the lie that is practiced unwittingly. At the juncture of the philosophical order and the social order only one lie may proceed, the noble lie of nature.

As opposed to the artisan who lies as he works, the philosopher claims to found the legitimacy of his own lie in the science of the true. But the situation of the lie is really the opposite, since it is the legislation of simulacra that founds philosophical legitimacy simply by decreeing its own genealogical myths.

Philosophy is fundamentally genealogy, a discourse on nature as a discourse on nobility. It should not be understood as a "pro-slavery" discourse designed to justify an inegalitarian social order or to shut men up in the "totalitarianism" of its idea. Its concern is less to lock others up than to protect itself from them, less to impose its truth than to safeguard its appearance. Nobility, we know, consists of that first and foremost.

Plato's order and delirium express neither philosophy's compromise with the established political orders nor its stubborn attempt to impose its own truth on the disorders of the city. They express, rather, the paradox of its very institution. Philosophy can trace the circle of its own autonomy only through an arbitrary discourse on nature and nobility, a discourse that makes possible its own tension by imitating its *telos*, perfect nature. But this imitation is forever destined to border on its own caricature. The philosopher-king is doomed to live with his apes.

The philosopher of Zarathustra will once more encounter this logic and this menace in the hopes and fears of the socialist age, but only at the price of speaking them against Plato. When Nietzsche glorifies the lie of life and the noble passion for appearance against the Socratic and plebeian passion for truth, he may only be prolonging the wrath of the philosopher-king against the plebeian Socrates of Xenophon the agrarian landlord, and against Antisthenes the popular philosopher. That truth derives its legitimacy only from the noble lie that distinguishes highborn souls from those born for the hammering of forges and the uproar of assemblies—this is the Platonic lesson that Nietzsche confirms.

But not without paying his own tribute to modernity by transporting the "Mediterranean" distinctions of the Greek myth to Bizet's Spain, and Agathon's banquet into the midst of the toreadors, soldiers, and female tobacco workers who frequent Lillas Pastia's tavern in *Carmen*. The essential thing, as we learn in the *seguidilla* dance, is that the tavern is at the foot of the rampart. Recall that the naïve (or wily?) Antisthenes had accused philosophers of refusing the protection of their rampart to the artisan folk, even though it had been built to protect them.

From what exactly, then, are the tobacco factory's workers supposed to protect the philosopher in the age of democracy and socialism? By what reversal does the factory come to work against the artisan, and the Venus of the crossroads to save the philosopher-artist's stake? If Bizet, contra Wagner, is to become the philosopher of Zarathustra, the reason is not simply that Carmen's dance is lighter than the Mass of the Knights of the Grail, but that there is something, perhaps, even more intolerable than the silly bombast of warriors such as Parsifal, Siegfried, and Lohengrin: namely, the modest poetic pretension of the shoemaker Hans Sachs.

11 :: Marx's Labor

I even decided to become a "practical man," and intended to enter
a railway office at the beginning
of the next year. Luckily—or perhaps I should say unluckily?—I
did not get the post because of my
bad handwriting.

> Marx, letter to Kugelmann,
> 28 December 1862

3 :: The Shoemaker and the Knight

IT MAKES NOT the least difference whether shoemakers sing in their shops or join choruses at popular festivals. The songs that lend rhythm to their work or occupy their leisure time help to maintain that semblance of love which, more than skill, keeps the worker at his post. And aesthetes in any case are not obliged to go and listen to them.

But in a scene from *Die Meistersinger* Hans Sachs does *something else*. He proposes that the people be allowed to judge music once a year. And, by this method, the first singer he wants to name as one of the masters is a knight.

The first of these mistakes is the more excusable since it is deemed natural that manual laborers reflect their judgments about the Beautiful in the clapping of their hands, confusing, in so doing, the unity of the Idea with the multitude of forms and voices. And it matters little if this is only a question of judging artisans' songs for the benefit of their fellow tradesmen.

But Hans Sachs does not indulge in that confusion. It is not his apprentice that he proposes for anointing by the multitude, but a knight. It is not a singer that he supports, but a poet. And with this poet-knight introduced by a shoemaker to the artisans of Nuremberg, everything seems to get scrambled: weapons, tools, and meters; trade, science, and inspiration; gold, silver, and iron.

THE INSURRECTION OF THE SHOEMAKERS

The confusion does not stem from a composer's Gothic imagination. The Festival of St. John (Midsummer's Day) staged by Richard Wagner in 1868 at the Munich Opera illustrates one of the themes that for several decades haunted the minds of experts as far as the philosophical, artistic, and political orders were concerned: the invasion of shoemakers into domains reserved for learned connoisseurs of the Idea of the Good and inspired lovers of beautiful forms.

The police, of course, have long been used to the fact that in the streets of Paris as in those of Nuremberg, apprentice shoemakers and tailors-in-training are the first to raise a ruckus. Which is in keeping with their concept, that of being the multitude par excellence: motley and boisterous number. The theater owners know this, too, and employ them as paid applauders.

There, perhaps, is the error, for the police are shrewd not to want such applauders in the theater. The greatest evil lies not in the mass as such but in its *decomposition*. For it is evident that these workers are acquiring a taste for the fancy dress in which they are decked out; for the aristocratic romances which they are paid to applaud; and for the theatrical illusion which they are invited to attend. As a consequence these workers are also flocking to secret societies where they dress themselves up in the hats and titles of the Republic, and to Saint-Simonian meetings where people of high society fraternize with the working class. And some are not afraid to continue ascending to the divine pleasures of the poet and the philosopher.

An insurrection of the shoemakers: the sociological orientation of historians would like to see in that the advancement of shoemaker virtue. The fierce pride of these skilled workers and their uneasiness over the new world of unskilled labor would strengthen the spirit and arms of the shoemakers as well as their inseparable acolytes, the tailors.

But the shoemakers, and indeed all workers, know very well that there is no shoemaker virtue. Or, to put it another way, theirs is a virtue that has not changed since Plato's day: the shoemaker is someone who may not do anything else than shoemaking.

This link between "status" and prohibition, which has become obscure to experts [aux savants], is no secret to workers for the simple reason that they are the ones who have inherited it. The link has become over centuries the rule of their internal hierarchy, their way of fulfilling their destiny and denying it simultaneously by dumping it off on a pariah, the shoemaker.

"Let no one enter here who is not a geometer."[1] Fellow journeymen have found their geometer-king in the carpenter, first in dignity among the offspring of those who built Solomon's temple. It was this carpenter who organized a universe of workers in which everyone—smith or cooper, locksmith or leather worker—finds his place and dedicates his life to the interminable apprenticeship of his art. These monotechnicians have no liking for imitators or for the mixing of metals. Hoffmann took revenge on behalf of poets by depicting Master Martin the cooper, who considers barrel making the supreme art and wants neither painter in his shop nor knight for his daughter.[2]

A world, then, of prohibition and hierarchy. After the geometer par excellence (the carpenter), one descends by degrees to lower levels where skill becomes increasingly crude and geometry increasingly superfluous, until one reaches finally the hell of the shoemaker. In the nineteenth century the shoemaker had not yet finished paying for his crimes against Plato's order. He is the dwarfish man ridiculed in journeymen songs for his huge apron, crude tools, and smelly pitch. He is the usurping slave fraudulently initiated into the secrets of the guild. The law of the carpenters orders every journeyman conscientious of his duties to kill the *sabourin* found wearing the guild's insignia.

By the middle of the nineteenth century this order was on its way out. But here and there one could still encounter the corpses of shoemakers punished for their audacity. In any case, the reality of the order of estates extends the prohibitions of the symbolic order. Shoemaking remains at the very bottom of the trades. If we find shoemakers in the first rank where workers of any kind should not be, the reason is that they are the most numerous, the least busy with their work, and the least deluded about the glory of the artisan. The insurrection of the shoemakers is not a battle *for* their status but a battle *against* it. A typical image of this rejection is the adolescent poet whose father, employed by a school, wanted to force him into the shoemaker's trade. Notes his biographer: "He resisted his father like a saint, broke the tools of a trade for which he had not been made, and became free again and his own man."[3]

There is the heart of the matter. Now anyone can make edicts about nature and judge for himself, independently of the external constraints that may compel him, whether or not he is made for the shoemaker's trade or for any other. The "nothing else" that had guaranteed the order of estates is contested here on two sides. There are workmen who discover in their migrations that it does not take much time at all to acquire a new skill, and that there is no harm in passing from one trade to another.[4] And there are workmen who perceive skilfulness itself as the other side of a prohibition and decide, rather, to appropriate for themselves the pleasures of appearance and the leisures of the dialectic. One joiner, for example, offers the following excuse for failing to pursue his work: "If I catch sight of Socrates at a distance, I suddenly let my duties go to hell and run after him, so that we may discourse together (often for a whole day) about the true goods of existence."[5]

We have here the routing of nature, the mixing of functions and metals, the passage of monotechnicians into the motley world of imitators where they encounter knights inspired by divine art and philosophers who hand over their secrets to the people. The proponents of order and of inspiration are equally disturbed by this disorder, and always put the same archetype at the center of their denunciations. In 1841 a Professor Lerminier, an early Saint-Simonian who saw the heresy at its birth, rebels against the homage being paid to these worker poets, in which he detects the symbolic presence of the shoemaker Savinien Lapointe. Opposing the republicans who celebrate them, he affirms the counsels of the father of the modern Republic: "I absolutely want Émile to learn a trade . . . I do not want him to be a musician, an actor, or someone who writes books . . . I prefer that he be a shoemaker to a poet."[6] All these things go together: aesthetic disorder, political disorder, symbolic disorder, real disorder. In a republic that would give the poet's palm to shoemakers, "the supreme power would have thousands of candidates and the law would have not one obedient subject."[7]

From the opposite perspective, the politically progressive editors of L'Artiste become disturbed, at the time of the Salon of 1845, by the democracy that is invading the arts. They, too, do not mistake the target: "Nature has not permitted everyone to have genius. It said to some, 'Make poems.' It said to others, 'Make shoes.' "[8] The rights of the inspired thus rejoin without constraint and inflect without violence the arguments of order's proponents. No petty fear animates the gentle Charles Nodier, who is bothered by these shoemakers writing tragedies like those by Corneille and offers his own diagnosis of the origin of this evil: the irrational democracy of writing which, having become the people's printshop and means of instruction, is everywhere turning "useful manual laborers and decent artisans" into "thieves, impostors, and forgers."[9] He then enunciates the solution that will satisfy simultaneously the government, the people, and the poets: return popular culture to the people, return to them the rationality of the myth first confiscated and then abolished by the philosophers. Halfway between the counterrevolution's anti-philosophical rancor and materialism's vigorous attacks on ideology, Nodier expresses in all its purity the return of a Platonism in which popular sentiment denounces a philosophy now identified with writing's dead letter.

All of which occurs as if the destiny of the modern republic were still representable in terms of this symbolic division, as if there should exist in it a class of individuals whose *trade* symbolizes the necessity for all tradesmen to do nothing else than their own business—a trade that recapitulates the necessity of labor insofar as it excludes the privileges, even the most ascetic, of leisure. Order is menaced wherever a shoemaker does something else than make shoes. By the same token, anyone who upsets the order of estates can be called a shoemaker. Thus the learned editor of the *Journal des économistes* has no hesitation about the identity of the German communist expelled by the French government for his incendiary writings. Mr. Karl Marx, he informs his readers, is a shoemaker.

THE NIGHT OF ST. JOHN

It is in this context that Richard Wagner imagines in 1845 the fable of the shoemaker and the knight, a fable intended, first of all, to refute his detractors. But when he stages this tale twenty-three years later, it is also meant to signal that the game is *over*. If *Die Meistersinger* is a unique opera in the repertory of the composer, the reason is that it is, precisely, a farewell performance. The insurrection of the shoemakers is finished. The artist is taking back full possession of the attributes of nature and genius which, in the turmoil of the 1840s, he entrusted to the people's care. Eva can always take the crown from Walter's head in order to crown Hans Sachs, but no one will be misled by that, and the outcome is exactly the opposite. The triumph of the shoemaker-poet is at the same time his abdication. It is the popular baptism through which the representative of St. John consecrates the inspired artist, returning to him the crown of the aristocratic *Minnesänger* that the artisans previously usurped. The alliance of shoemaker and poet in the cult of the people and of woman is over as soon as it began. It was power for a single day, the royalty of carnival exercised just long enough to restore the supremacy of genius over technique, inspiration over mnemonics. Only one intermediary is needed—

Beckmesser, the town clerk and the mastersingers' "marker," the man with the overly punctilious memory. He is the sophist of modern times. Or rather, he is less than a sophist since he can neither learn something correctly by heart nor make his own shoes. This discount sophist is now called a petty bourgeois.

As an aesthetic and progressive refinement of the new dream of "popular culture," this "Gothic" opera represents one of the dominant forms of our modernity. Between *Tannhaüser* and *Die Meistersinger*, between the singing contests of Wartburg and those of Nuremberg, a shift takes place in the Saint-Simonian and Feuerbachian homage paid to the people and to woman. The positivizing of artisanal virtue is accompanied by a game of tit for tat [*prêté et rendu*] in which the inspired artist attributes to the popular *ethos* a genius, a *daïmon*, that the people immediately cede back to him, thereby consecrating the artist of the people, worker and knight, in his difference from the mechanical imitator. This consecration of the artist is then proposed in turn as a model for the politician and expert. Where the old Platonic order asserted itself in the horror of ragout and motley jumble, the Nuremberg carnival embodies a modern kind of mixture that abrades the colors of metals and the visible contours of the old orders, offering the guardians and those inspired by the modern age a new legitimacy based on the only powers that now are said to matter, the ones from below.

Ironically, the one critic who sensed better than anyone else the scope of this operation was the young revolutionary, Richard Wagner. In *Opera and Drama* (1851), he offered the most felicitous analysis of these round-trips to the heart of the popular spirit that injected new life into opera: Auber's mad gallop through the display stalls of Neapolitan fishermen; his rival Rossini's promenades to the sound of Alpine flutes; the promotion of the masses on Meyerbeer's stage.[10] To be sure, these are simple cookbook recipes compared with the representative machine set in motion by the shoemaker Hans Sachs and his apprentice.

There are at least two philosophers whose classical tastes find this sort of popular culture repugnant—Friedrich Nietzsche and Karl Marx. Nietzsche submitted for a while to the popular charm of the St. John's Day celebrations. It took him some time to arrive at a diagnosis that strangely recalled old Plato: the theatrical resolution of the shoemaker insurrection is still the triumph of the shoemakers, for the simple reason that it is theater. Theatrocracy, exactly echoing the *Laws*, is the concept used by Nietzsche to settle the "case of Wagner." It matters little that the fable of the shoemaker serves only the consecration of the artist. For it is precisely the power of the imitator-artist—of the actor [*comédien*], says Nietzsche—that inaugurates decadence so far as music and hence philosophy and politics are concerned. To subject the rules of music to the judgment of artists is, in the short term, to have them fall back into the hands of the people. "The theater is a revolt of the masses."[11] The figures of the Platonic phantasm find their echo in the images used by Nietzsche to pummel Wagner's theater in Bayreuth: it is an enchanter's cave where highborn youth are corrupted. But it is also an "institute for hydrotherapy," its contemptible hygiene reminding us of the public bath where the fugitive slave had been grooming himself. The result scarcely differs from Plato's diagnosis that the actor's reign can issue only in the destruction of the "instincts by virtue of which the worker becomes possible as a class."[12] Against which there is hardly any other recourse but the circle of cicadas in the midday sun.

The Ideologue, the Shoemaker, and the Inventor

South against north: a certain geography of the defense of thinking against the simultaneous advent of the imitators and the masses. But the Marxian landscape is organized differently. For the native of Trier and inhabitant of London, the south does not represent civilization as opposed to northern barbarism. Barbarism makes all territories equivalent, and civilization is only the stream of exchanges that flows from them. Nuremberg is the south, the land of cramped little towns, antiquated junk, and south German sentimentality as opposed to the large estates, militarism, and bureaucracy of the north. An immobile contradiction reflected for Marx in the comedy of the German revolution, which is summed up perfectly in the complementary characters of the two "heroes" of 1848, Marx's twin *bêtes noires*: the adventurist militarism of Lieutenant August Willich and the sentimental grandiloquence of the poet Gottfried Kinkel.

Just after the revolution Marx finds himself talking about Nuremberg and its shoemaker-poet in a review of a book by Friedrich Daumer called *The Religion of the New Age*.[13] Against the decadence of the "culture" now under siege by contemporary barbarism,

Daumer proposes a new human religion based on nature and woman. To his hostile reviewer, this "nature" is merely the inane idyll of the small-minded citizen reciting Klopstock odes to embellish his Sunday strolls, and the rehabilitation of woman simply follows the model of women of letters from the preceding century. But Daumer's complaints about decadence indicate a rather different source:

> The "culture" whose decay Mr. Daumer laments is that of the time in which Nuremberg flourished as a free *Reichsstadt*, in which Nuremberg's industry—that bastard (*Zwitterding*) of art and craftsmanship (*Handwerk*)—played an important role as German petty-bourgeois culture perished along with the petty bourgeoisie. Where the decline of former classes such as knighthood could provide material for great tragic works of art, philistinism (*Spießbürgertum*) can achieve nothing but impotent expressions of fanatical malice and a collection of maxims and precepts in the style of Sancho Panza. Mr. Daumer is the continuation of Hans Sachs, but dried out and stripped of all humor. German philosophy wringing its hands and weeping on the deathbed of its foster-father, German philistinism: such is the touching scene unfolded to us by *The Religion of the New Age*.[14]

The judgment appears to be simple and returns us to two major themes in Marxian thought. First is the critique of ideology as the inability to comprehend the development of productive forces. What follows is the opposition between two theatrical figures of history: the tragic, authentic expression of the struggle between the old world and the new, and the comic, derisory repetition of a history already played out and of values already dead. Daumer thus becomes the representative of those ideologues who go "no further" in their thinking than the petty bourgeoisie go in their practical life, who are just as incapable as the petty bourgeoisie of perceiving the liberating element in the ruptures of the industrial age, and who, like the petty bourgeoisie, have nothing to oppose to those ruptures but the dream of an impossible return from this side of capitalism. In short, a grotesque repetition of a fight against history that knighthood had already lost in the days of Don Quixote.

A simple reading, but Marx is never stingy with false openings. We all know from him that 1848 was a farcical repetition of the tragedy of the great Revolution that had used ancient disguises to free the new bourgeois world from its feudal shackles. But here the matter is different. The comedy of philistinism is not a repetition of the tragic; it is a repetition of itself. Daumer is grotesque because he repeats, in degrading it, an already ridiculous social figure. And that ridiculous figure is not the futile struggle of knights errant, but the productive activity of Nuremberg industry in its golden age.

Marx's target here, in effect, is neither the caste system of the corporations nor the narrow-mindedness of trade idiocy. It is the flourishing industry of one of those free cities of the Middle Ages in which progressive historians customarily locate the first seeds of the new world of bourgeois domination and popular emancipation. For these historians, only one thing caused the downfall of this metropolis of nascent capitalism: its unfortunate geographical position, far from the great rivers and sea lanes but right in the path of devastating armies.

Curiously, however, the father of historical materialism reasons otherwise. For him this obsolete industry had been stillborn—a double thing, a hybrid, a bastard. It was the mixture of two contradictory natures, industrial activity with artistic creation. But in his own time this union is not exclusively the dream of now-outmoded artisans; it is also to be found among social and industrial innovators, promoters of industrial art. Even the moribund culture of Nuremberg can still interest progressive men. At the World Exposition of 1867, the worker delegates, bowing in admiration before Nuremberg's mechanical toys, opposed the scientific education such toys can provide to the silly dolls that teach French children the softness and corruption of the declining classes.[15] In short, the industrial arts and toys of Nuremberg could offer more convincing models to the "polytechnic" education of the future communist world than the ironic variations on ambiguous pastoral themes to which Marx at times abandons himself: a world where there no longer will be painters but merely individuals who, among other things, paint; a world where the individual can be, at his pleasure, a fisherman, a hunter, a shepherd, a critical critic . . .

But Marx interprets progress differently. For him the overcoming of the Platonic prohibition is neither the shoemaker-poet, nor industrial art, nor the mechanical toy. The future of bourgeois liberty and popular emancipation did not lie, in the days of Hans

Sachs, with the flourishing industry of the free cities of the Empire. It began in England or the Netherlands in the purifying hell of the textile mills set up on the shores of the sea of exchange. There we have the anticipation of the revolutionary marriage of fire and water, a union finally realized when the inventions of the watchmaker Watt and the jeweler Fulton opened the way for large-scale industry and the world market: "Ne sutor ultra crepidam! Let the shoemaker stick to his last! This nec plus ultra of handicraft wisdom became sheer madness and a curse from the moment the watchmaker Watt invented the steam engine, the barber Arkwright the throstle, and the jeweler Fulton the steamship."[16]

It is not, then, by becoming a poet or industrial artist that the shoemaker escapes his curse, but by inventing the machine. The paradox, of course, is that now the shoemaker, far from making more than his footwear, has every chance of making even less. The machine revolution means that the worker in a trade or in manufacturing, performing a limited task, now performs an even more restricted one. In short, madness and curses can outstrip the old wisdom only if these now apply to everyone. A curse for the bourgeoisie, to whom these ingenious artisans bring prosperity in the short term and death in the long term, because large-scale industry itself shall, "under pain of death," replace the fragmented with the complete individual, and it can do that only by first stepping on the bodies of the bourgeoisie. A curse for the proletarians, who will achieve this world of complete individuals only at the price of abandoning their competence and freedom as artisans for the frenzy of the bourgeois factory. The artisan inventors free their brothers by forcing them to commit suicide. The artisan must consent to be stripped of all his positivity in dragging the bourgeoisie into the infernal cycle of his suicide.

This history of deathbed lamentations may have been only a trompe l'oeil. For history "advances" precisely where it confronts death, and where there are no longer wringing hands or jeremiads but madness and cursing. The death of Hans Sachs or of Nuremberg industry is, on the contrary, merely a comedy, a caricature of death. After all, philistine Nuremberg is just at the dawn of its industrial heyday, and the "sentimental ass" Liebknecht will turn it into one of the strongholds of the Marxist worker party. That is precisely what characterizes backwardness: it has a hardy life. Thirty years later Engels will remind Bernstein: "We have always done our utmost to combat the narrow petty-bourgeois philistine mentality within the party because, having developed since the Thirty Years' War, it has infected *all* classes in Germany. . . . It prevails on the throne no less frequently than in a cobbler's dwelling."[17] Backwardness is not a history that has become obsolete but one that has gotten off on the wrong foot. It is bad history, the sordid or wayward kind that doubles legitimate history. Bastardy is the bad figure of Two, that which does not split itself apart but contents itself with its duplication—as if it found, in the mixture that constitutes its indignity, strength to survive in escaping the fire of contradiction. The baseness of this history is its false nobility: its *mixture* of art and craftsmanship, fabrication and imitation, usefulness and leisure, base and precious metals. Bastardy is as much the skill of the copper workers of old Nuremberg, who perfected a way of imitating goldwork, as it is the triviality of the worker-philosopher Proudhon, who desires useful works of art. For his own part, Doctor Marx is in favor of separation. He loves Greek art and the classical masterpieces. His daughters have dolls rather than mechanical toys—and to amuse them, he plays horse on his hands and knees and tells them Hoffmann's tale of a magician who could not pay his debts, had to sell to the Devil the marvelous objects he made but always ended up recovering them.[18] As for his naïve pastoral about the communist of the future, perhaps it, like the eschatology of the *Phaedrus*, is most important, finally, for what it excludes: there is in it neither industrial fabrication nor artistic imitation, which is certainly the most radical way of not mixing the two together.

Bastardy, on the other hand, is the force of the lie at the very heart of production, and on that point the theorist of productive forces agrees with Hoffmann's fantastic stories. Nuremberg industry can always be modeled on the workshop of Master Martin which, unbeknownst to him, is peopled with journeymen who—all the more perfect—simply pretend to be coopers: the painter Reinhold, the sculptor Friedrich, and the knight Conrad. A closed world, locked up in the repetitive games of same and other—a world of fabricator and imitator, artisan and ideologue. If Nuremberg culture is decadent, it is not because it is old but because it is of minimal value and always has been so. If today it seems shabby juxtaposed to the factory world of Manchester, the truth is that it already was so, even in its prime, when compared with lost battles of knighthood in decline and the "great tragic works" that reflect them.

Good history is on the side of tragedy, *there where the tragic hero fights against history*. Here is where Marx, despite his reference to Hegel, sharply distinguishes himself from him. For Hegel tragedy has to do not with decline but with the ascending phase of the world order. The tragedy par excellence, that of the Greeks, marks the moment when the powers of nature clash with those of the law of the state, when Antigone opposes Creon or Athena absolves Orestes for a crime against his mother's blood that is justified by his desire to avenge the paternal order of the family.

For Hegel, knighthood in decline is the subject matter of the novel. Or rather, it is the very subject of the novel as a historical genre, the tale of the wanderings of Christian subjectivity in a world that escapes it on all sides. The Romantic hero par excellence is surely Don Quixote; the champion of a world in decline, he is doubled by a servant called upon to become the master of the future—Sancho Panza, the man who represents the prose of the new bourgeois world.

For Marx, however, the novel changes meaning in becoming tragic history. It embodies the opposition between history's tragic grandeur and comic pettiness. The distance between Marx and Hegel is best indicated by something too often disregarded despite its strangeness: in Marx's work it is Sancho Panza who battles windmills. Here, as in The German Ideology, the ideologue of hollow dreams—of backward illusions, empty phrases, and imaginary battles—is not Don Quixote but Sancho Panza, the ploughman's son who thinks only of his stomach and speaks in proverbs. The ideologue is precisely someone who seemed fully to incarnate, like Hans Sachs or the free Nuremberg artisans, the world of the productive and prosaic future as opposed to the knightly reveries that justified the feudal order of castes. In The German Ideology, in fact, Sancho has become the master of his master. The ideologue is not the chimerical dreamer but the strong spirit who "demystifies" knightly illusions. And perhaps that is why he understands nothing about history—whether about the tragic struggles of his masters, or the hellish and progressive work of the artisan inventors of large-scale industry, or the foolishness of workers launching "an assault on heaven," or Doctor Marx sacrificing everything to the great book of their liberation.

Marx's critique of Sancho Panza approaches the insurrection of the shoemakers the other way round. It sees in their poetic dreams only the pettiness of artisanal duplicity. For Marx, the shoemaker-poet is the man of bad history, the man of the double as opposed to the man of contradiction, the worker who wants to improve his status when he must sacrifice it—the man who, in the world of manufacturing, makes prosaic the great pastoral dream of the poet Antipatros, in which working girls take their leisure while Nymphs turn the water wheel.[19] On the contrary, workers for Marx must leave behind in the "archaic" distance the divine life of leisure in order to recover that life through the sacrifice of machine, science, and combat.

The clear genesis and simple evaluation of political and ideological forms, with their basis in the history of productive forces, double themselves here in a discrete but implacable genealogy of values close to that of Nietzsche, at least in the division [*partage*] that opposes the artisans of comic decadence to the knights of tragic decline. Tragedy is the grandeur of life in death, comedy the pettiness of death in life. For Marx, as for Nietzsche and Plato, there are two ways to be born and to die, and history's apparently unique direction lies similarly in the imbrication of two movements. Plato's *Statesman* offered the myth of the opposing rotations of a world sometimes governed by the law of the One and sometimes left to the neglect of the Many. Marx's text shows us the imbrication of two modes of the Many, two cycles of life and death: the corruption of mixture and the incandescence of contraries. In the face of those who denigrate decadence, the supposed optimism of the theory of productive forces is immediately ripped to pieces by the play of two contrary powers: the grand tragedy of water and fire, of production and destruction, and the low comedy of earth and air, of fabrication and imitation. One may talk as much as one likes about Marx's "Promethean" theory, but the body of Prometheus is fragmented from the outset. The materialism of history and the dialectics of revolution run the risk of never encountering each other in it.

4 :: The Production of the Proletarian

YET THE BULKY manuscript of *The German Ideology*, abandoned to the "gnawing criticism of mice," would like to prove to itself and us that things are very simple and that history has only one principle. Whoever wants to start off from earth, and not from the heaven of Ideas, must note this simple and constraining truth. One first must live in order "to make history": "But life involves before everything else eating and drinking, housing, clothing and various other things. The first historical act is thus the production of the means to satisfy these needs, the production of material life itself. And indeed this is an historical act, a fundamental condition of all history, which today, as thousands of years ago, must daily and hourly be fulfilled merely in order to sustain human life."[1]

"Daily and hourly": a curious echo of the Platonic rule concerning the absence of time whose function is no longer to attach men of iron to their place but to recall this point to knights and philosophers who think themselves kings. In effect, the commandment of "nothing else" shifts its place as the worker's rule of life becomes the golden rule, the very rationality of discourse. The impossibility of "anything else" becomes the general law of history that resounds obsessively through the rhetoric of *The German Ideology* or the *Manifesto of the Communist Party*. We know "only one science," the science of history. History is "nothing but" the succession of generations, each exploiting the materials transmitted to it by the preceding generation. The history of every society down to our own day "has been merely" the history of class struggle. The ruling ideas are "nothing more than" the ideal expression of the dominant material relations. Modern government "is but a committee" managing the common affairs of the whole bourgeois class. Ideologues go "no further" in their thinking than the petty bourgeoisie in its practice. Communism is "only" the real movement that abolishes the present state of things. And these proletarians who "have nothing to lose but their chains" will simply be transforming their own condition into a general social condition when they eliminate property.

"Only," "merely," "nothing but," "no further," "simply": these adverbs and similar phrases, if they are not to be the lonely agents of the monotonous labor of demystification, must form the other side of the positive principle that unifies the historical process, production.

THE ORDER OF PRODUCTION

This is where the grand affair of the reversal of heaven and earth must lie. Would it be worth the trouble, otherwise, to make such a commotion in proclaiming the simple discovery that human beings, in order to live, must eat, drink, have clothes and housing and do a few other things, which are not listed here in any more detail than in book II of the *Republic?* For the inflexible law of trivial necessity suffices to make the point. The novelty of the reversal cannot consist in the reminder of these evident facts, any more than in the reversed direction traveled on the road between heaven and earth. It lies wholly in the insistence on a concept that is posited as the essence of all "earthly" or "heavenly" activity, *production*. Humans differentiate themselves from animals "as soon as they begin to *produce* their means of subsistence." "By producing their means of subsistence, human beings are indirectly producing their actual material life." People "are the producers of their representations, their ideas." They also alter, in "developing their material production and their material intercourse, along with this their real existence, their thinking and the products of their thinking." The satisfaction of needs that is the "production of material life" is necessarily prolonged in the "production (*Erzeugung*) of new needs" and in the form of production known as procreation. All these productions are necessarily bound up with a mode of cooperation that is also a "productive force" and that must be studied before we arrive at consciousness, which is "from the very beginning a social product, and remains so as long as men exist."[2]

Thus the reversal of heaven and earth does not lie simply in the inversion of the journey's direction but in the persistence of the point of departure. There is no leap from the state fit only for pigs to civilized society, or from the seeding of soil to the formation of experts [*savants*]. The order of cities and the order of discourse are each as much *products* as the footwear of the shoemaker. Production is the essence of every activity, the measure of labor, war, and thinking, and it knows only transformations. From the worker's labor to the development of the productive forces, from the productive forces to the interests of a ruling class, from ruling interests to ruling ideas, and from ruling ideas to the rule of ideas: one can always reconstruct the chain which guarantees that in the gold of thinking there will never be anything but a certain transformation of the iron of production. However, this transformation also apparently works to the advantage of the man of iron. The philosopher is a producer like everyone else, but his production is not like the others. It is the limit of a process in which production is transformed into its own imitation. Its gold is nothing more than a demonetized money, a vain reflection of the exchangeable metal of productive activity.

THE OTHER CAVE

Now the man in the cave would be Plato's chief imitator, reduced to the rank of the most backward of producers. For in the philosopher's dereliction there is, apparently, something more to consider than the simple mechanism of inverting objects in the camera obscura of ideology. According to Marx, the German philosopher resembles the French peasant in his love for grottoes. *The Eighteenth Brumaire of Louis Bonaparte* tells us, too, of the sixteen million French peasants who live in troglodyte dwellings. Marx's correspondence repeats the tale of a visit that Bruno Bauer paid to him before returning to Germany to lead the life, far from the center of London, of a dirt farmer in the "pigsty" inhabited by his brother Edgar. The abode par excellence of the philosopher in chains is Berlin, since the city is surrounded by fields and has no outlet to the sea of industrial exchange. A wooden barrier (stone undoubtedly would be too much of a luxury for our troglodyte) detains him at a gate—not any gate but the one leading off to Hamburg, the industrial and commercial center where Marx will have *Capital* published. In that cave, the "pure thought" of the German philosopher boils down to its exact opposite, the pure drive of animality:

> In the case of a parochial Berlin schoolmaster or author, however, whose activity is restricted to arduous work on the one hand and the pleasure of thought on the other, whose world extends between [the Berlin suburbs] Moabit and Köpenich and ends as if stopped by a crude wooden barrier behind the

Hamburg Gate, whose relations to this world are reduced to a minimum by his pitiful position in life, it is certainly inevitable that his thought becomes just as abstract as he himself and his life. . . . In the case of such an individual the few remaining desires, which arise not so much from intercourse with the world as from the constitution of the human body, express themselves only through *repercussion*, i.e., they assume in their narrow development the same one-sided and crude character as does his thought, they appear only at long intervals, stimulated by the excessive development of the predominant desire (fortified by immediate physical causes such as, for example, [stomach] spasms) . . .[3]

We find here the philosopher-slave enchained, his body and soul injured by the mechanics of his craft and the baseness of his condition. To Plato's bald smith who washed himself at the public bath, dressed up as a bridegroom, and went off to court the noble orphan girl, there now corresponds the forlorn philosophy of "a widow of faded looks who puts on makeup and adorns her withered body now reduced to the most repugnant abstraction, and who heads out all over Germany in search of a suitor." And to the "critical critic," in whose eyes "the worker creates nothing" because his activity is enclosed in the singularity of need and its satisfaction, the young champion of materialism and the proletariat returns the compliment: "Critical criticism creates nothing, the worker creates everything; and so much so that even his intellectual creations put the whole of Criticism to shame."[4]

But putting criticism to shame is not, perhaps, the heart of the matter. If the king has taken the place of the slave, we still need to know which attributes the slave received from royal power. And it is here that things become confused, due perhaps to a certain excess of "clarity." For as soon as "any philosophical problem is resolved . . . quite simply into an empirical fact," it is clear that "a self-sufficient philosophy [die selbständigige Philosophie] loses its medium of existence."[5] So there is no longer a philosophical order from which the shoemaker could have seen himself excluded, but neither is there one to which he could have had access. A place is no longer reserved for science, but perhaps science no longer has an assignable place in a universe where all are fabricators and imitators, where the abode of truth is identical to the abode of *doxa*. The absence of time to do anything else than his work may have become the absence of place to produce anything else than the illusion of his craft.

THE SCAFFOLDING OF WORK

So now it is simply a matter of conceiving things "as they actually are, i.e., as they act, produce materially." But the question is knowing who can devote himself to the "empirical observation" of this history. If everything is production and if people are producers of their ideas at the same time as their material life, it may be pointless to assure us that the phantasmagorias of the human brain are the simple results of the "empirically verifiable" process of material life. The human beings who "perceive" the process are also the ones who "appear to themselves" in the phantasmagoria produced by this process. In other words, *there is no German ideology*. Bauer and Stirner must see "things as they are." Unfortunately, "you cannot have any experience of these things across the Rhine." They misread history but the fact is that in Germany "history has stopped happening."[6] If there are only phantoms, then the philosopher of phantoms is a good observer. To see something different or to see the same thing differently, one has to be elsewhere, one has to examine the hubbub of the German scene "from a vantage point outside Germany." Even if that means discovering in Paris that the reality of the class struggle is also the reality of political illusion, or discovering in London that the reality of modern industry is also the reality of economic illusion. While it is true that *The German Ideology* was written in Brussels, there is, apparently, less illusion there, but perhaps less to see as well.

Ideology, in other words, simply may be the fact that each does "his own business" in a universe where fabrication and imitation, truth and *doxa*, exchange their powers. Seeing, not seeing, and seeing upside down become here equivalent terms that also render equivalent the phantasmagoria of the imitator and the clairvoyance of the fabricator. So Proudhon "sees things upside down, if he sees them at all."[7] But this is also because he sees what is, not what will be. He sees in the machine the liberation it is not (recomposed labor) because he does not see what will be: the complete individual who will be born, instead, out of decomposed labor and the total loss of the worker's status. But this faulty view of the ideologue is nothing but the short view that is the worker's own virtue, the consecration of craft idiocy.

The ideologue is not a person of leisure, the heavenly dreamer who falls into a well while looking up at the stars. He is someone who toils, a drudge who—like Proudhon, the modern Hippias: typographer, riverboat clerk, philologist, economist, and philosopher—tries painfully to raise scaffolding between the earth of work and the heaven of science. This backward fellow truly does not see that we are no longer living in the days of Thales, that truth no longer dwells in heaven. It is here on earth where it is only a matter of observing, but where no one sees.

For if "seeing" is not the production of illusion added by each category of producers to the production of "one's own business," then it has become an unassignable activity in a world where, moreover, the task is not to "contemplate" but to "change" things. Like Proudhon, the drudge will never get beyond the second level of the scaffold. He will always fall off the side. He will fabricate where he should see, and contemplate where he should change.

So the vice of the ideologue may be merely the worker's virtue. His phantasmagoria reveals in magnified form the way in which all know-how [savoir-faire] forges a vision of the world. Any opposition between the "intellectual creations" of the worker and the wild imaginings of the philosopher in chains is completely illusory. Industry may well be "the open book of man's essential powers,"[8] but the letters that compose it cannot read themselves. All the nobility of humanity may shine on the brows of Parisian workers who meet for study, but the commodity itself presents a more obtuse face. It does not have written on it that it is the "sign of the division of labor that marks it as the property of capital" except in the form of hieroglyphics that cannot be read by workers who wear on their brows the sign of a people both chosen and condemned.[9] The "intellectual creations" of tailor Weitling—he is the person in question—can always put criticism to "shame." But that is all they can do: prove to the bourgeoisie that workers can do as well as, or better than, the professional ideologues. The proof is given only too well when it is addressed to workers. Taught by Weitling to the shoemakers and tailors of the League of the Just, repeated by some artisan suffering from intellectualism and then memorized by his proselytes, Weitling's "creations" reveal themselves for what they are: *fabrications* produced and reproduced in the manner of petty bourgeois ideologues which, in turn, are no different from the needlework of the shoemakers and tailors who learn them by heart. In short, Beckmesser and Hans Sachs are one and the same character. Ideology is just another name for work.

THE NON-PLACE OF SCIENCE

So the chaining of the ideologue is also that of the worker. To escape from such constraint, there must emerge from the productive universe a philosopher who is no longer a philosopher and a worker who is no longer a worker: a scientist [*savant*] and a proletarian. To German poverty is hence opposed a view from exile that is its non-place.[10] To the schoolmaster of the cave in Berlin is opposed his former fellow student, the scientist no longer narrowly confined to any place in the division of labor.

What this science lacks, however, is the explanation of its own course. If it keeps on accumulating "empirically verifiable" items of evidence, it is because it is unable to answer this question: what makes it possible for science to tear the tissue of the production of material life as well as of its imitations? The *Communist Manifesto* responds with an extravagant geology: when the class struggle approaches its crucial moment, the process effecting the decomposition of the old society detaches and drops into the militant proletariat "a small fraction of the ruling class . . . specifically, the portion of the bourgeois ideologists, who have raised themselves to the level of comprehending theoretically the historical movement as a whole."[11]

This confusion of precipice and summit makes it clear enough that science is an inexplicable phenomenon. Ideology is explained, even overexplained. It is the fabrication of imitations, the imitation of fabrications, the banality of factory reality as social order. Science itself is an accident, an improbable throw of the dice in the orderly play of fabrications and imitations. It is the unlikely nonplace of all places: the power to see not simply "truth" behind appearance but death in life and nonbeing in being. The power of *dissolution*. Doctor Marx does not write books of philosophy, history, politics, or political economy; he writes only books of *criticism*.

Only one text in all of Marx's works proposes the theory concerning this power: "A Contribution to the Critique of Hegel's *Philosophy of Right*: Introduction," published in 1844 in the *Deutsch-*

französiche Jahrbücher. This paradoxical theory tells us that it is precisely the backwardness of Germany that makes solvent-criticism possible with its practical powers of dissolution. Prevented from living modern history in reality, Germany has had to live it in thought. Hegel fashioned the theory of the modern political state, a state that actually exists only in England or France. Hence the critique of his theory is already the critique of the quintessence of the modern world, the necessary anticipation of the human world to come. In short, German backwardness establishes philosophy as the absolute non-place of the old feudal world and the new bourgeois world. And the same backwardness that prevents any specific class from carrying out its own political revolution in the name of others also draws in outline the future subject of the human revolution, that is, the proletariat, which is the pure dissolution of classes, the pure identity of being and nonbeing.

The curious geology of the *Manifesto* is now explicable: it is the philosophical and political paradox of criticism planed and sanded by *The German Ideology*. The historical and materialist law of the "nothing else" forbids German poverty from producing anything other than a philosophy of poverty. But the emergence of revolutionary science has no other explanation to offer. Marx cannot change the interpretation of criticism; he can only erase it. As a consequence science remains based upon its unassignable difference, though now it runs the opposite risk of being nothing more than the science of things "as they really are," the positive science of philistinism. It is instructive, of course, to explain to the bucolic Feuerbach that the cherry tree before his eyes was not always there; that it was imported in specific historical circumstances; and that it, like everything in this world, is hence the "result of the activity of a whole succession of generations, each standing on the shoulders of the preceding one, developing its industry and its intercourse, and modifying its social system according to its changed needs."[12] But at its limit the solid philosophy of these improvements in arboriculture is very close to a morality of history attacked by the young Marx: that of the philistine Plutarch, who related with satisfaction how the corpses of the "great and noble" Cimbri proved to be an ideal manure for the orchards and vineyards of "the philistines of Massilia."[13] According to Marx, histories of descent are often histories of decadence. Those who stand on the shoulders of giants, and sometimes on their backsides, are generally dwarves. And the demystification of bucolic vistas in the name of positive history can be left to the philistines, who will always know how to make use of them. That was already the trick of the jurists of the Romantic school to justify the state of things "as they were." The ethics of demystification is that of preservation; the ethics of critical science is that of destruction.

In the history of production, then, one must recover the instance of decisive justice, not that of formative labor. If production recurs obsessively in The German Ideology, another reason may be the elimination of the concept that competed with it in the Economic and Philosophical Manuscripts of 1844: labor. From now on labor's point of view is the theory of others, the theory of ideologues. It is the theory of the worker-sophist Proudhon. Making him the spokesman of an obsolete artisan class is but meager consolation. Creative labor will also be the first word of modern German social democracy, the word that will seal its fate: confidence in the unlimited accumulation of productive forces. Marx's often iniquitous tenacity in dissecting one or another person's words and underlying motives is, first of all, a way of exorcizing the inherent contradiction in the materialist theory of history. Marx tells us that in Feuerbach's work, history and materialism never encounter each other; what remains to be seen is how the materialist history of superimposed generations will itself rejoin the revolutionary dialectic. For if history "is nothing but the succession of the separate generations, each of which exploits the materials, the capital funds, the productive forces handed down to it by all preceding generations,"[14] it is hard to see how it will ever know the fire of division. The sole viewpoint of the "transformation of circumstances" is that of the bourgeoisie which, much to the detriment of Quixote-like spirits, never stops revolutionizing the instruments of production in creating wonders that surpass the Egyptian pyramids, the Roman aqueducts, and the Gothic cathedrals. It is the viewpoint of a bourgeoisie that will never stop making its revolution: the Absolute Bourgeoisie, in the manner of Hegel's Absolute Spirit.

Curiously enough, it is there that some often look mistakenly to find the Hegelian ancestry of Marxism, there in the edifying theory of the formative work of culture: thus the slave, who at first submitted to serving an "alien being" out of fear, masters him through the discipline of labor, the instrument that the *Aesthetics* regards as superior to all the beauty of nature since it is an achievement of the spirit. The industrious happiness of the Dutch bourgeoisie is reflected in the brilliance of household objects shining in their still life paintings. Prometheus, citizen of Delft.[15] There, too, is the labor of history in childbirth, the succession of too-fragile shells shattered by Spirit until the cunning of reason finds its "good infinity" in the Sancho Panzan prose of the bourgeois world: constitutional monarchy; the representation of economic interests; and the university realm of spirits where the philosopher scoffs at the beautiful souls who pursue no career, the young people who have finished their wild years of apprenticeship, and religious beliefs in the hereafter (though he derides the last only in whispers to a wary listener while looking around to make sure no one else can hear).[16]

The Hegelianism of master and slave is precisely that: the discreet charm of the radical bourgeoisie. After his *Economic and Philosophic Manuscripts of 1844*, Marx will give up trying to find the force of Hegelian negativity in labor. What interests him henceforth is the Hegelianism of the *Logic*, which does not talk any more about formative labor or reason in history but about the conflagration of being and nonbeing or the leap from quantity to quality; and where it matters little if one goes astray in hazardous anticipations of the philosophy of nature, or in speculations on electricity and magnetism. A thinking of fire and water, of a production whose force derives solely from bearing within itself the anticipation of destruction. The encounter between materialism and the dialectic, the socialized leisure of the great media of circulation and exchange born of industry, can occur only beyond the break [*la coupure*]. On the contrary, labor "forms" proletarians only by stripping them of all social property.

The history of production, then, must be cracked in two. On the one hand there is the labor of generations, the accumulation of transformations, compost and grime. On the other there is revolutionary justice that "gets rid of" (*beseitigt*) labor—a justice executed by a class that is no longer a class, not only to overthrow the ruling class but also to "succeed in ridding itself of all the muck of ages and become fitted to found society anew."[17]

That is how we must understand "the stern but steeling school of labor."[18] It is not labor but its disappropriation that forms the proletarian. What he learns at work is to lose his status as a worker. The apprenticeship comes to an end where labor has become completely an *alien* power—a lot of good this may do him! If the proletariat comes to be the agent of history, it is not because it "creates everything" but because it is dispossessed of everything—not only of the "wealth" it "created" but especially of its "creative" power, i.e. the limits of the "dedicated" worker realizing himself in "his" product:

> When socialist writers ascribe this world-historic role to the proletariat, it is not at all, as Critical Criticism pretends to believe, because they regard proletarians as *gods*. Rather the contrary. Since in the fully formed proletariat the abstraction of all humanity, even of the *semblance* of humanity, is practically complete . . . since man has lost himself in the proletariat, yet at the same time has gained theoretical consciousness of that loss . . . it follows that the proletariat can and must emancipate itself. . . . It is not a question of what this or that proletarian, or even the whole proletariat, *regards* as its aim at the moment. It is a question of *what the proletariat is* and what, in accordance with this *being*, it will historically be compelled to do.[19]

So nothing could be more grotesque than imagining a class consciousness based on the virtue of the laborer. It is not "doing" that determines being, but the opposite. The proletarian is someone *who has only one thing to do*—to make the revolution—and who *cannot not do that* because of what he is. For what he is, is the pure loss of every attribute, the identity of being and nonbeing, which is not at all the empty identity of Hegel's *Logic* but an identity that has gone through the school of labor, i.e. through the opposition between the *nothing* of the laborer and the *everything* of wealth. This pure coincidence is presented here with all the bluntness of the dialectical pivot: *at the same time* (zugleich). It is this same coincidence that Marx will oppose to Proudhon's culture of labor: "The moment that every special development stops, the need for universality, the tendency toward an integral development of the individual begins to be felt."[20]

"At the same time," "the moment that": the locutions of the

revolutionary dialectic come along to redress the "nothing else" and the "only" of materialist history. The other time of the revolutionary dialectic is the pure time of the reminiscence of the negative. The proletarian is Meno's slave: the *tabula rasa*, the blank surface on which—on the condition that the *Manifesto* gives him existence as a subject—the Revolution will inscribe itself with the same necessity as the diagonal of a square.

Thus the proletarian is nothing else than the negation of the worker. He is the anti-ideologue precisely insofar as he is the anti-worker. By the same token, the worker who is *not yet* a proletarian can be baptized with a variety of names that are all equivalent: artisan, *lumpen*, petty bourgeois, ideologue . . . Supposed to interject itself between the worker and the consciousness of his state, this baleful third party has no consistency. The worker-fabricator and the ideologue-imitator are brothers, like the "liberated" student and the robust mechanic who share the favors of a Berlin midwife and the paternity of a little bastard named Proudhon-Fourier.[21]

If it amuses them, some may indulge in the grave recital of the "objective conditions" delaying the development of proletarian consciousness, but delay is not a historical category. The "consciousness" in question does not belong to the development of "objective conditions." Artisan, petty bourgeois, *lumpen*: these sociohistoric categories are merely comic masks disguising the distance between worker and proletarian, the noncoincidence of the time of development and the time of revolution.

Thus are redistributed the terms of the prohibition of the "nothing else" that linked the specific virtue of the artisan to the absence of time. In principle, Plato's commandment had been overturned in the promotion of *technē*. But *technē* divides itself immediately into two. It will become what it is in itself, production, only through the fire of destruction. And this fire is not that of the worker's forge. To gain access to the communist realm of the Many where his free activity will be identified with the leisure of the philosopher, the artisan first must become the pure negation of himself. The barrier that separated him from the philosopher is now the barrier of the revolution he must carry out. But access to this barrier involves confrontation with its own paradox, with the exigency of a self-subtraction that is even more devious than the one that was supposed to change the hairy man into a bald one. When will the artisan be sufficiently stripped of his status to become the subject of the *nothing else* of the revolution?

Thus the barrier of the orders forms itself again inside the materialist "reversal." No one erects it before the artisan except the artisan himself. The worker-artisan of the development of productive forces, the proletarian-warrior of the revolution, and the producer-philosopher of the communist future are three personages belonging to different times.

THE BACKWARD WORKER,
OR THE PARADOX OF COMMUNISM

The Marxist tradition identifies that heterogeneity with the simple weight of the past, with the hold of the dead on the living. The obstacle would come from backward artisans attached to crafts swept away by modern industry, and to little shops condemned by the world market. The Weitling tailors who debate whether they should chain down their communal knives and forks, the joiners who repeat by heart theories that their leader learned from Grün, who got them in turn from Proudhon: these all would be false proletarians, artisans of the old mold who want to return to the time of the journeymen of yesteryear known in Germany as *Straubinger*.[22]

This explanation is ridiculous and Marx knows that very well. What attracts tailors to Weitling or joiners to Grün is neither the prospect of sewing or planing fraternally nor of taking their finished clothes to a counter to receive in exchange some finished pieces of carpentry. It is the desire to do something else besides making clothes or casement windows, to establish themselves as a society of friends of wisdom. Marx himself noticed this in Paris with all the enthusiasm of a revelation: "When communist *artisans* associate with one another, theory, propaganda, etc., is their first end. But at the same time, as a result of this association, they acquire a new need—the need for society—and what appears as a means becomes an end. . . . Association, society and conversation, which in turn has association for its end, are enough for them; the brotherhood of man is no mere phrase with them, but a fact of life, and the nobility of man shines upon us from their work-hardened bodies."[23]

But here is the problem that is likely to transform the enthusiasm of the communist into the despair of the revolutionary—the nobility of humanity *already* shining on brows that should have lost even the appearance of it in order to produce the future nobility of humanity. The propagandist Friedrich Engels, who comes along two years later looking to persuade these shining brows of humanity, could know what to expect. The principal obstacle to his mission is not the influence of his petty bourgeois rivals. It is the very nature of this new need which, not content to add where it should subtract, had also the impertinence to find its satisfaction *hic et nunc*. The obstacle to the transformation of *Straubinger* communists into revolutionary proletarians is not their status as artisans but their status as communists—not the heavy weight of their journeyman past but the lightness of their anticipation of the communist future.

In short, Marx's science has exactly the same problem as Cabet's utopia: *how is one to make a new world with those who desire it?*[24] For Cabet this involves squaring the circle. To build Icaria Cabet needs men of order and fraternity, but only Icaria could educate such people. Those who present themselves to found Icaria are disordered and combative, revolutionaries that the old world had fashioned in its own likeness. Icaria will die, then, without ever having begun. The communist revolution faces the same problem from the other end. Those who intend to effect it have the fault of *already* being communists. They are not necessarily fools who argue in the land of plenty about their knives and forks; they are, simply, men who transform means into ends and ends into means, who pretend to be already living the ideal of the future to which the young revolutionary science has not yet found anything superior: the Swabian, sentimental, south German—in a word, Schillerian—ideal of *the aesthetic education of humanity.*

A Communist among the Lapps

The propagandist's mission, then, resembles a game of "loser takes all." Engels will leave the tailors to Weitling the *Straubinger* and wrest the joiners from the petty bourgeois Grün. But what good does that do if the new *goal* he gets them to vote for (by a margin of 13 to 2) immediately becomes, for these natives of Swabia, the *means* to imitate the sociability of the future? The only result will be to have enlarged the *Straubinger* army in the party of the proletariat, which will never lack for them.

For all these "backward" joiners, tailors, and shoemakers are only too inclined to hear modern theory preaching farewell to the "old rubbish" of needle, plane, and shoemaker's pitch. They will always be eager to depart for a world in which machines will produce large quantities all by themselves. The problem for the theory does not come from journeymen set in their ways in the practice of their craft, for they will always be the best soldiers of organization and production. It comes from workers whose sense of the vanity of their trade has carried them farthest along in the stripping away of the old artisanal character from those who fit most closely the definition of a proletarian. The problem thus comes not from those who combat theory but from those who adopt it enthusiastically and are always ready to abandon tool and workshop to propagate it. We need only note the pleasure with which the best of the *Straubinger*, the London communists, follow the mission of a propagandist who had set out to spread their doctrine in Scandinavia:

> From an emissary sent from here, who went from Helsinger to Sweden and traveled the country on foot, we have received a letter from Uppsala dated May 23. Since he had no possessions, he had filled his bag with communist tracts that he was fortunate to get over the border into Sweden. He writes us that in all the cities where there are German workers, he paid visits to the latter in their workshops, handed out our literature, and found a big response to his propagandizing. Unfortunately, since he found no work, he could not remain anyplace long enough to found communes. In Stockholm he handed over to the local branch (our communist outpost in the North) the first two circulars of the central authority, and that news fanned the ardor of our brothers there. From Stockholm he went to Uppsala, and from there to Gävle where he labored for a time. He is now on route to Umeå and Torneå. A communist emissary among the Lapps![25]

In all likelihood, this propertyless worker no longer counts on meeting any German workers in Umeå and Torneå, for whom he would not have any tracts remaining anyway. As for his finding work there, it is rather his pure being as a communist that he is showing off in the solitude of the north. Communist propaganda finds there its truth: a headlong rush to fraternity, travel satisfied with its own enjoyment [*jouissance*]. A Lapp himself, this traveler of the "bad infinity" finds the privileged place of his wandering in the expanses of Scandinavia viewed as the land of barbarism by the people of the Rhine. See what Engels tells his friend Marx: "The whole country has only two proper towns, à 80,000 and 40,000 inhabitants respectively, the third, Norrköping, having only 12,000 inhabitants and all the rest perhaps 1,000, 2,000, and 3,000. At every post station there's one inhabitant. In Denmark things are scarcely better, since they have only one solitary city there, in which the guilds indulge in the most ludicrous proceedings, madder even than in Basel or Bremen . . . There's also a frightful number of Hegelians there."[26]

One need not be a Danish Hegelian to understand the dialectical necessity of the reversal that links infinite dispersion to corporatist narrowness. The territory of the bad infinity is also that of the immediate, and the propagandist who delights in traversing it belongs to the same world as the most barbarian Scandinavians, among them the Norwegian who "rejoices in the fact that at home in Norge exactly the same stupid peasant economy is dominant as at the time of the noble Canute," or the Icelander who "continues to speak exactly the same language as the unwashed Vikings of anno 900, swills whale oil, lives in a mud hut and goes to pieces in any atmosphere that does not reek of rotten fish."[27]

A FALSE EXIT: CLASS AND PARTY

That, then, is the basis for the backwardness of the *Straubinger*—nothing else than their communism. The first obstacle on the road to the communist revolution is posed by the communists themselves, and apparently one can *do nothing* about it. From his relations with the London communists Engels draws his disabused conclusion: "We have learnt from this business that in the absence of a proper movement in Germany, nothing can be done with the Straubingers, even the best of them. . . . Vis-à-vis *ourselves*, these lads declare themselves to be 'the people,' 'the proletarians,' and we can only appeal to a communist proletariat which has yet to take shape in Germany."[28]

It is too hard a task, even for the best dialecticians, to prove to communist proletarians that they are not communist proletarians by invoking a communist proletariat whose only fault is that it does not yet exist. So the materialist takes over with his solution, the materialist solution par excellence: waiting. It is futile to refute theoretically communists who have no theory. The only thing to do is to leave things alone, put communist workers and communist correspondence on ice, and wait for the coming communist proletariat and its organized movement.

Like every materialist solution, this is a simple one. But like them, too, it is ineffective. The artisan's barrier is also the philosopher's. If we must wait for modern industry to produce a communist proletariat, then the scientist may be no more advanced than fraternity's pedestrian. Industrial development could certainly create a modern working class. Yet what is needed is *not a class*, even a modern one, but a *non-class*. Every class is itself a caste, a survival from the feudal and slave-based past. The proletariat will be a revolutionary "class" only to the extent that it is the dissolution of all classes and above all the "young" working class itself.

So let our nostalgic friends celebrate today, near the end of the twentieth century, the "fusion" of "Marxist theory" and the "labor movement." Before the end of 1847 Marx and Engels, for their part, realized that they were faced with a different task, the union of the *formation of a class* and its *dissolution*.

For a question is very much in order: why did they change their minds? Logically, the *Manifesto of the Communist Party should never have existed*. Marx and Engels should have quietly let their correspondence with the *Straubinger* of London go dormant. And yet Marx and Engels join with those very people to publish with great fanfare the manifesto of the communist party. *What* communist party? The party of the as yet nonexistent proletariat? The party of the *Straubinger*? Some might suggest that in the interval the *Straubinger* mended their ways and assimilated Marxist ideas. And then? After all, a Marxist *Straubinger* still remains a *Straubinger*. This perverse breed is characterized by its very ability to "assimilate" every idea that comes to hand. As a disabused Saint-Simonian priest put it, they are "eaters of ideas." People who "digest" things quickly tend, periodically, to worry Marx and Engels.

So why make a party with people who decidedly will never be true proletarians? Perhaps precisely because they never will become such. Because first of all the purpose of a party is not to unite but divide: "Proletarians of all countries, unite!" That also means: "Workers of each country, divide!" The alliance of science with this ridiculous vanguard is, first, division *in actu*. The party is essentially the point at which is materialized the principle of the proletariat as division, under its double aspect. It represents the proletariat as absolutely *One*, constituted as such by the hatred of all the powers of the old world. But it is also the dissolution of this *One*, the non-class that attacks class from within.

In a sense, then, the party can be summed up in the trenchant words of the philosopher. The pure power of division finds its universality in the opposition of its singularity to all the forces of the old world: "I told them straight out that we owed our position as representatives of the proletarian party to nobody but ourselves; this, however, had been endorsed by the exclusive and universal hatred accorded us by every faction and party of the old world."[29] The philosopher is himself the party only as the tragic power of the negative. Whatever gathers around him—this irresolute mixture of *Straubinger* with intellectual pretensions and half-pay intellectuals—is doomed comically to repeat a text that is not its own and that it can only distort. A court filled with jesters whom the philosopher-king in exile would gladly let pass. Note Engels's jubilation when it comes time to bury quietly the party that had been baptized with so much solemnity: "At long last we gain the opportunity—the first time in ages—to show that we need neither popularity, nor the SUPPORT of any party in any country. . . . Haven't we been acting for years as though Cherethites and Plethites were our party when, in fact, we had no party, and when the people whom we considered as belonging to our party, at least officially, *sous réserve de les appeler des bêtes incorrigibles entre nous* [French in original: "with the reservation that between ourselves we called them incorrigible fools"—Trans.], didn't even understand the rudiments of our stuff? . . . And what have we . . . to do with a 'party,' i.e. a herd of jackasses who swear by us because they think we're of the same kidney as they?"[30]

The Genius of the *Straubinger*

But the philosopher cannot bypass those incorrigible fools. The pure nonbeing of division must have a body to anticipate the proletariat that has not yet been formed in Germany, but it also must divide this class that will always be quick enough to constitute itself with its common interests and their modern representatives. The International is perhaps that, first of all: the union of workers as a *non-class*, a weapon against the modern organizations which—in England, France, or Germany—express only too well the interests of workers *as a class*. For that purpose, nothing could be better than the clowns of the party in general and the *Straubinger* in particular. To counter the organization of German worker associations, the sentimental south German ass, Liebknecht, will go to Leipzig. To check on Liebknecht, who has distributed no more than six membership cards for the International throughout Germany, the old conspirator Becker in Geneva. To keep an eye on Becker, the tailor Eccarius (the Marxist *Straubinger* par excellence), this "son of toil" who in his London exile has learned how to write but not yet how to punctuate, and who is only too happy to find in his new life as a leader and publicist his revenge for a life lost in "the hell of needlework."

They are clowns, assuredly, but for their respect due to the indomitable Becker. They can hardly undertake any initiative without botching it. But for this reason they can be trusted to do the job of *representing nothing*. They are irreplaceable for playing the role of the people in the burlesque way that their colleague, the joiner Snug, plays the lion in *A Midsummer Night's Dream*. They are poets, *daimonic* men. So it is with the tailor Ulmer, a nondescript man under the inspiration of a certain "genius." And when indignation turns him into a poet, his genius sends him into trances and has him sow terror at meetings of democrats: "And what is more, the communist's fierceness has made him infallible."[31]

Promoting dissolution and undermining codes of representation, such men are Shakespearean individualities in contrast to the types employed by the Schillerian Lassalle, in whose play *Franz von Sickingen* "the principal characters are representatives of specific classes and tendencies." Engels may well be thinking of his own "party" when he reproaches Lassalle for omitting from his drama the whole "Falstaffian backdrop"—the "vagabond beggar-kings, hungry mercenaries and adventurers of all kinds" characteristic of "this period's dissolving feudal ties."[32] The literary question of tragedy is also the political question of revolution in the 1850s, when the bourgeoisie "has for the second time experienced its 16th century."[33] To arrive at the tragic dimension of the revolution, the bourgeois drama of representation—Schillerian, Lassallean, and social democratic—must be doubled with the Shakespearian tragicomedy of dissolution. The legitimacy of "the first-born sons of modern industry" must be doubled with the bastardy of the mendicant philosopher-kings and mercenaries—*Straubinger*—of communism. Similarly, the rationality of the development of productive forces must be doubled with the legend of the mole of revolution. The latter, who is sometimes confused with his Hegelian companion, the cunning of reason, is also a Shakespearean character. But there has been a shift of scene. Hegel borrowed his mole from the tragedy of Prince Hamlet, in which he saw the first tears in the fabric of the new bourgeois individuality. The materialist Karl Marx seems to prefer fairies. At a banquet honoring the "first-born sons" of English industry, he rebaptized and rejuvenated the old mole. Its name, he said, is Robin Goodfellow, or Puck, the sprite of *A Midsummer Night's Dream*.[34] The modern figure of the daimon Eros, son of Poros and Penia, Puck is the genius of a history that is no longer cunning but simply ironic.

5 :: The Revolution Conjured Away

A FEW DETOURS are needed, then, if the proletariat is to exist through its party and the party through its manifesto. But all the manifestos of science and party must repress such detours behind the optimistic rationality of a history that is and does "nothing else" than what everyone can see plainly. This work of effacement gives the *Communist Manifesto* its discursive cast as it plays with its two meanings, proclaiming that there is nothing to proclaim except what is manifest to everyone's eyes. "We find," "we witness," "we see," "we have just seen," "we saw": history until now has been simply the history of class struggle, which means, in the last instance, a history of productive forces that developed on the basis of certain property relations. Those relations became fetters hindering the development of the aforementioned forces; they had to be broken and they were. Other relations replaced them but these, too, became fetters and were broken in turn, and so on until the final moment of appropriation/disappropriation. This is the work of a grave-digging proletariat produced by a bourgeoisie destined to be buried as if by an earthquake: "The proletariat, the lowest stratum of our present society, cannot stir, cannot raise itself up, without the whole superincumbent strata of official society being sprung into the air."[1]

Doctor Marx likes geology and geological metaphors. Their application here indicates a total confidence in the soil of modern society that supports the proletariat and in the bourgeoisie who fertilize it with its progress and its waste. If the *Communist Manifesto* displays an optimism out of proportion to the communist experience of its authors, it is precisely because the possibility of communism is founded in the text not on the power of a proletariat still absent from the scene, but on the power of the bourgeoisie. It shifts the whole force of development and contradiction to bourgeois action and passion.

It begins with the *mise en scène* of the subject of the *Manifesto*: the communist party. If that party exists, it is certainly not as a result of the *Straubinger* communes, but neither is it due to the virtual power of the children of large-scale industry. Its exists because of the terror of its specter felt by all those in power. The text would meet "this nursery tale of the Specter of Communism with a Manifesto of the party itself." But "the party itself" exists only as the other side of the tale. Its power stems from being the specter feared by everyone in power. Its legitimacy—even inverted— derives from the pope and the czar, from Metternich and Guizot, who are united in their efforts to exorcize it.

We need only reverse the specter to get the subject. This short-cut avoids Feuerbach's detour, since his reversal of the divine specter did not give us *Mankind* but only *men*, the multiform reality of difference. This gearing down constituted the force of his reversal (i.e., it no longer was reversible), but also the weakness of the move itself: essence no longer existed except as a sum to be added up, thereby making communism the bad infinity of fraternity. "Only the *sum total* of humans know nature. Only the sum total of humans live the human."[2] The itinerary for an infinite journey in the manner of Anders the Lapp.

Logically the Marxian reversal should produce the same result. In *The German Ideology* we found "living individuals" opposed to speculation. In the *Manifesto*, however, the refutation of the communist specter, in itself, would lead back only to the sad reality of actual communists. Further, the materialist principle of addition and multiplication, of "living individuals" and unceasing generations, must itself be joined to a dialectical principle of death: division, which alone can do the trick because it presupposes the unity, the All, that multiplication never attains. What is needed is a *One* that is a *Two*, a totality presupposed by its very division.

That is what is provided by the bourgeoisie's fear of the specter, which gives birth to *the party* as the One to which all others are opposed. This fear has nothing to do with the terrors of children or old people. The power that invents the communist specter is the same power that invented the railroads. The bourgeoisie is afraid because it recognizes the proletariat more or less confusedly as its own double, the other side of the pact it sealed with the god—or devil—of the productive forces. Its fear is still another manifestation of its power. If bourgeois passion sustains the existence of communism, this is because bourgeois action sustains the existence of the proletariat.

For in the *Manifesto* the bourgeoisie alone has the power of agency. It is the agent of a civilization of the universal whose cities, factories, railroads, ships, and telegraphs are breaking down all barriers of caste and nation and wiping from the earth all traces of primitive savagery and peasant backwardness. It is also the agent of its own destruction, too imbued with its own tragic power to evade the destiny that compels it to keep revolutionizing the instruments of production and unchain the forces that are to drag it down into the abyss. The *Manifesto* is an act of faith in the suicide of the bourgeoisie.

In this drama there is no way that the proletarians can be gods. At most they might play bit parts. Gravediggers, not even assassins. Everything they are they owe to bourgeois action or passion. They are mere soldiers of industry, instruments of labor, appendages of the machine. Human only by virtue of the competition that divides them or the artisanal backwardness that sets them against the machine, they must receive their power from sources outside themselves. They owe their growing unification to industrial concentration, the leveling of skills, and the speed of the railroad. They have received their status as political subjects from the bourgeoisie, who brought them into their own fight against the feudal order. And their ongoing political education is bound up with the dissolution of the ruling class, which constantly sends them masses of combatants trained in its school and philosophers to lead their fight.

One privilege, at least, should remain to the proletarians: that of the "nothing," the disabused look peculiar to people stripped of all status and for whom property, family, religion, and nation have no further existence. But even that is the doing of the bourgeoisie. The relations of the proletarian with his wife and children are said to have "no longer anything in common with the bourgeois family relations," but bourgeois marriage is itself already "a system of wives in common."[3] The proletarians have no homeland, but the bourgeoisie can exist only as a universal class, and it has battered down all the "Chinese walls" defending national interests and routines. To the proletarian, "law, morality, and religion are so many bourgeois prejudices behind which lurk as many bourgeois interests," but the bourgeoisie has already drowned all tremblings of religious ecstasy and moral enthusiasm "in the icy waters of egotistical calculation."[4] The *lack of status*, which is pure passivity in the case of the proletarian, is in the case of the bourgeoisie the force of spirit in perpetual motion that sweeps away all fixed determinations along with all the old decay. The bourgeoisie is revolutionary not just because it created large-scale industry but also because it is already the movement dissolving all classes—all fixed, ossified determinations. It is already the class that is a non-class, the tragic identity of production and destruction. Simply the double or reverse side of the bourgeois revolution, the proletariat merely sanctions this identity of life and death. Its action is not dialectical but simply materialist. The gravedigger sanctions the completion of the bourgeois revolution.

THE BOURGEOIS BETRAYAL

Thus the *Manifesto of the Communist Party* entrusts to the bourgeoisie the task for which no proletariat conforms to its concept: the identification of *materialist* demystification with *dialectical* destruction. The credit that the text gives to bourgeois radicality goes hand in hand with its confidence in the political readability of history.

But this confidence was doubly disappointed by the revolution of 1848. That revolution is a botched representation, a tragedy turned into a farce that could be called *The Demystifier Mystified*.

Yet all the conditions had been present to confirm the "findings" of the *Manifesto*. June 1848 turns book truth into street spectacle: the visible division [*partage*] of classes on one side of the barricade or the other. And the republic rebaptized in the bloodshed of repression is very precisely the dictatorship of the bourgeoisie as an entire class, now stripped of the old tinsel that masked the nature of power.

Up to this point everything confirms the theory of the observer of *Class Struggles in France*. But from that point on, everything becomes confused. We expected to see bourgeois domination fulfill itself and political history prove to be the open book of class struggle. But the book that was to be the *revelation of the manifest* is now covered with hieroglyphics. The political stage is purged of its rightful actors, bourgeois and proletarian, making way for a troupe of substitute comedians whose burlesque performance reaches its climax in the triumph of the clown Louis Napoleon.

The apparent victory of name over things, conjuring over production, backwardness over history.

This succession of theatrical or circus effects on the stage of revelation has a precise meaning: it conveys the general incapacity of classes to exist at the only level that would give them the right to be called classes, the level of their political representation.

It was to be expected that the proletariat, caught between the old and the new, the not yet dead and the not yet born, could not measure up to its task in this matter. It was still too weak to play its role; it could only display its interest *alongside* the interest of the bourgeoisie in February 1848, and then carry out its funereal "solo" in June. The problem came from the class still bearing the force of revolution, the bourgeoisie. The troubling event of 1848 was the absolute incapacity of the bourgeoisie in power to accomplish the business of the bourgeoisie in power. This conquering class, unleashing the forces of modern industry and its demystifying political and ideological enchantments, gives way to a seducer who is not even a proper sorcerer. It abandons its power without putting up a fight to a swindler, a leader of a society of parasites, a boor whose representative capacity derives, aside from the pickpockets surrounding him, solely from the backwardness of old peasant France.

There is a materialist explanation for this turn of events, of course, which is fear. At the June barricades the bourgeoisie saw too closely the visage of its own death. It saw that the "pure" form of its political domination was unleashing class struggle in all its nakedness and clearing the ground for the final confrontation. It was afraid of a victory presaging its own death. It realized that its own self-interest dictated that it "should be delivered from the danger of its *own rule*."[5] To preserve intact its social power, it entrusted its political power to a supposedly imbecilic figurehead. But Louis Bonaparte caught the bourgeoisie in a trap and forced it to abdicate the *reality* of power, of which it wanted to grant him merely the appearance, and in return he gave the bourgeoisie a propitious order to its affairs. In short, the bourgeoisie simply sacrificed its *political interest* for its *social interest*.

But this explanation only pushes the problem further back. Prudence is a materialist virtue, to be sure, but for a dialectical agent of history it is a declaration of bankruptcy. Can we still apply the name "class" to a grouping of political interests that trembles at the idea of exercising its political role in the class struggle, and thinks it possible to entrust that role to the first adventurer who comes along? The bourgeoisie of the *Manifesto* was something else: a radical class obliged to carry out to the end its historical task of exercising fully its power of production and destruction. Here, on the other hand, we see it shrinking back when it is still at the beginning of its task. Anyone could understand that a class at the end of its course might grasp fearfully at any means to ensure its own survival. But the industrial bourgeoisie is still not in power in France: "The industrial bourgeoisie can only rule where modern industry shapes all property relations in conformity with itself, and industry can only win this power when it has conquered the world market."[6] Protectionist France is still far away from that.

Thus the bourgeoisie is behaving like a senile class before having attained its maturity. It is recoiling not only from the exercise of its political domination but also from its own business, the development of productive forces: "The proceedings on the Paris-Avignon rail line, which began in the winter of 1850, were still not ready to be concluded on December 2, 1851."[7] The conquering class seems to be decomposing between the backwardness of its past and the fear of its future.

So the tale of the demystifier mystified is not simply that of "the sprinkler sprinkled" [l'*arroseur arrosé*].[8] It displays rather the inconsequence and inconsistency of classes as such. The triumph of the most grotesque individuality—the reign of a pure proper name in the hour of the universal bourgeoisie and the world market—is not simply a prank of history. It is rather the limit of a process of decomposition attacking every class at the point which should be that of its exemplary manifestation. At this point each class appears to be doubled, decomposed by its own caricature or, more precisely, its *lumpen*.

THE TRIUMPH OF THE LUMPEN

This decomposition that doubles every class has generally been recognized only in the description of the *lumpenproletariat*: the "passively rotting mass" of "the lowest layers of old society," according to the *Manifesto*; "the breeding ground for thieves and criminals of all sorts, living off the garbage of society," according to *The Class Struggles in France*, which adds that this subproletariat provided the troops for the Mobile Guard in June 1848 that would put down the insurrection of the true proletariat.

Marx's sociological explanation is completely incoherent. If we check the facts, we find that the Mobile Guards belonged to the élite of the proletariat rather than to its scum.[9] The *lumpen* is not a class but a myth—the myth of a bad history that comes to parasitize the good. In that sense it is inscribed in an already constituted political mythology: bourgeois denunciations of thieves, prostitutes, and "escaped galley-slaves" as the hidden force behind all worker and republican disturbances; worker denunciations of self-interested confusions between the truly laboring, militant people and the equivocal fauna of Parisian streets and barriers. Marx had clearly read Cabetist denunciations of coffeehouse revolutionaries,[10] and the term *lumpen* itself may have come to him from Heine. Analyzing in 1832 the connection between legitimist agitation and the ragpickers' rioting against the new garbage carts, Heine saw in this the emblematic fight of all the defenders of the corporatist past, of the champions of "traditions of crap," "rotten interests of all sorts," and, in general, the "medieval manure" that was poisoning life today.[11]

For Marx, however, this rottenness is not simply the garbage of the past piling up on the streets. It is the product of a decomposition of classes that can take two opposed forms. There is the *active* decay, the good decomposition that attacks the caste order and pushes the classes toward their death. And there is the *passive* decay, the bad kind that causes classes to fall short of themselves. The "lumpenization" of a class is its return to the strict conservation of itself and, at the same time, its decomposition into a mere aggregation of individuals. The *lumpenproletariat* is opposed to the proletariat as bad decomposition to good decomposition, the class that is *not even a class* to the class that *no longer is one*. The phantasmal image of a vagabond army in the pay of the bourgeoisie masks a more formidable secret: it is always possible to recruit from the working class an army against the working class. The exceptional betrayal of the Mobile Guards' firing on their "brother" workers is justified *a posteriori* by the ordinary betrayal of workers whom the industrial prosperity of 1850 prevents from reacting against the law that deprives three million of their fellow workers from voting : "By . . . forgetting the revolutionary interests of their class for momentary ease and comfort, [these workers] renounced the honour of being a conquering class."[12]

Every class, insofar as its members defend their own "social interests," is virtually its own *lumpen* to itself.

The rout of the bourgeoisie cannot be explained otherwise. The paradox that makes it lose its power at the very moment when it is absolute refers to the same process. The bourgeoisie continually falls short of itself, destroying its political interests to secure its social interests. It keeps sacrificing its *class interests* for the *material interests* of its members. As with the dissolution of the proletariat, this bourgeois decomposition bears the name of a double. Where we think we see the bourgeoisie going against its concept, we must recognize instead its own *lumpen*. The modern industrial bourgeoisie is being eaten away by a parasite, which has a name— the *finance aristocracy*, a class of conjurers that lives off productive wealth. Thus the so-called "bourgeois" monarchy of Louis-Philippe in fact had been the vampirization of the true bourgeoisie by the finance aristocracy. It was this finance aristocracy that "made the laws, was at the head of the administration of the state, had command of all the organized public authorities"; it imposed on society as a whole its own principle, the principle of anti-production, the orgy of generalized mixing:

> The same prostitution, the same shameless cheating, the same mania to get rich was repeated in every sphere, from the Court to the *Café Borgne*, not by production but by pocketing the already available wealth of others. Clashing every moment with the bourgeois laws themselves, an unbridled assertion of unhealthy and dissolute appetites manifested itself, particularly at the top of bourgeois society—lusts wherein wealth derived from gambling naturally seeks its satisfactions, where enjoyment becomes *crapuleux*, where money, filth, and blood mingle together. The finance aristocracy, in its mode of acquisition as well as in its pleasures, is nothing but the *rebirth of the lumpenproletariat on the heights of bourgeois society.*[13]

One would expect, quite logically, that the Republic of 1848 would sweep away this *lumpen*-aristocratic parasite for the sole benefit of the agents of the development of the bourgeois productive forces. Unfortunately, the opposition of the true productive class to the false unproductive class is belied immediately. In the context of the bourgeois republic, the so-called finance aristocracy shows itself for what it is, which is nothing else than the bourgeoisie itself, the democracy of "a countless number of people from all bourgeois or semi-bourgeois classes" who profit from the national debt.[14] The vampirism of taxes and rents that keeps alive, at the expense of industrial capital, the government machine and the finance pseudo-aristocracy is not simply the price that the latter pays for the order it needs to dominate. It is the process of decomposition whereby the bourgeois class undoes itself and becomes an aggregate of atoms living at their own expense. The ruling bourgeoisie proves itself to be what it is: not the force incarnate of modern industry but simply a mob of individuals eager to fill their purse by any means. They are not even concerned with calculating what the government costs in capital and what it yields in return; they simply go about their own petty affairs. If they accept this state vampirism, they do so, on the one hand, so that they can calmly pursue their illegal speculations and, on the other hand, because they themselves are vampires eager to make up "in state salaries" what they cannot pocket "in the form of profit, interest, rents, and honorariums."[15] The so-called "social interest" for which the bourgeoisie sacrifices its political interest is merely the sum, the crowd, of "the narrowest and most sordid private interests" of its members.[16] This would be the true meaning of the victory of the Bonapartist swindler and his band of crooks: the glorious class of bourgeois industry is only a band of speculators. The industrial development of the Second Empire will also be "an orgy of stockjobbery, finance swindling, Joint-Stock Company adventures . . . a pandemonium of all the low passions of the higher classes . . . the glory of prostitution."[17] The modern bourgeoisie is still merely a backward mob replicating the villainy of the criminal underworld, the rottenness of the Middle Ages, or the pigsty of the peasantry. In the spring of 1871, the defender of the Commune will contrast to it the "manly aspirations" and "herculean power" of the working class.[18] But has he not already demonstrated that even the latter does not escape the general fate of classes—their virtual dissolution into the simple collection of their members? The phantasms of the villainous orgy are merely the imaginary currency of this fall into the universe of addition and dispersion.

THE SWAMP FLOWER

This additive decomposition takes two mythical forms: the small-holding peasant and the Napoleonic mobster. Marxist tradition has turned the passages on the peasantry in *The Eighteenth Brumaire* into the archetype of the Marxist analysis of social class. But one could just as well see it as the very opposite—as the total derision of any political explanation in terms of class. Marx's hallucinated description of this unnameable and innumerable mass of savage beasts living in habitations without windows on the world, and his scorn for these populations that can only increase their numbers like so many potatoes, have nothing evidently to do with any sort of economic, sociological, or political analysis. Marx clearly counts the doors and windows of peasant homes through the tax declarations of their named inhabitants, and judges the modernity of cultures on the basis of political attitudes. The region of Les Cévennes suggests the future of French agriculture to a scientist [*savant*] who only recently had considered a summons to live in the Morbihan a disguised death sentence.[19] The unnameable agglomeration of these troglodyte peasants who find themselves represented only in the single person, indeed the single name, of Louis Napoleon simply expresses this phantasm of bad dissolution, a phantasm figured also by images of medieval decay and sums of pure addition. And for good measure Marx again doubles the "flower of peasant youth" with the "swamp flower of the rural subproletariat."[20] But the demonstration had already been sufficient: the backward peasantry is the revealed secret of "modern" classes, their continuing dispersion into the real of pure preservation, their common incapacity to respond to the exigencies of their concept.

The so-called materialist analysis of different social classes is thus a myth manifesting the perpetual flight of identities and the common dereliction of classes. We already knew that the laborer was ever only a petty bourgeois, the ideologue a swineherd, the *Straubinger* a Lapp. Now we learn that in every entrepreneur of modern industry there is also a troglodyte of the Vendeé swamp, an Icelander fond of rotten fish, or a dozing king of mobsters. The bourgeoisie as well as the peasantry is represented in the person of the boor Louis Napoleon. Just like the comedian-intriguer Thiers, Louis Napoleon could work his spells upon the bourgeoisie only because he is "the most consummate intellectual expression of their own class corruption."[21] The comedian is the undistorted reflection of a history reduced to the simple comedy of preservation.

The defeat of the revolution is thus the *other side* of the class struggle. Instead of the All divided by the agents of history, the revolutionary farce delivers only the grotesque sum of their doubles. That is just what we find in the Napoleonic underworld of the Society of December 10:

> Alongside decayed roués of dubious means of subsistence and of dubious origin, alongside ruined and adventurous offshoots of the bourgeoisie, were vagabonds, discharged soldiers, discharged jailbirds, escaped galley slaves, swindlers, mountebanks, lazzaroni, pickpockets, tricksters, gamblers, maquereaus, brothel keepers, porters, literati, organ-grinders, ragpickers, knife grinders, tinkers, beggars: in short, the whole indefinite, disintegrated mass, thrown hither and thither, that the French call la bohême.[22]

A list as unverifiable and unfalsifiable as the account of troglodyte dwellings. The vertigo of an enumeration proceeding by redoubled blows. This underworld is also the motley crowd of the Platonic polloi. This imaginary album in the style of Gavarni illustrates phantasmatically the pure non-sense of a history ruled by the law of addition alone. A Platonic myth of the world upside down, of the reign of mixture, of those masses of the theater that aesthetic and political modernity has turned at once into actors and spectators—like the applauders that the comedian Louis Napoleon parades everywhere so that they may play enthusiasts in the same deliberately false way that the joiner Snug plays the role of the lion.[23]

THE COMEDIAN KING AND
THE BEGGAR KING

The paradox that allows the Napoleonic clown to triumph at the supreme hour of the class struggle, or that engorges the state vampire at the moment when bourgeois economic rationality demands cheap government, is not due to any historical delay that can be localized in the conscientious study of social structure. It is pointless to lose oneself in analysis of the causes of French backwardness. In modern England as in troglodyte France, the evil stems from birth: "The bourgeoisie does not possess the qualities required to rule directly itself."[24] The state lives off society like a parasite in the same way that society lives off itself like a parasite, constantly dissolving into the collection of "living individuals" who, "before they make history," must *first* eat, drink, get clothing and housing, reproduce, and do a few other things of which one never sees the end. The backwardness at the core of the historical tragedy is the comedy of the materialist preliminaries to its advent. The revolutionary dialectic of production and destruction is corrupted by the materialist history of preservation and reproduction. The political derision of the *doubling* of the class struggle is also the ironic reversal of science. The contradiction inherent in the materialist dialectic sees itself caricatured in the derision of its object. Louis Napoleon and his Bohemian court are symbols as well as caricatures of materialist theory. The reduction of political and ideological illusion to economic reality takes on the burlesque shape of an individual obliged to "make history" to escape his creditors.[25] In the fatalism of this clown-king convinced that human beings are governed by such irresistible forces as cigars and champagne, cold poultry and garlic sausage, the philosopher-king sees the caricature of his science. The crowned conjurer is the double of the demystifying scientist, for in his own practical and specific way he carries out the program of the materialist science of history: the return to earth from heaven, the reduction of great political conflicts and ideological spectacles to the unembellished reality—"*sans phrases*"—of individual interests. "He considers the historical life of the nations and their performances of state as a comedy in the most vulgar sense, as a masquerade where grand costumes, words, and postures merely serve to mask the pettiest knavery."[26]

This fascination with the derisory identity of the clown-king and his Bohemian court reflects the questions posed by science concerning its own proper place and identity. The Bonapartist *lumpenproletariat* so complacently described—this "artificial class" that liquidates the French revolution—is also the metaphor for the society in which Marx himself lives: the society of revolutionaries in exile. It is not for nothing that Marx gives Louis Napoleon the nickname Crapulinski, which he borrowed from Heinrich Heine, another German in exile, who so caricatured the Polish knights in exile. But Crapulinski is also Marx's *bête noire* in London: the "president *in partibus*" of the future German republic, Gottfried Kinkel, admirer of all the old artisanal junk, the false poet and true comedian who runs after grocers to read them his poems and organizes for polite society poetic excursions to the lakes with obligatory declamations of Schiller. The derisory traits given to the

Bonapartist lumpen are also the buffooneries of the fauna of Bohe-mians, the parasites and castoffs of the German revolution in exile: the hippopotamus Schapper, coffeehouse companion of the "knight of the noble conscience," Willich; Marx's "secretary" Pieper, who gives lessons at the Rothschilds, courts for financial reasons the greenish daughter of a vegetable merchant, contracts syphilis from less honorable companions, and continues in all circumstances to regard himself as a genius; Marx's brother-in-law Edgar von Westphalen, who set out to play the woodsman in Texas and will come back with the sole dream of returning to Texas to open a wine store or a cigar business; the "genial" Ulmer with his trances; the "rascal tailors" who left to find gold in California; their colleague Rumpf, who stayed behind but has since gone mad and proposes to Marx to solve the social problem by making him prime minister; Anders, the famous "Lapp," seized with an attack of *delirium tremens* on the public road; Conrad Schramm, nick-named *Lumpazius*, whose chaotic existence will be interrupted by consumption; the schoolteacher and bohemian Biskamp, who left his village school to wage, in a journal modestly entitled *Das Volk*, "the struggle of labor against capital," and who is a mixture of "the moral sense à la Kant and unreserved mirth"; the jackass Liebknecht, who displays more of an appetite for Marx's bacon than for his books, and who has not really managed to do anything in his London sojourn except make a little Liebknecht. And per-haps should be mentioned here, too, the fancies of the purest of the pure: the "courageous, loyal, and noble pioneer" of the pro-letariat, Wilhelm Wolff, who gets himself thrashed by pimps in a Manchester brothel; or Marx's friend Engels, who chases after *grisettes* in Paris and hunts the fox in Manchester, dishes out blows with his umbrella to a drinking buddy, and never manages in Manchester to hand out more than two membership cards in the International. And what, in the midst of this universe, is one to think of the position of the philosopher-king of bohemia, Karl Marx? He divides his days between writing articles on the Turkish question for American readers and taking desperate steps to have the due date of his bills pushed back, sometimes ironically regret-ting that he, as a simple individual, lacks the means possessed by bankers or prince-presidents to rid themselves of their creditors.

So the answer is necessarily double. In liquidating his "party" even before the revolutionary comedy was finished, Marx made a choice in order to devote himself to the work of science. Since, this time around, the economic crisis was reabsorbed, one must wait for its return to enlarge the field of conflagration and make the history of productive forces coincide with that of revolution: "The solution begins only at the moment when, through the world war, the proletariat is pushed to the head of the people that dominates the world market, to the head of England. The revolution, which here finds not its end but its organizational beginning, is no short-winded revolution. The present generation is like the Jews whom Moses led through the desert. It has not only a new world to conquer, it must go under in order to make room for the men who are fit for a new world."[27] At the cost of a "sacrifice," then, the history of development can coincide with the genealogy of values. The present generation is a generation of substitutes. For want of a bourgeoisie equal to the task, Louis Napoleon will play the sorcerer's apprentice of productive forces, orgy will make the bed of mass production and destruction, and the Jew Karl Marx, in the desert of his non-place, will labor at the science put to work only by new men equal to the new world.

In a sense, then, the absolute One of science is affirmed, amid the motley mass of revolutionary parasites, as the sole representative of the coming revolution. This is attested to in the "incredible" response given by Marx and Engels to the delegation of bumpkins who wanted, on the basis of elections, to reconstitute the management of the party: it is from themselves alone that Marx and Engels owe their designation "as representatives of the proletarian party."[28] Only science concentrates the cutting edge of contradiction, which is forever socially postponed and always politically stolen away. But this singularity of science also marks its belonging to the Quixotic and Falstaffian world of dissolution and rebirth. The comedy of the London exile confirms science in the paradoxical status that the *Deutsch-französische Jahrbücher* had granted philosophy: that of being the pure non-place produced by extreme backwardness. And the comedy of the revolution conjured away cannot be attributed solely to the cunning of reason. It affirms the Shakespearean side of history in this new sixteenth century, a second one that should lead the bourgeoisie to its tomb just as the first sixteenth century brought it into existence. It affirms, moreover, the power of dissolution to lead to their death those classes retreating into the backwardness of their afterlife. Finally, it affirms the power of individualities in a century when "the victories of science seem bought by the loss of character,"[29] and when the division of labor, transferring differences to individuals and classes, has produced such social monotony that Leibniz would have difficulty discovering any *differentia specifica* and Shakespeare would find it impossible to recognize his fellow countrymen.[30] The revolutionary tragedy could be only a tragicomedy. The double alliance of science, with the rationality of modern productive forces and the madness of knights errant, is not simply at the mercy of circumstances. Science is part of these same "circumstances." It may be necessary to wait until circumstances are ripe. But the work of science belongs to "immature fools who have still not recovered from their revolutionary fantasies."[31] It belongs to the beggarly army that gnaws away at the order of classes and its factory rationality even as it is gnawed away at by that order. Karl Marx is the magician Hans Röckle, who must sell his inventions to the devil to pay the devil and the butcher. He is also the beggar-king who lives at the expense of capitalists and laborers. In Manchester the employees of the firm of Ermen and Engels also work so that the partner Engels can use the earnings of capital to keep the scientist Karl Marx from having to take a "job," allowing him rather to devote himself to the work that will bring the proletariat into being as the pure subject of the destruction of capital.

6 :: The Risk of Art

THE FAILURE OF the revolution puts science back in its time. The secret of the revolution conjured away may be that it was, itself, a bit of conjuring. After all, the Parisian revolution of February 1848 was nothing more than a "*coup de main*" against a society that was on the verge of overcoming its economic crisis.[1] And so, with the return of prosperity, it could only move backward. But as in the Platonic myth of the *Statesman*, this backward movement is also a rejuvenation, time moving in reverse from old age to birth and clearing a place for the return of the normal order in which generations are born, die, and transform the forces of production. The conjuring away of class struggle by the prestidigitator Louis Napoleon returns the world to the normal temporality of economic cycles and crises. The triumph of the backward underworld over bourgeois political rationality permits France to make up for its economic belatedness in comparison with England. Similarly, in 1866, the unexpected triumph of the old Prussian "roguery" over Austrian civilization will force squire Bismarck to unleash, in turn, the bourgeois forces of production with their proletarian double. The French imperial parody and the German nationalist comedy are, for these two countries, the means of access to the normal "English" march of history.

In its exile in London, which is the center of this development, the singularity of science follows the movement that transforms, in universalizing production, the singularity of economic interests and political intrigues. It makes use of "the ghastly period of peace" for its own accumulation.[2] It observes the signs of the future, the expansion of production and destruction that is to offer the revolution a theater worthy of it.

First, there is Marx's and Engels's great dream, the expansion of production and exchange in the new world being born on the shores of the Pacific. Drawing up his balance sheet from the 1848 farce, Marx does not forget to hail the birth of his publisher's son: "Good luck to the new world citizen! There is no more splendid time to enter the world than the present. Come the day when people can travel from London to Calcutta in a week, both our heads will long since have rolled or started to roll. And Australia and California and the Pacific Ocean! The new world citizens will be unable to comprehend how small our world once was."[3] But the narrowness that had always oppressed our two citizens of the Rhineland is already being overcome: "In six months' time the circumnavigation of the world by steam will be fully under way and our predictions concerning the supremacy of the Pacific Ocean will be fulfilled even more quickly than we could have anticipated."[4]

There is also the fever of the great means of communication and fascination with the linking of the oceans that are to be the motor of the great destruction: "Russia is importing capital and speculation and, given these distances, these hundreds of miles of railways, the gamble may well develop in such a way as to come to an early and sticky end. Once we hear THE GRAND IRKUTSK TRUNK LINE WITH BRANCHES TO PEKIN, etc., etc., that will be the moment for us to pack up. This time the CRASH will be quite unprecedented; all the elements are there: intensity, universal scope, and the involvement of all properties and ruling social elements."[5]

But the water of exchange and the fire of destruction do not let themselves be given away so easily in marriage. Speculation hesitates to plunge headlong into the routes of the Pacific; those who do plunge in bear on their backs all the old rubbish of peasants and lumpenproletarians. On the banks of the Pacific we find not only the intoxication of the new world and the *hybris* of crisis but also the magic of gold and the riffraff of prospectors. The rationality of economics, as with any political representation, has its own *roguery* that both doubles and gnaws away at it. The conqueror of the new world finds his caricature in the California prospector, and the latter his caricature in the Australian convict.

"California and Australia are two cases which were not foreseen in the *Manifesto*."[6] This lack of foresight takes two forms. First, it is a countertendency to the logic of crisis. Australian gold rids the European population of its surplus and establishes a new market eager for the products of the Old World. It also prompts the population to neglect the sheep whose wool had been inundating Europe. But this countertendency to normal historical development is also the production of a caricature history ensuring the triumph of the *lumpen* instead of global conflict between bourgeoisie and proletariat: "our predictions concerning the supremacy of the Pacific Ocean will be fulfilled even more quickly than we could have anticipated. When this happens the British will be thrown out and the united states of deported murderers, burglars, rapists and pickpockets will startle the world by demonstrating what wonders can be performed by a state consisting of undisguised rascals. . . . But whereas in California rascals are still lynched, in Australia they'll lynch the *honnêtes gens*, and Carlyle will see his ARISTOCRACY OF ROGUES established in all its glory."[7]

So the fire and water of economic modernity are subsumed within the same process of degeneration that affects the earth and air of political decrepitude. The *backwards march*, the comedy of the *lumpen* also parasitize the "royal road" of the "last instance." The Beggars' Opera plays on the stage of the theater of the Universal. And there, too, the rogues' apotheosis is made into a metaphor that takes us from periphery to center. The phantasm of the Bonapartist underworld became a metaphor for the *decadence* of the bourgeoisie, for its decomposition into simple individuals who bear bourgeois material interests. The image of the Australian underworld, in turn, becomes a metaphor for the decomposition of the working class. This decomposition is not to be understood as its simple dispersion but as its possible compaction into a sum of individuals united by "common" interests that they also share with the bourgeoisie.

In effect, the corruption of the European working class takes two forms. First, there is the betrayal of the militants attracted by the New World's gold. The matter seems important enough to warrant discussion in the *Inaugural Address* of the International. But these deserters are also the trees that hide the forest. The truly radical corruption is the integration, the unilateral constitution into a class, of precisely those British workers who were supposed to carry out the task of leading the worldwide revolution. Relieved of its excess population and benefiting from the new markets, the British working class becomes a willing party to the bourgeois order: "the English proletariat is actually becoming more and more bourgeois, so that the ultimate aim of this most bourgeois of all nations would appear to be the possession, *alongside* the bourgeoisie, of a bourgeois aristocracy and a bourgeois proletariat. In the case of a nation which exploits the entire world this is, of course, justified to some extent. Only a couple of thoroughly bad years might help here, but after the discoveries of gold these are no longer so easy to engineer. For the rest it is a complete mystery to me how the massive overproduction which caused the crisis has been absorbed; never before has such heavy flooding drained away so rapidly."[8]

So it all fits together. The working class has become too bourgeois to seize the crisis in a revolutionary way, and the crisis that should have radicalized it has been reabsorbed more or less equivocally. The Justice of the crisis, too, is the domain of mixture. Its logic of destruction is parasited equally by a logic of conjuring. Here again we can identify the same features as in the political conjuring away of the revolution. Speculation becomes frightened in the face of the economic equivalent of the confrontation of June 1848: the great, suicidal Trans-Siberian venture. The nearby stock exchanges and markets step in to take the place of defaulters the way the classes took on the task of their neighbor.[9] The creation of "fictitious markets" corresponds to the "artificial classes" of state parasitism. And at the center, at this development's point of departure and return, conjuring once again triumphs. There is not, there cannot possibly be, a revolutionary proletariat in England: "You ask me what the English workers think about colonial policy. Well, exactly what they think of any policy—the same as what the middle classes think. There is, after all, no labour party here, only conservatives and liberal-radicals, and the workers cheerfully go snacks in England's monopoly of the world market and colonies."[10]

The insularity that puts England at the center of exchange simultaneously isolates it from the fire of revolution. The sea of exchange, too, becomes a swamp into which are deceitfully dumped commodities whose accumulation should have been explosive, and in which the class in charge of destruction "flounders" in the "shallow waters" of preservation. England is a center only for the decentering of science. As for the proletariat, it must happen elsewhere.

CAVALRYMEN AND COMEDIANS

Science and revolution are decidedly in league with backwardness. This truth of 1844 is still a truth in 1884, the year Engels will explain to Bebel and Kautsky the new form taken by the German paradox. In France and England the industrial revolution has been accomplished for the most part. The break between industry, handicrafts, and agriculture has taken place. The proletariat's living conditions have stabilized in a setting in which capitalist development is stronger than the counterpressure of labor. So there is no opportunity or moment to be seized by revolutionary surprise. If this chance exists at all for Germany, it is because it experienced its industrial revolution in the most unfavorable circumstances. In Germany modern conditions ran head first into the disjointed limbs of the old handicraft and peasant orders, the result being a disequilibrium affecting every social identity and plunging them all into a general imbroglio. Domestic handicraft workers are now fighting against machines; bankrupt small peasants are launching themselves into domestic handicrafts; and to round out their income, day laborers are going in for the cultivation of potatoes. But to this imbroglio, which recalls classic images of backwardness, Engels gives a wholly different name: for him it is a "direct revolution of all the conditions of life." Through it the whole of Germany finds itself swept into a "social revolution" that "ultimately leads to the expropriation of the peasants and artisans." To this German structure always corresponds the same paradoxical chance. This revolution is taking place "at the very time when a German . . . was destined to elucidate the whole nature . . . of capitalist production."[11]

But how exactly is this coincidence to be understood? What is the place of science caught between the corruption of development and these occasions of backwardness? "If I were merely to consult my own private inclinations, I would wish for another few years of superficial calm. There could, at any rate, be no better time [than the present] for scholarly undertakings."[12] The ambiguous knowledge of the revolutionary responds to this desire of the scientist [savant]. Economic or political crisis provides an opportunity to resolve cases in which the classes have not yet stabilized: "I think that in a fortnight the storm will break in Prussia. If this opportunity passes without being used, and if the people allow that to happen, we then can calmly pack up our revolutionary paraphernalia and devote ourselves to pure theory."[13]

In this case there was little need to pack because the expected opportunity—Prussia's defeat by Austria—came out backwards on the battlefield of Sadowa. And Marx could speak ironically about the irony of any theory of kairos: "Beside a great Prussian defeat, which perhaps (oh but those Berliners!) might have led to a revolution, there could have been no better outcome than their stupendous victory."[14]

But interpretation of that victory lends itself to ambiguity. Marx sees in it the ironic but indisputable confirmation of materialist theory. It was the Prussian needle-gun that brought victory: "Is there any sphere in which our theory that the *organization* of labor is determined by *the means of production* more dazzlingly vindicated than in the industry for human slaughter?"[15] Marx urges Engels, as a specialist in military matters, to write an appendix on this topic for *Capital*. Engels promises "to do that thing on the massacre industry." But he takes a curious interest in a different aspect of the issue: the loading of guns through the breech. And almost in passing he completely muddles the materialist theory that pairs progress in armaments with the decline of chivalry. Engels predicts: "When breech-loading becomes general, the cavalry will come into its own again."[16]

A hidden polemic between Marx the scientist and Engels the horseman [*cavalier*], one that poses at the same time a question of science and ethics. The scientist is quick to reproach his friend for his riding prowess because he hardly thinks that horsemanship is the "specialty" in which Engels will be "of greatest service to Germany."[17] Engels replies to this twice—on the level of *doxa*, that it is Bonaparte's reputation as a horseman that accounts for his prestige (even though he does not jump as well as Engels himself); and on the level of *science*, that horsemanship is "the material basis for all my military studies."[18]

War certainly is not the scientist's strong suit. His passion for the necessities of geology is the antidote for his friend's pleasure in equestrian risks. While Engels is studying the causes and effects of the Prussian military victory, Marx develops a passion for a book by Pierre Trémaux that had been published recently in Paris, *Origine et transformation de l'homme et des autres êtres* [Origin and Transformation of Mankind and Other Beings]. As Marx sees it, Trémaux's work provides the scientific basis for Darwin's theory: it is the difference in soil composition that explains differentiations in the evolution of animal species and human races. In vain does Engels object that Trémaux "knows nothing about geology, and is incapable of even the most common-or-garden literary-historical critique."[19] Marx takes no account of this demurral: "Trémaux's basic idea about the *influence of the soil* . . . is, in my opinion, an idea which needs only to be *formulated* to acquire permanent scientific status."[20]

This may be the right moment to suggest that Sartre and some others have been quite unfair in claiming that Marx's historical dialectic was corrupted by Engels's scientism. As regards the science of nature, Engels is often more circumspect than his friend Marx precisely because he believes less in science and more in history. His impatience as a horseman creates the patience of the scientist. One can put off deciding about evolution if the decision is a question of terrain. And there is no paradox in the fact that this reserve is accompanied by the risk of creating a *Dialectics of Nature*. For that, first and foremost, is a military operation designed to preserve for revolutionary action the terrain menaced by the incursions of science. The "naïve" lover of the science of nature is Marx, not Engels. Marx's geological materialism is a way of seeking to exorcize the comedy that gnaws away at history. Here it is the revolutionary's doubt that creates the scientist's impatience. The geological theory of races *must* prevail over their theory of Darwinian warfare—just as the party "everywhere springing up naturally out of the soil of modern society" *must* reduce to nothingness respectable workers' associations and little bands of knights errant.[21] Just as the earthquakes of the mode of production must bring justice to the revolutionary comedy. And for the disabused scientist, the science of the soil must provide the unambiguous testimony of history's stormy weather.

For the basic risk that menaces revolutionary action is not the threat of defeat or death in combat but the threat of comedy. As Hegel showed so well, in dialectics *ridicule kills*. Lucian's satires brought the Greek gods to their tomb. As for the modern revolution, it is being attacked from within by the comedians who serve as its actors.

In principle, revolutionary action is one that "arises from the class struggle itself."[22] But a different rationality imposes itself on this terrain. The revolution by definition *does not obey social laws*, and neither does it obey the simple rules of military strategy. The rationality of revolution belongs to physics, the spectacular physics of whirlwinds instead of the chemistry of soils: "A revolution is a purely natural phenomenon which is subject to physical laws rather than to the rules that determine the development of society in ordinary times."[23] Into this whirlwind, notes Engels, representatives of the party may be dragged despite themselves. It is better in such situations to preserve the freedom of those without a party, but that is reflection after the fact [*après coup*]. On the terrain of the German revolution in 1848, as in the preparatory stages accompanying every crisis that offers revolutionary hope, we find indeed that the opposite appears to be the case. It is in vain that scientists and strategists try to be "objectively" more revolutionary than "phrase-mongers," because the latter are already on the scene.[24] Objectivity always comes too late. A mixture of Prussian brutality and south German histrionics is—more than the civility of Rhenish science—the virtue needed to seize the revolutionary opportunity by the hair, even if it means transforming it into a mere occasion for putting on a comedy. The comedian-kings, always and again: men who spend their lives rehearsing and waiting for the right moment to step on stage, strike a pose, raise their voice, or brandish their banner. Thus in 1858, the crucial year that swells the exiles' hopes, Marx observes a little trick that has every chance of submerging once again the voice of science: "All these people sense THAT THERE IS SOMETHING MOVING AGAIN. And, of course, are pushing their way onto the stage bearing banners of liberty. . . . Moreover, my wife is quite right when she says that, after all the misère she has had to endure, the revolution will only make things worse and afford her the gratification of seeing all the humbugs from here celebrating their victories on the continent. . . . She says, à la guerre comme à la guerre. But THERE IS NO guerre. Everything is bourgeois [Alles bürgerlich]."[25]

THE DUTY OF THE BOOK

Neither the development of production nor the outbreak of war can, by itself, produce difference in a universe where everything is bourgeois. The whole of difference must be concentrated in the science of the party to come, for science alone entails the negation of the bourgeois world. Science is at once the absolute leisure of the philosopher and the total dedication of the militant.

The time of science is not only the interval between two crises that allows one to dedicate oneself to research and writing. It is also the absolute distance, taken in the very midst of poverty, from the occupations of the multitude: "what has happened over the last ten years must have increased any RATIONAL BEING's contempt for the masses as for individuals to such a degree that odi profanum vulgus et arceo has almost become an inescapable maxim." The brutality of this statement is, to be sure, immediately corrected: "However all these are themselves philistine ruminations that will be swept away by the first storm."[26] But this correction is not just the revolutionary's repentance in the face of the philosopher's secret demons. In the Century of Production, leisure is *work* [*oeuvre*], and work is the absolute sacrifice of the author.

There are two men at least, one on either side of the English Channel, who ponder this absolute of the work-sacrifice [*l'oeuvre-sacrifice*] that absolves its author from all participation in the bourgeois comedy. The two men are infinitely remote from one another and yet very close. One is the reactionary *rentier* Flaubert, securely shut away at Croisset. The other is the freelance journalist Marx, living in his two-room flat in Chelsea and grappling with his crowded family, dying children, creditors to be repulsed day after day, and recurring illness. But both men are equally convinced by the revolutionary farce that there is only one thing left to do: the work that will be the total negation of the reigning baseness, the bourgeois world denied by its reproduction.

This proximity is exorcized throughout the many pages in which Sartre attempts to mark an agreement between Flaubertian nihilism and the desire of the bourgeoisie, contemplated in the confrontation of June 1848, to put proletarian and revolutionary subjectivity to death.[27] But how can one not be struck by the way that these two lovers of Cervantes engage themselves, at the same time, in the quixotic project of the absolute work, which requires the absolute sacrifice of its author? To be sure, the project of Marxian science goes beyond Flaubert's nihilism which, through the sacrifice of the author, brings the work into existence as the negation of the bourgeois world. Marx's sacrifice aims to bring into existence not only the work but the party, the reality of division *in actu*. But Flaubert's counterexample shows clearly what the Marxian sacrifice *is not*. It is not, as good souls believe, a matter of simple devotion to produce the science destined to arm the proletariat with knowledge of the "objective conditions" of their struggle. The proletariat does not need the science of capital to become educated. It needs it to exist. The proletariat exists only by virtue of its inscription in the Book of Science, and that inscription is, first of all, the account of a journey into hell: "Among the motley crowd of labourers of all callings, ages, sexes, that press on us more busily than the souls of the slain on Ulysses, on whom—without referring to the Blue Books under their arms—we see at a glance the mark of over-work, let us take two more figures whose striking contrast proves that before capital all men are alike—a milliner and a blacksmith."[28]

An astonishing vision. Evidence suggests that the dead souls of the capitalist hell do not carry Blue Books under their arms. On the contrary, it is Marx who found their faces in the Blue Books of investigators and factory inspectors. And the overwork he recognizes at a glance is also his own. As Marx confides to Engels, these lengthy pages on the descent into proletarian hells are the fruit of the infernal hours when illness and fatigue do not permit him to pursue his scientific investigations.[29] They are not, for all that, mere padding designed to give the author and his public rest from the aridities of science. Rather, they present the myth of science. The latter is the work of absolute sacrifice, of the descent into hell required to give to the voiceless mass of dead souls the Book that will redeem it from oblivion, ushering in the Proletariat subject in place of the motley crowd of laborers. Science is, first of all, *reminiscence* in the strongest sense of the word.

To put the proletariat in the place of dead souls is essentially to make *Capital* the inscription of contradiction. In that sense the book has *only one thing* to say: that capitalist production and even simple commodity production carry in themselves the explosive power of the identity of opposites. This proof is given right at the start in the early passages on the market. The crucial thing here is not the exposé of surplus value; everyone knows that secret, and scrupulous distinctions between the value of labor and the value of labor power have no importance *in this context*. The crucial thing is destroying in advance Proudhon's solution to surplus value, which is the free and equal exchange of labor between producers. Economic heresy, perhaps, but above all the collapse of the great logic of production and destruction into the baseness of the economy of *labor*. In that sense, everything is played out in chapter 1, where "the relative form and the equivalent form are two intimately connected, mutually dependent and inseparable elements of the expression of value; but, at the same time, are mutually exclusive, antagonistic extremes—i.e., poles of the same expression."[30] Once he has established that the equivalent form of the commodity is an *exclusive* form, the game is over. Proudhonism is impossible. In a sense, then, what Marx wants to demonstrate in the book is achieved already in the very first chapter.

But the book is also the inscription of the proletariat—or, what amounts to the same thing, the party—in science. And that makes the work infinite. For this alone is the cutting edge of the party and must be unassailable. And it can be that only if it examines, from crisis to crisis and from document to document, the form that capital takes in each instance to escape its death. The death notice inscribed in the first chapter of book I must be suspended so long as capital finds ways to escape its destiny. For capital, it seems, is more Leibnizian than Hegelian; it will not move on until it has exhausted all its possibilities. And the scientist who has sacrificed his life to the science of the proletariat must keep returning to work to achieve his sacrifice at the end.

THE UNKNOWN MASTERPIECE

An interminable work. There are several ways to take it. The physician's viewpoint is simple. Doctor Kugelmann never ceases to be irritated: why does Marx allow himself to be distracted constantly from the only important work in this century of science triumphant—the completion of *Capital*? If he is sick, then let him get well once and for all!

The Marx family does not like these moral lessons. Her honor as the patient's nurse affected, young Jenny replies dryly: "In truth, it is the book that precludes any thorough cure."[31] Marx will not abandon it to take care of himself. A pure sacrifice to the "noble cause of the proletariat"—such is the second volume of a work, "the first volume of which the great German nation has not deigned to read."

Marx himself likes to recall that point. He makes light of the so-called "practical" men who turn their backs on the sufferings of humanity and look after their own skins. He understands "practical" in a different sense: "But I should really have thought myself *impractical* if I had pegged out without finally completing my book, at least in manuscript."[32] But there is more than one way to conciliate everyone, Engels suggests many times. It really may not be necessary to have read all the materials on ground rent in every country to publish his study of the reproduction of capital. Why not print his results in fascicles as he goes along? To this Marx must reply with a different reason. His *Capital* is not a scientific book like others: "Whatever shortcomings they may have, the advantage of my writings is that they are an artistic whole, and this can only be achieved through my practice of never having things printed until I have them in front of me in their entirety. This is impossible with Jacob Grimm's method which is in general better with writings that have no dialectical structure."[33] A word to the wise, then! The artist Karl Marx does not work the way philologists and authors of dictionaries do; he is not a hack.

On, then, with the painstaking examination of ground rent! And for that, Doctor Marx has found accomplices hard to beat: the Russians. Before he can disentangle the agrarian question in Russia, the artist must take his time—and the Russians are not miserly about documents. Then there is the Russian language to be learned. Indeed, he confides that "the bulk of materials I have received not only from Russia but from the *United States*, etc., make it pleasant for me to have a 'pretext' of continuing my studies, instead of winding them up finally for the public."[34]

"Folly consists in wanting to conclude": it is, again, Flaubert who said this. Marx, of course, is much more inclined to refer to Balzac. Is it because Balzac, "even though reactionary," succeeded in demonstrating the class struggle? The matter may be a bit more devious. It is not *Les Paysans* [The Peasants] that Marx recommends to Engels but *Le Chef d'oeuvre inconnu* [The Unknown Masterpiece], the story of an absolute work concealed from every jealous gaze and destined to perish with its creator as soon as anyone's glance might pierce its secret—not because it is naked like the king but because it is *invisible* by virtue of its enhancement with the true forms and colors of nature.[35]

The book that is to give the party its identity is a work of the same sort, a work held back indefinitely because its author *does not want* to deliver it to the public. Engels will have confirmation of that fact after Marx's death; he discovers that the work is almost completed, but also left systematically incomplete.[36] Without which it would not be the absolute sacrifice. Without which, too, it would become imitable, repeatable, prostituted: a *Marxist* work.

Marx, as we know, is not a Marxist—which does not mean that he is not "dogmatic." It means he is not a member of his own party. Engels will make the same point to Bernstein: he is not his "comrade." Every member of a party imitates, repeats, transforms the work of art into a comedy and a technique. Which is another reason why this "undogmatic" scientist is so touchy about his formulations. Why does he invest such maniacal care in correcting the *Gotha Programme*? Because the class struggle often might turn on a misunderstood word, and errors in theory might have "serious" practical consequences? To think that would be to believe that politics in the nineteenth century was still a part of the art of breeding, and Marx has no illusions on that score. Even if the program is irreproachable, Liebknecht will apply it the wrong way. And if the program of the French party must be *dictated* to Lafargue and Guesde, the purpose is not to guarantee its strict application; the purpose is strictly to guarantee the program through all "applications." The program is there for reminiscence. The text must be scrupulously respected *for its own sake*, even to the point of simply *copying* what one does not understand.[37] For the text in itself is the thing that appeals to the future, to a revolution that will make a mockery of the "right" or "wrong" actions of the clowns who are party leaders. And the text makes this appeal insofar as it is an inimitable work of art.

To say art—and this, too, marks a change since the days of the shepherd-kings—is to say anti-technique, anti-imitation, anti-labor. Among the "theoretical errors" with "serious" practical consequences that irritate Marx the most are always those involving the word "labor." Thus in his *Critique of the Gotha Programme* he fiercely opposes the paragraph that, in *overlooking nature*, proclaims that work is "the source of all wealth." He is vigilant lest any abuse of language transform the "*value of labor power*" into the "*value of labor*." In practice, to be sure, no one makes a mistake on this subject. The whole question is one of principle, of ontological dignity, and no one will confuse a commodity with a principle. Pure production calling out for revolutionary destruction possesses the same character that distinguishes art from labor: *it is priceless*. A work of art, a work of nature. Marx tells us this himself in that curious passage of his *Theories of Surplus-Value* that uses seemingly disconcerting examples of productive work: "Milton produced *Paradise Lost* for the same reason as a silkworm produces silk. It was an expression of *his own* nature. Later on he sold the product for £5. But the Leipzig proletarian of literature (*Litteraturproletarier*) who assembles books (such as compendia of political economy) under the direction of his publisher is a productive worker, for his production is from the outset subsumed under capital, and only takes place so that capital may valorise itself."[38]

We see in what sense *Capital* is a "critique of political economy." It is a critique of productive *labor*. True production lies with Milton and the silkworm, with those who produce without bosses or calculation. This quixotic work finds its exact counterpart in the Parisian revolution of 1871: a revolutionary scaling of heaven, a government of "simple workingmen" replacing the "richly paid sycophants" of the state and doing their work, "as Milton did his *Paradise Lost*," for a few pounds.[39] Paradise lost and regained, the paradise of the anti-wage earner whose leisure-work is to produce *reminiscence* in the interval, in the *other time*, that separates singular moments of revolutionary irruption.

The Errant Science

A singular relationship between the time of the work [*l'oeuvre*] and that of revolution, far beyond all rationality of economic development and the constitution of class. There is no *political art* that makes the blade of science coincide with the cuttings of social history. German poverty, which gives the science of capital its chance to be produced in London, also seals its erratic destiny. This science is not the mastery of any object or the formation of any subject. By proclaiming the primacy of production, it paradoxically shuts itself up in the solitude of an art henceforth situated at an infinite distance from all technique. The materialist "reversal," the return from heaven to earth, has the unexpected result of destroying the space of *practice*. No more *right opinion* there, where every circumstance depends by right on science but where science is condemned always to interpret, after the fact, the reversal of circumstance. No more political art capable of effecting the happy intertwining of social characters. It would certainly be strange to find a weaver-king in the new age inaugurated by the mechanical loom, but it is even stranger that the radicalness of the revolutionary future is presented here under the archaic image of the silkworm revolution.

The silkworm is indeed the unity of two opposites. On the one hand, it represents the nobility of free nature, the activity of the poet, unconcerned about wage earnings. On the other, the silkworm represents the inverted image of the mechanical worker, and lacks only the latter's speech. This hieroglyph of the identity of opposites is a figure for the destiny of a science whose power is remanded to the absolute risk of art confronted with the density of the bourgeois world.

"Everything is bourgeois." One need not take this to mean that bourgeois prosperity puts consciousness to sleep or that "bourgeois ideology" clouds it. As I have tried to show, this "ideology" about which there has been so much fuss is only the banality of the laboring order. "Everything is bourgeois" means there is no *outside*. There is no other place from which to raise another army, an army for which science would provide the training. Everything takes place within the sublime and grotesque tragicomedy of the bourgeois era. And revolutionary justice can come about only as the product of a double annulment, of a perpetual reversal between the normality of historical development and the pathology of its decomposition. In this play of reversals science by itself does not have the power of decision. It is pointless to ask of science whether we should place our confidence in the god of productive forces and the spontaneity of the soil from which will spring the party of destruction, or risk it all in the dice-throw of revolutionary decision.

The fact is that nothing could be more ridiculous than trying to extract from Marx's writings arguments to justify the reformist approach or the revolutionary approach. Science does not teach its usage. Its point of arrival resembles its point of departure, the time when the philosophy student Karl Marx submitted to his examining committee the following thesis: the physics of Epicurus, which is regarded as the simple continuation of the physics of Democritus, is actually its opposite. And in this opposition must be seen two antagonistic visions of the world. On the one hand the man of science, on the other the man of practice. The one in love with the science of the true, to the point, we are told, of blinding himself in order to escape the sensory illusions fatal to physics. The other was satisfied, for the practice of philosophy, with any explanation that chases away myth and saves phenomena. The one was impassioned by the scientific observation of a sensible world he regarded as pure illusion; the other was unconcerned with exploring this world, which he regarded nonetheless as the sole truth. In this century of technological royalty and the destruction of what Nietzsche in the *Zarathustra* called the *Hinterwelt*,[40] the uses of science may well be even more undecidable than in the days of Greek philosophy. One can always write out *Capital* on note cards, as does the self-taught bookbinder Most. But one will never have anything more than external marks without life, written discourse, dead discourse—"incapable of helping itself," as the old lesson of the *Phaedrus* put it—but susceptible to rambling all over the place and causing the heads of those not made for science to drift from one side to the other. So Most and his bunch are kept flung around by the text, which is mute to them, between wait-and-see scientism and anarchistic outbursts. The sanction of a knowledge lacking the science of ends.

But the science of ends is not taught now any more than it was in the age of Plato—or rather, it is taught even less. There are no more academies or banquets for it. In the age of demystification it has paradoxically become pure miracle. Strange as this may seem to us after decades of Marxism, we must state the facts as they stood for its founders: *everything is a matter of individuals*. Marx's theory is not a guide for any sort of action, be it violent or peaceful. None of the theses of science teach us whether we should study in our room, stand instead for elections, or prepare weapons for an insurrection. Science teaches only one thing, not knowledge but a way of being. It teaches those who study it to be *equal to the new world*. As with the work of genius in Kant's aesthetics, the work of science does not offer laws, only models. They must be copied, not in the manner of mnemotechnicians but in that of apprentice painters who train their gaze and hand by reproducing the works of those chosen by nature to impose on art the rules that distinguish it from the routine of technique. The work of art entitled *Capital* can teach people to *judge* whether they should act as a scientist or general, poet or diplomat, because it is the reminiscence of the great revolution, the only one worthy of the name, that was effected in the sixteenth century by a handful of men—of giants, rather, who were *all that* at once: "It was the greatest progressive revolution that mankind had so far experienced, a time which called for giants and produced giants: giants in power of thought, passion and character, in universality and learning. . . . Leonardo da Vinci was not only a great painter but also a great mathematician, mechanician, and engineer. . . . Albrecht Dürer was painter, engraver, sculptor, and architect, and in addition invented a system of fortification. . . . Machiavelli was statesman, historian, poet, and at the same time the first notable military author of modern times."[41]

And so the stage and play are set. Everything is resolutely played out in the land of paradox and advanced backwardness—in that Germany which, since Luther, has always been a hundred years ahead of the thinking of other countries and a hundred years behind their practice. Everything is played out on the stage of Nuremberg between the descendants of the shoemaker-philosopher Hans Sachs and those of the artist-scientist Albrecht Dürer, between the dwarves and the giants. But to represent the missing giants, to train new humans fit to be diplomats or horsemen, scientists or artists, there is only the work of art and reminiscence: the musical score with which to "make petrified relations . . . dance"; the fantastic tale "to teach the people to be terrified at itself in order to give itself *courage*";[42] the monument of science, on the model of which one must exercise one's eye and pen to cure philistines of scientistic demystification and the comfortable criticism of "utopias"; the dramatic masterpiece that one must learn to interpret to thwart the comedians and to play one's proper role in the tragedy of the future.

The application of science can only be this: learning to *interpret* the work on the stage of revolution. There is no escaping from the theater. One must do it better than the comedians, and even take their place. In the Marx family, where one learns to recite Shakespeare from early childhood, the head of the family has a favorite prose writer: Diderot, author of the *Paradoxe sur le comédien* [The Actor's Paradox].

One must train actors who are anti-actors. Another man of the theater, Brecht, will dwell on this problem for a long time: where is one to find the "grand method"—the art of learning to play, on the stage of the theater as on that of the revolution, not only their opposition but also their identity? Brecht, too, will need to go into exile to see the root of the problem: the question of the actor does not revolve around the art of showing but the art of living. It concerns the public only insofar as it concerns the actor himself. For in the final analysis, the pedagogy that "raises consciousness" by unveiling exploitation and its mystifications is a very impoverished virtue. The great virtue that must be learned by the public with the actor is *humor*, the art of performing on stage where opposites never cease to interchange themselves.

The art of becoming *historical agents*. No longer the simple "bearers" of social relations, whose misfortune is not being unaware of real conditions but of not being *equal* to what they bear. "Everything is bourgeois." Let us remember that to stage Shakespearean drama there are as yet only *comedians* like those whom Prince Hamlet engages: uncivilized boors, hams from provincial troupes, performers of bourgeois comedy for whom the alliance of the sublime and the grotesque comes down to an alternation between Schillerian tirade and vaudevillian buffoonery. That is why, to save the play, there is no solution but to recall each time the old bit part that captures the quintessence of bourgeois theater—the old Hegelian handmaid known as "the irony of history."

History will be ironic until we see the birth of the new actor, the anti-comedian, the historical character who alone is worthy of the modernity of the big-budget production: the young proletarian who, endowed with humor, can send into retirement the old handmaid with her whole cast of extras.

The Testament of the Artist

Humor is the art of distance that is learned at a distance. So it is pointless to try to know if Marx and Engels are truly prohibited from residing in Germany, where, after all, they would be in a far better position to preserve the Party from deviations of all sorts. It is pointless to ask whether it is really Bismarck's anti-socialist laws that oblige the Party to have its central organ in Zurich after the German section of the International had had its office in Geneva. Science, in any case, can act only at a distance. And as long as the new actor is not yet on the scene, it operates as his proxy. It replaces the absent hero, occupying the interval of time needed for his arrival. But it also makes use of the waiting time and a whole system of substitutions to constitute the elements of his "education."

This *mise en scène* is very precisely regulated by the elder Engels when Marx's death makes him the heir of the science of the future. First he must put together the monument of the work, making books II and III of *Capital* out of the formless mass of hieroglyphics left by the author of the Unknown Masterpiece, which is to say, consuming both his eyesight and the time allotted him to achieve the sacrifice. Then he must teach the reading of these hieroglyphics to two scribes, Bernstein and Kautsky, endowed with the necessary qualities and defects needed to play the flattering and sacrificial role of the *two Marxists* (no more than two of them are needed). Then he must publish widely those works of self-popularization (e.g., the *Communist Manifesto*) that are fine for copying as long as they cannot be understood. He must prevent any comedian from coming along and altering the text of the actors of the future. But he must also hold the stage and prevent any other text from taking its place there, even if that means pursuing Dühring and his gang onto the shaky grounds where they discourse upon every knowable thing and a few others besides.

Preserving the purity of the text for the actors of the future also means consolidating the double power of science and class. It means profiting from Bismarck's repression to set up in Zurich the board of the *Sozialdemokrat* and its theoretician Bernstein as representatives, among the German militants, of the science preserved in London and as critics of their parliamentary representation. But it also means sharpening the dialectical—humorous—capacity of German workers by means of the very gap between their political representation in Germany and their literary representation in Zurich. It does this by means, moreover, of the criticism that the Marxist writer Bernstein makes of the transgressions of the Social Democrat parliamentarian Liebknecht, as well as through the criticism that the worker-organizer Bebel makes of the Marxist scribe Bernstein.

The art of contradictions. The last lesson of the pedagogue Engels will be his curious preface to the new edition of Marx's *Class Struggles in France*, glorifying the legal and parliamentary victories of socialism (to please the party leaders) but reminding them (to make them gnash their teeth) that this legal approach is merely one of the ironic forms of revolutionary art.

A lesson lost? The heirs definitely have no humor. They proceed to act the same way that the scientist Marx reproached the worker-philosopher Proudhon for acting. They hold onto the *good* side of Engels's preface and suppress its bad side.

One can say, of course, that these little acts of cowardice are of no consequence. The conclusion of Engels's preface denounces in advance the ridiculous fears of these pusillanimous spirits in the face of the anti-socialist laws. These laws will be about as effective as Diocletian's fierce persecution of socialism's ancestor, the Christian revolution: "It was so effective that seventeen years later the army consisted overwhelmingly of Christians, and the succeeding autocrat of the whole Roman Empire, Constantine, called the Great by the priests, proclaimed Christianity as the state religion."[43]

What is he thinking of? A new autocrat? A new state religion? He says these things only in passing, but nothing follows except for his final period. Thus was completed the theoretical testament of Marx's legatee. For Friedrich Engels, suffering from cancer of the throat, it is time to think of retirement. It is time for the artist to withdraw from his creation. Cleanly and without a trace. On 27 August 1895, four people—Eleanor Marx, her false husband Edward Aveling, the Marxist scribe Eduard Bernstein, and the old *Straubinger* Friedrich Lessner—will take Friedrich Engels's ashes on their boat. The urn will rest at the bottom of the sea, below the cliffs of Eastbourne.

The final fusion of fire and water, imitating in reverse the fate of the poet Shelley some seventy years earlier, who was washed up by the sea and cremated by his friend Byron on the beach of Viareggio. Even as Engels, whom all his dear friends called "the General," would have us know in parting that he was, first of all, a poet.

There remains in Highgate Cemetery the other tomb, built out of stone and adorned by proletarian posterity with the bust of the prophet. Artists do not escape the power of comedians.

III :: THE
PHILOSOPHER AND
THE SOCIOLOGIST

Against the clerics and scholars
Tintoretto would readily call himself a proletarian if we could whis-
per the word to him, even though
his ambitions impel him to rejoin
the bourgeoisie. In any case, he is
"people," he is the people.

SARTRE, "The Prisoner
of Venice"

7 :: The Marxist Horizon

WHAT REMAINS WHEN the tomb of the scientist [du savant] has been erected and the artist's ashes thrown into the sea? Very obviously, Marxism. Though not, to be sure, Marx's thought. Marxism is what remains when the creator has withdrawn from his work, when we find annulled the imperceptible distance, the accepted share of non-sense, the humor whereby the philosopher escapes the status of the objects of his science and the enumeration of the members of his party.

When one suppresses this *nothing*, there remains, certainly, *everything*. The total intelligibility of a world entirely defined by the laws of production and circulation, the great solid masses that form the everywhere-recognizable landscape of our world and the misrecognized reason of our thoughts: the being that precedes consciousness; productive forces that bump up against the constraining wall of the relations of production; the windmill that produces feudalism, the watermill inaugurating capitalism; the bourgeoisie unleashing and restricting the forces of steam, electricity, and democracy; the proletariat coming to consciousness and organizing itself in the light of science and on the edge of combat; the petty bourgeois spinning around in the shadowy circle of ideology. A world of transformations and reflections in which there is room everywhere to produce and everywhere to decipher.

THE DÉCOR OF PRODUCTION

Simplistic illustrations [images d'Épinal], some say, with regard to the complexities of the open science. They would denounce those unhappy windmills whose ridiculous arms cast their shadow on the book of science.

The only problem is that the mills do not belong to the bad illustration of science. They are part of its founding myth, which binds Antipater's pastoral to Arkwright's hell.[1] And since Don Quixote's time, they form part of an obligatory décor or setting that marks the boundary separating the science of the new industrial world from the feudal reverie of the old world. For that is what Marxism is, above all: the scene set with the rationality of the new technological world. Marxism, Sartre will say, is the unsurpassable horizon of our time. That horizon is décor: line of flight reduced to backdrop, from which we perceive the scene. It matters little in this respect that the trees, windmill arms, or factory chimneys punctuating the horizon possess the garish banality of chromolithographs. The horizon of science need not be scientific. It is not primarily a matter of what we know but of what we see, of the *doxa* that constitutes the décor of the new science.

The Marxism-horizon is preeminently the imperious décor of production. Hard and clean as the lines of concrete and steel. Severe as the labor of pistons and the effort of their servants. It was not Rousseauist pity or messianic apocalypse that the philosophy of our era first experienced in the Marxist text. Nor was it detained by the glory of the producer, the demystification of the ideologue, the reign of Science or Humanity. What caught its attention first was the rigid metal and implacable line of the new décor: the cold edge of polished steel, the solid line of unadorned concrete, the precise work of the machine. Victory of the hard over the soft and of the straight over the curved. Nearly everywhere in our philosophy we hear the same cry of joy over being freed by new machines and materials from the sluggish digestions of consciousness and syrupy musics of the soul. The décor of production restores to consciousness its freedom as a "thing among things"; it attests that everywhere "it works [*ça fonctionne*]." Everywhere there are productive bodies liberated from the "prison of the soul." Everywhere there is meaning at work: thought at work in the stone and iron of machines and buildings, matter at work in the words of the thinker. And the interworld of *doxa* is gradually populated with new machines and novel circuits—with arts of making [*de faire*], apparatuses of power, economies of meaning, textual machines, productions of desire, etc.[2]

A world of generalized production, of a philosophy furloughed, released from duty. It no longer has to stand guard since now there is a new guardian, represented on stage in front of the chimneys on the painted backdrop, but active above all in the wings to keep the stage itself in good operation: the worker-machinist. Philosophy can enjoy the new form of its leisure; it no longer has any hills to climb, suns to contemplate, or souls to educate. It sings the democracy of productive bodies. That may not be exactly what the shoemakers were hoping for, but the soul and its education do form part of the shoemaker's archaic faith—that of the self-taught humanist of the library of Bouville, the clerk who reminds the philosopher of the son of the shoemaker Guéhenno.[3] Man of the dead letter, which is now to say, *man of the soul*.

An unexpected reversal of the hierarchy of souls. The scene has turned around the philosopher and the shoemaker, but only the philosopher has noticed this. He is now with the men of steel and concrete, of the machine and production. As for the shoemaker, he finds himself endowed with that soul which is *without value*, which now is backwardness—the productive body's distance from itself. Henceforth the hierarchy takes this new form: there are more or less productive bodies, organs, and productions more or less liberated from the soul, *which is to say*, from anti-production.

A question of music as in Plato's time, but in a new sense. For Plato there was the noble lyre and the Dorian mode of the Muse's friends as opposed to the vulgar flute and the Lydian rhythm prized by the populace. Now there is the good and bad worker, the good and bad organ for performing the same music, for turning it into the swelling lungs of the soul or the sharp-edged metal of the productive body.[4] Music of "the soul," music of the shoemaker. Music of the body, music of the future technician. To the chorus of cicadas responds the modern dream in which the men of the workshop are those who expel the popular consumers of the soul, which is to say, themselves: "we can imagine that—eventually?—the concert will be exclusively a studio, a workshop, an atelier from which nothing—no dream, no image-repertoire, in a word no 'soul'—will overflow and where all musical doing will be absorbed into a praxis with *nothing left over*."[5]

The Sun and the Horizon

But the new theater of philosophical enjoyment, the workshop of praxis with *nothing left over*, is not for tomorrow. The Marxist horizon is not only this factory décor that, replacing the sun of science, gives the objects and actions of our universe their new lines and colors. The horizon in philosophy is not simply the backdrop of science. It is also the paradoxical site where science and *doxa* redistribute their powers. Thus in the seventeenth century, one of the favorite settings of philosophical combat was the horizon of the rising sun or moon.

The problem is well known. In their rising, the sun and the moon appear to us as enlarged disks. While the scientist may know that the disk is the same at its rising and its zenith, the peasant nonetheless continues to see its diameter vary in its course and philosophers continue to fight over the reasons for this appearance.[6] But it is a curious debate because the basis of the quarrel already had been voided. In the seventeenth century all philosophers already know, and all peasants soon will know, that the sun does not rise or set in any case. So why waste time over the appearance of an appearance?

There are circumstantial reasons for doing that. Those who take the liveliest interest in these questions during the seventeenth century, for example Father Malebranche and Bishop Berkeley, have concerns that fall naturally in line with their vocation as churchmen. They want to give to each its share—peasant, scientist, and God. They want to validate each gaze in its place: the "naïve" gaze of the peasant at his sun, the learned gaze of the scientist through his telescope or microscope. They want to denounce illicit crossings, superimpositions of gazes that place the substantial world of the peasant at the end of the scientist's lenses or the geometrical world of the scientist on the horizon of the peasant, thereby producing a self-sufficient world of ideas and things subsisting in themselves outside the activity of God and humanity. The crucial question, in effect, is not the criterion of the true but the nature of the visible, and the main evil to be repulsed is not error but passivity. When he asserted, for the good of his cause, that the spectacle of the sensible is entirely assimilable to the activity of divine speech, the much discredited idealist Berkeley placed himself in the front rank of the inventors of our productive modernity. In the age of empirio-criticism, Lenin will have to face the consequences.[7]

For beyond circumstantial compromises between science and religion, there is the matter of the long-term future of philosophy. In the slow collapse of eternal truths, this future may well lie in the substitute for eternity that science assures it of being: the permanence of optical illusions, the necessary non-concordance between what the scientist knows and what the peasant sees. *Doxa* henceforth no longer will be the world that philosophy must traverse to reach the light of the true; it will be the colorful horizon of philosophy's domain. The coming philosophy will be the *reason of doxa*: the knowledge of the gap between science and representations, but also the knowledge of their *familiarity* in a world no longer acquainted with Nietzsche's *Hinterwelt*,[8] a world in which both illusion and circumstance depend on science. Even at the price of developing a split personality, of emancipating under surveillance the modern knowledge of the individual and society as the knowledge of the conditions that widen the gap between *doxa* and science. Even at the price of turning against itself the weapon of this semi-emancipated knowledge, of affirming that the truth of the philosopher is the great optical illusion clouding the work of science and the enjoyment of appearance.

At this horizon where a larger sun rises that also does not, in this place where science will never replace *doxa*, is set the modern stage of the conflicts and complicities between philosophy and social knowledge. The stage of that *philosophy of the poor* populating our theories, our politics, our social sciences: that perpetual coming and going that unceasingly sends the empty gaze of the heavenly ideologue back to the substantial gaze of the peasant, marking in so doing the gap that separates this substantial gaze from its own truth. Our social knowledge is that, first of all: a thinking of the poor, an inventory of illegitimate modes of thinking, a science having for its object the thinking that has *no time* to be thought. A knowledge denouncing the vanity of philosophical leisure that is, at the same time, relegated to the ersatz function of philosophy.

An ersatz that philosophy cannot do without, since in order to preserve its role in the legislation of legitimate thoughts, it is itself obliged to produce a discourse on non-philosophy, on illegitimate modes of thinking. Whence the permanent exchange, the porous space of competition and complementarity between a diminished philosophy of the legislation of the true, and a philosophy of misrecognition and the social knowledges of acculturation. We have here the strange scene of modern scientific opinion, where a servant-mistress philosophy continually crosses and recrosses social knowledges at which its generosity tenders as many prohibitions as they claim to wrest illusions from it.[9] Which it does even at the price of recovering from the other hand the very same prohibitions metamorphosed into "inescapable" social positivities, while of course reserving for itself the epistemology of "methods" and the critique of the "instruments" of their "production." The scene of a Platonism denied, that is, sociologized, where the artifice of the *absence of time* will become the unremitting constraint on the productive universe; where the declared lie concerning the difference between natures made for production and those made for the leisure of science will become the democratic law of a history that humans "make" only on the condition of misrecognizing it; where the divisions [*partages*] of science and misrecognition will be identified with the tribunals passing judgment on true and false workers.

THE PARADOXES OF PRODUCTION

Marxism has come to organize the scene by contributing a necessary modification to the horizon of the visible, by changing the rustic décor in which the philosopher on holiday observed the peasant mistaking the size of his sun. And so the *Theses on Feuerbach* are, in the first place, the promptings of a theater director. In Feuerbach they incriminate the philosopher of the countryside who thinks he can liberate humanity and science by demystifying the speculative sun, turning the heavenly divinity into the sensible fervor of earthly love.

The *Theses* make clear that in confining itself to this critique of representations, the good will of philosophy, seeking to become the world, remains shut up within the horizon of impotent contemplation and interminable education. The critique of optical illusions will always be less potent than the illusions themselves. The peasant will go on not knowing what he sees, and the scientist will go on not seeing what he knows. The meeting point will always be missing unless it is given at the very start. That meeting point is practice, the activity of transformation that gives rise at once to the décor of production and the perception of the actors: the gaze of the producers of history upon the productive machine replaces the passive gaze of the bucolic philosopher upon a cherry tree come from who knows where . . .[10]

Subjects *in actu* within a décor itself created by subjects *in actu*: the theater of production opposes its true actors and regulated mechanics to the flickering shadows projected in bygone days onto the wall of the cave. The whole force of the system lies in the words "make" or "do" [*faire*] and "history." There is in this way no remainder and there always is one. People "make" history but they "do not know" they do so. The formula can be developed *ad infinitum*. The world is populated by people who "do," who only express what they are in what they do and what they do in what they are, but who cannot "do" without fabricating for themselves a knowledge that is always besides what they are. It is impossible to do without misrecognizing that one does, and it is impossible for this misrecognition not to "do" something in turn. It is due to the very same movement that all is *technique* under the jurisdiction of a science of the machine that demystifies, and that all is *doxa*, artifice of the machine in which the gaze is caught. In the theater of history, every illusory effect hearkens back to the science of machinery. But the machine is also what sustains the décor, exhausting its powers in the visibility of the spectacle. Thus science and *doxa* trace in a disenchanted world the figure of the new enchantments of *paradox*. These practices that misrecognize what they do, these misrecognitions that take action [*agissent*] themselves, these knowledges of misrecognition that lead in turn to misrecognition—they all inscribe in the prose of the world what once had been the weapon of the rhetorician and the sophist.

Long ago, in the presence of Socrates, the sophists and fencers Euthydemus and Dionysodorus amused themselves by posing a trick question to panic young Clinias: how can you learn what you do not know? You must know already what you do not know in order to be able to learn it. But by the same token, you always know already what you say you are learning because what you know is just a collection of words.[11] Such is the rhetorician's ploy, which is always just the thing for misleading frightened adolescents. Simple wordplay based upon the deliberate vagueness of the words "learn" and "know." But at the horizon of *technē*, this is something else entirely. Sophist paradoxes, blind practices, and self-ignorant forms of knowledge now are grasped in the texture of things and played for good on the stage of history: absences that operate in the mirage of their presence; secrets that stay hidden only when written out in full; false prohibitions that compel action [*à faire*]; recognitions that cause misrecognition. They are at work everywhere, these illusion machines that turn technical demystification into generalized simulacra. The world of absolute functionality is also that of universal suspicion.

We know how Marx approached this theater of paradox—paradoxically. Too classical for the world he invents, Marx continues to love the science of Truth more than the demystification of *doxa*, literature more than the theater, and knights errant more than machinists. The inventory of ways in which the truth of the machine is distributed in *doxa* effects, the science of the gaps between what people do and what they "imagine" they do, the interplay of presence and absence, of the spoken and unspoken through which these subjects make and miss the truth of the social: Marx, with the distant generosity of those who have better things to do, leaves all this to the philosophers and sociologists of the future. The cycle of *Class Struggles In France* and *The Eighteenth Brumaire* is a perfect example in this connection. The buffoonery of the revolution conjured away demonstrates the absolute rationality of the paradoxes of political representation. But it is also the part of the irrational that preserves the distance between the science of true movement and the sublunary accidents of the political universe.

And there is still, perhaps, a more radical problem. This practice that is the common constitution of subject and object and this world that is wholly the work of acting subjects: both resemble (a bit too much, perhaps) what Bishop Berkeley once desired for his declining religion, and what the young engineers of souls, in the service of new autocrats, will want tomorrow for their new religions of state. The dangerous obstinacy of locating dialectics in nature may be, first of all, the safeguard against a more formidable peril, the thought of decadence that weighs upon practical, productive modernity. The objectivation of dialectics in nature is a response to the same concern we saw in the return of Shakespearean subjectivity within history. This is not the concession to scientism denounced by Sartre but an attempt to restore the grand physics of production which is inseparably physical and metaphysical as in the days of Democritus,[12] and which by that very fact is distinct from the labor of engineers and the prestidigitations of politics. One can always get the better of a scapegoat named Dühring or Bogdanov, but one does not escape thereby one's own logic. And the engineers of souls will always know how to consign their shares to the dialectics of nature and history as the needs of the new autocrats dictate.

Here, then, is the other side of the game, for the world in which making or doing [*le faire*] is proclaimed as the law of being is also a world in which it is no longer distinguished from its simulacra. To be sure, the preoccupation of this distinction may refer to the backward musics of the soul and the shoemaker. But what is abandoned easily on the side of truth returns insistently on that of justice. The enchanted philosopher would like in vain to leave it up to the seeming innocence of the modern productive machines, but such innocence is strictly doubled by the paranoia of the engineers of souls. The *doxa* machines are in the first place machines of confession. Elsewhere the gay science of unchained appearances becomes the "justice" of the worker state condemning saboteurs who are recognizable by virtue of the fact that they do *not* sabotage to hide all the better their sabotage. The question of music turns around, then, and the philosopher–art lover—astonished to see the guardians of the worker state reject the music of the new technical age—becomes the moralist caught in the cross-reasonings [*les raisons croisées*] of generalized culpability: "You know as well as I do, the Communists are guilty because they are wrong in their way of being right and they make us guilty because they are right in their way of being wrong."[13] Between the philosopher-become-servant and the new guardian, the cross-plays [*les jeux croisés*] of justification begin all at once.

8 :: The Philosopher's Wall

THE PROBLEM IS the following: the new guardian who justifies the philosopher's word is a curious functionary. He is there and he is not there; he is here and somewhere else.

Such, typically, is the cross-relation [*le rapport croisé*] in which Sartre's philosophical and political itinerary is engaged. We can grasp it by starting from the lesson he gives Camus. Sartre reproaches Camus for claiming to speak "in the name of poverty"; that, says Sartre, is the demeanor of a rhetorician or actor [*comédien*] leaning up against "the wings of the scenery."[1] The philosopher *could* do that too: "And suppose I were to summon as witness an old Communist militant, after having taken care first to burden him with years and troubles sure to stir the heart, suppose I make him appear on stage and make this speech to you: 'I am sick of seeing bourgeois like you furiously going about destroying the Party, which is my sole hope, when you are incapable of putting anything in its place.' "[2]

That is what the philosopher would do if he were trying, as the rhetorician or actor would, to win by acclamation the vote of the assembly of shoemakers. Instead of that, he is a philosopher as Socrates understands it: a unique witness speaking to a unique witness. So he does not do it.

Or at least he says he does not do it. He does it in his way of not doing it. But this paralepsis is not simply a stylistic device pitting a rhetorician against a better one. It is the half-turn that transforms the rhetorical powers of the gesture designating the shadows of the stage into the powers of the machine exchanging presence and absence. The old militant who will not come is actually the young machinist who is the invisible motor of the stage. Effective insofar as he is not there, and insofar as he will never be.

THE TIRED GUARDIAN

Young Clinias, then, should not be mistaken about the real meaning of the refutation of the rhetorician. The worker *whom one need only have gotten to speak* is a worker one will *never* hear speak. So how could young Clinias hold a verifiable discourse about his thinking? On the day after an abortive communist demonstration, for example, he says that the worker has grown "tired of being the plaything of Moscow."[3] But how does he know that? "Have you heard him complain *with your own ears?*" In all honesty he must admit *he has not heard him*, though he may indeed have heard *some workers*. But *the worker*—what ear could hear him? He is now trained enough in philosophy to know that the concept of dog does not bark; only dogs bark. Through all the workers he could interrogate, the silence of *the worker* would resound even louder—the worker who they are not, the one who is the negation of their empirical dispersion.

Let there be no mistake here. The relation of *the worker* to the empirical multitude of workers no longer resembles what one learned in the school of Socrates: the difference between beauty and a catalogue of beautiful things, between virtue and examples of virtue. "The worker" who is absent here is not the common essence of which empirical workers supposedly partake. It is that strange, unheard-of figure in the order of discourse: the heavenly constellation *that is and is not* a barking animal; the concept that clothes itself in flesh and bones to chase away the shadows of speculation—flesh and bones that cannot be found in the collection of empirical individuals; the body absent from all bodies; the voice absent from all discourse. *What would speak* in the worker whom one could always question would be only the absence of the worker. But they do not speak in any case. They do not have time. *They are too tired.*

Which is actually the secret of the new guardianship. The new guardian who has relieved the philosopher is not himself at his post. He, too, is off duty, but for the opposite reason: he has neither the time nor the leisure to exercise his function. "At first sight there is not in principle the least difficulty in an unskilled worker's making an excellent militant: the only serious obstacle would seem vulgar and circumstantial: it is fatigue. Only there it is: this fatigue is not an accident; it accumulates without melting, like the eternal snows, and it *makes* the unskilled worker."[4]

Eternity once more recovered where one was not expecting it—*in the absence of time.* The worker-divinity of the disenchanted world is not, in the first place, technology but fatigue. Henceforth the guardian is someone *who has no leisure,* who cannot have any leisure. Not by virtue of any prohibition, but simply because in the age of mass production it is less possible than ever for a person to do two things at once. There is no longer any commandment, only a *sufficient reason*. It is enough to note this vulgar *circumstance*, this prosaic *kairos* called fatigue that is not content to distinguish worker-being [l'être-ouvrier] but actually *makes* it. Plato's artisans did not have time to treat themselves to the illnesses of the rich. Sartre's unskilled worker does not have time to treat himself to the luxury of criticizing his party. He cannot treat himself to the luxury of "freedom of thought" in which the intellectual glorifies the vulgarity of his leisure. An unskilled worker who thinks would "damage" the machine.[5] The labor of negation is a separate full-time job; it cannot be done in the *lost moments* of the worker's labor. The law of the absence of time imposes itself on all the agents of the productive world. The bourgeoisie itself, when it acts as a class, has nothing to do with thinking freely. And there is all that snow weighing down the body of the unskilled worker, the twenty tons per day that crush the body of the female metal worker [la *metteuse en plaques*]. Young Clinias and his friends, those "intellectuals pale and soft as young ladies"—would they dare to go and speak with her face to face about the freedom that Soviet metal workers should possess to criticize Lysenko's theses? They are not in any danger of incurring a violent reaction from her. She, like the others, will have no other response than to disclose what constitutes her—fatigue: "Don't be afraid: she won't hit you; she's too tired."[6]

Nothing else. According to Sartre, only the nostalgic sophists of anarcho-syndicalism persist in putting people on the wrong track. Against the dazed worker and the union boss cut off from the masses they set the skilled worker, master of his machine as of his thinking, who leaves the factory with the awareness and energy needed to go out and breathe life into his union meeting or to write for its official organ. But that machinist-king is a vestige of the past. Before the age of Taylorism he was the man of the "universal machine," the mechanic of the end of the nineteenth century idealizing in the reign of producers his own suzerainty in the milieu of his peers. That worker is no more. Or if he still does exist, it is as a hostage of the bourgeoisie, of the plan of *continuous extermination* through which the bourgeoisie *makes* the working class. Indeed, for Sartre, that is the key to our social history: the famous bourgeois fear over the face-off of June 1848. Marx saw it leading to the tragicomedy of a revolution conjured away. Sartre, however, does not like mixed genres, preferring historical tragedy. Like Lady Macbeth, his bourgeoisie lives with the obsession of the proletariat that it did not kill enough of in 1848 or exterminate sufficiently in 1871. Failing to finish it off with fire and sword, it decided to choke the proletariat in the iron collar of Malthusianism by maintaining regressive productive structures. The proletariat is the work product of bourgeois mourning. In this play the machinist-king is merely an extra on the stage of the performance. Below there are nothing but the tons of iron and snow that make the guardian what he is: a prisoner, *a dead man reprieved from death.*

The Party, or Continuous Creation

There are only . . . *there would be only* . . . if this radical absence of the guardians did not define precisely, in opposition to them, the pure nonbeing, the pure power of their representation. The party consists of that, the pure and simple negation of worker-being fashioned by bourgeois mourning and the snows of fatigue. It is the pure act of the proletariat, representing under the form of its absolute negation the pure fatigue of the proletarians, the immaterial bond of their pure dispersion. The party is reminiscence *in actu*, the continuous creation of a Cartesian God who produces the *nonbeing* of the proletariat in response to the bourgeois continuous extermination that made the worker's *being*.

We are familiar with the implacable logic of this pure act. It is absolutely sovereign because no member of the class of which it is the party can oppose it without denying himself as a member of this class, without falling back into the dust from which he was drawn. And if all the members of the class were to oppose it, that would simply mean that the whole class would have fallen back into dust. It exists only through its pure act. And it is clear that this act must be unique, for otherwise it would not be the negation of dispersion. Only the Communist Party could oppose itself to the Communist Party. The workers, for their part, can only exclude themselves from it, as from their class.

But this absolute sovereignty has another aspect pointed out already long ago by Aristotle: no one is bound to obey it. The party is absolute Exigency, necessity that does not trouble itself with the feelings of tired individuals. But ultimately this absolute Exigency commands only itself. This eternal life of the proletariat is affected in return by the eternal snows of proletarian fatigue.

The logic is simple. Fatigue demands that the workers be represented by a party. At the same time it demands that this party *absolutely not* represent them since they are pure passivity and it must be pure act. So it is logical that the party, in its directives and watchwords, does not take account of the needs of those workers whose needs it expresses. But it is also completely logical that they, in turn, do not feel the need to obey the watchwords of the party that expresses their needs. Thus, on 28 May 1952 the working class did not appear at the demonstrations organized by its party against General Ridgeway's arrival in Paris. The pure act of the party had then to become street theater: a demonstration put on by party hardliners for the masses about what they should have done if they had not remained precisely what they are—the masses. The party had performed for the masses their own power so that they might forget their fatigue. But the masses were too tired to be represented with such power, thereby confirming in the most striking way that the solitude of the party is indeed their unique power.

To put it another way, there cannot be anything else but pure power [*puissance*] and simple impotence [*impuissance*]. If the masses were not at the street demonstration of May 28, if only 2 percent of the workers went on strike June 2 to demand the liberation of their leader Jacques Duclos, who was arrested during the demonstration, there cannot be any positive reason for this. The absent masses simply manifested their being: fatigue. Not the fatigue of "their" party since, by definition, the party is their non-fatigue. Simply the "vulgar" fatigue that constitutes them, a fatigue reinforced by the "anemia" that the exterminating will of the bourgeoisie imposes on the whole social body. And the solitude of the party clearly proved what, in any case, *could not but be proved*— that it alone makes the proletariat into the negation of worker fatigue.

Thus each is found to be right [*avoir raison*], but for a reason not its own.[7] The party is right to call upon the masses to demonstrate, masses whose reason consists in not being able to show up. But it does not know why it is right. It is right for reasons that are not its own [*il a raison pour des raisons qui ne sont pas les siennes*]. It takes itself for the positive expression of the working class when it is the pure nonbeing of the proletariat. Only the philosopher knows why the party is right.

But by the same token the reason of the philosopher is closely bound up with that of the party. The philosopher can be right only *in the reasons* of the party. And he cannot speak this reason either to the masses, who lack the ears to hear it, or to the party, who could not recognize it as its own. It is only among his peers, the "viscous rats" of the left intelligentsia, that he can be right—that he can have an oblique reason for forbidding others to seek out the reasons of those who bear on their bodies the sufficient reason that makes them the absent guardians of the philosopher's world.

A discourse of circumstance, say those content to laugh at it or excuse it. But it really is something else, a discourse *on* circumstance in a world where there are, indeed, *only* circumstances. Sartre's *The Communists and Peace* implements a concept of circumstance that has nothing "circumstantial" about it. The worker law of our world is identified with a Sartrean idea of freedom that is also a philosophy of creation: a telescoping of act and thing, of instant and eternity, of the true and the artificial—a Cartesian theory of continuous creation.[8]

The privileged interlocutor of these "discourses of circumstance" is not mistaken: "There is theory precisely in this way of treating the event as ineffaceable, as a decisive test of our intentions and an instantaneous choice of the whole future and of all that we are. . . . Not to speak of the proletarian, of the class in itself, and of the eternal Party is here to make a theory of the proletariat and of the party as continuous creations, that is to say, as the dead reprieved from death."[9]

For Merleau-Ponty, the Sartrean discourse of circumstance is the annulment of the historical dialectic in a series of acts both immediate and eternal: the gaze of the most disadvantaged proletarian, from which one reads the mute exigency of the human; the pure act of the party, creating and re-creating the class in the instant of decision; the unshakable confidence of the proletarian in the party, without which he would be only dust; the pure choice of the philosopher that allows, as sole guide in the aleatory nature of meaning, the gaze of the most disadvantaged proletarian that renders interpretation ridiculous; and as the sole means to read this gaze, the act of the party that brings it to light.

And so opposites are united: the extreme idealism of the Exigency that is to come, and the extreme realism of confidence in the material instance incarnating this Exigency. The mythology of a reminiscence frozen in the eternity of its recommencement and of an end indefinitely pushed back to the horizon. As if the philosopher could feel at ease only in the face-off between "the brute will of the leaders" and "the opaque necessity of things."[10] As if his own status were bound up with the rejection of the universe of mixture lying between the two: an in-between world of uncertain techniques and the reflections of *doxa*, of "open, incompleted meanings" and "indecisive actions" that "run off the track along the way or even change into their opposites as soon as they are put into circulation."[11]

A world, then, of Platonic right opinion or Aristotelian *prudence* on which the philosopher and the politician have lost their grip. This realm of hybridity and ambiguity rejected by Sartre is, for Merleau-Ponty, nothing less than the dialectic itself: the dynamic of relations between persons transformed by the mediation of the things in which they are inscribed. Sartre's *Critique of Dialectical Reason* is merely a long response to that verdict.

THE DIALECTICAL SEAL

This interworld raised as an objection to Sartre, this universe of meanings overturned by the reality of things will become the very fabric of his *Critique of Dialectical Reason*, the play of passive syntheses serving as the basis for the dialectic of groups. And Sartre will show that this theatrical confidence, this *oath* whereby the rule of the party stops the seriality of the ensemble of workers, is not the grace of a God present, like Christ, "wherever two workers gather together." Such things depend on the same rationality as the *seal* [*sceau*] in worked matter that seals [*scelle*] the first unity of workers outside themselves. Condemning these latter to revolving games of seriality but also tearing them away from ahistorical tepidity and adialectical adhesions of reciprocity, the seal hurls them onto the great wheel that launches needy, working people onto the road of the group and History.

The critic, then, is taken literally. The dialectical praxis that serves as the basis for political action is precisely, for Sartre, the becoming-thing of humanity and the becoming-human of things:

> Significations are composed of matter alone. Matter retains them as inscriptions and gives them their true efficacy. In los-

ing their human properties, human projects are engraved in Being, their translucidity becomes opacity, their tenuousness thickness, their volatile lightness permanence. They *become Being* by losing their quality as lived events, and insofar as they are Being they cannot be dissolved into knowledge even if they are deciphered and known. Only matter itself, beating on matter, can break them up. The meaning of human labor is that man is reduced to inorganic materiality in order to act materially on matter and to change his material life. . . . The future comes to man through things in so far as it previously came to things through man.[12]

That, in sum, would be Marxism finally realized: an entirely materialist dialectic, an entirely dialectical materiality. A world in which there would be only transformations, subjects acting on things and things resulting from the action of subjects—the formula developed in the *Theses on Feuerbach* doing away here at last with the unbridgeable gap between nature and history to the benefit of the history of humanity. There are only *things* precisely to the extent that there are only *ends*. But only the shock of matter against matter will transform the material condition permitting the existence of the human subject.

With a closer look, however, this nice optimism begins to blur. There is a true and a false dialectic. The dialectic of worked matter on which is inscribed human projects is in fact only a simulacrum of dialectic. Things give the people who devoted themselves to them no future other than repetition. In one sense the first part of Sartre's *Critique* is merely the demonstration of this trap: the dialectical magic that worked matter has stolen from human praxis is something it will never give back, under the form of reason, to practitioners.

THE PHILOSOPHER'S WINDOW

The "dialectics in things" is in reality theft without restitution. Let us beware of complaining about that. Worked matter is right [*a raison*] in having the same sort of reason as the party that has no ears for the weariness of those whose matchless power it expresses. What would they be without it? Of what dialectic could they be the subjects? Without the hard, sharp block of this matter, what relations could needy, working subjects sustain besides "adhesions of a colloidal sort," human relations as viscous as the roots of the public garden of Bouville or the "rats" of the left intelligentsia.[13] It is this adhesion, this viscosity, that is the absolute evil, the glue (peasant or Lapp) of bad history. "A few acres of ground, a decent wife, children, the modest freedom of the craftsman at work, of the peasant in the field—in short, happiness": a happiness, in other words, that is the renunciation of the "great enterprise" of the dialectic.[14]

Even before worked matter enters the scene, the philosopher has protected himself against this colloid. He has built a wall in the décor of rustic and peasant happiness: "From my window I can see a road paver on the road and a gardener working in a garden. Between them there is a wall with bits of broken glass on top protecting the bourgeois property where the gardener is working. Thus they have no knowledge at all of each other's presence."[15]

The broken glass and the bourgeois property are there for ambiance. The décor itself has another purpose. Sartre wants to show that in their separation and mutual ignorance there always exists between two workers relations of *interiority*; but also and above all, that these relations never exist except through the mediation of a *third*. Thus, in the perception where the man at the window is figured as object, the two men outside become the "hemorrhagic center" of the object, each of them united with the other at the point of the gaze: "The mere fact, for each of them, of seeing what the Other does not see, of exposing the object through a special kind of work, establishes a relation of reciprocity in my perceptual field which transcends my perception itself: each of them constitutes the ignorance of the Other. . . . They are ignorant of one another *through me* to the precise extent that I become what I am *through them*."[16]

Clearly the philosopher at his window, too, feels someone's gaze on him: the ironic gaze of his privileged opponent. And he also insists that no one is going to get him to say that he is a transcendental subject constituting others in his own perception. He is not the philosopher-master; he is not the Leibnizian God of action at a distance. He is merely an intellectual on vacation, a petty bourgeois who does not know how to weed flower beds, how to crush pebbles, and against whom is already exercised the mute complicity of these workers who are ignorant of each other.

But this modesty is useless, or misleading. The philosopher's act was not the dissolution of the stone wall in order to "interiorize" the two workers. It was the erection of the wall to put them in the true element of the dialectic: not the colloid of reciprocal relations but the steel and concrete of worked matter that seals meaning in consigning backward workers to their solitudes, their turnings in place, or their aphasic dialogues. Much more than *The German Ideology*'s laboriously demonstrated historicity of the cherry tree, the philosopher's rustic wall engages humanity on the road of the productive dialectic. When the two workers have entered the workshop, the philosopher at the window will give way to a more severe figure of the dialectical Third: the timekeeper, a pure representative of the Exigency of worked matter.

THE WORKER AT HIS MACHINE

For worked matter has again taken on the character that not long ago permitted the philosopher to recover his reason in the reason of the party: it is Exigency, the categorical Imperative, depriving even subjects of leisure from knowing whether they should obey. Worked matter is Idea—its own Idea that disallows room for another thought in the body that it subjugates.

Such is the logic of the wall constructed by the philosopher: it is not possible or even conceivable that bodies at work could ever earn the least liberty *by themselves*. To prove it, there is no longer any need for the female metal workers whose burdens make viscous rats lower their eyes. The working women of the *Critique of Dialectical Reason* seem to be more alert. Lulled by the rhythm of the machine, they evade the dullness of labor in the pleasure of erotic reveries. But such sexual abandon is, precisely, a false evasion: it is the exact level of vigilance required for a job where neither active thinking nor total absence would be appropriate. The working women believed only that they were dreaming: "It was the machine in them which was dreaming of caresses."[17]

As we already know, the same holds true for the "humanism of labor" in which the anarcho-syndicalists dreamed of the future royalty of workers. It was merely the projection of their *de facto* suzerainty in the workshop of the universal machine.[18] They found their idea of honor-work inscribed in the inertia of the worked thing. Through them it was simply Worked Matter that became its own Idea, as Spanish gold did in the days of Philip II. The worker's thought will ever only be the dream of a dream of matter: his freedom is precisely the "means chosen by the Thing and by the Other to crush him and transform him into a worked Thing."[19] In Spinoza's Latin this freedom is called *amor fati*.

Dialectic of machines. Simulacrum of the dialectic. The praxis incorporated in things never has reason to make the leap that would turn it back to needy, working people. The enchantments of worked matter, the whirlpools of seriality that they orchestrate, the dreams of freedom reflecting it: how could they not be as eternal as the bourgeois enterprise of restrained extermination, the eternal snows of fatigue, the pure act of the party, and the pure choice of the philosopher? "The worker will be saved from his destiny only if human multiplicity as a whole is permanently changed into a group *praxis*."[20]

Nothing but this everything. But what lever could lift "the turning ensemble of unfortunate materiality" into the eternal life of group praxis? Surely not the factory lever with which the human being "becomes a thing to act upon things." What eternity will he ever earn outside the eternity of *amor fati*? Where could change ever begin?

Yet the first definition is there to assure us that at the origin of everything, there is always the free praxis of individuals. A "translucent" praxis recovered through any surrender to opacity. The female worker is not content merely to dream; she is also the minor deity of continuous creation who freely decides each morning to go to the factory, who freely chooses to have or not to have children. Except that the machine has decided the *meaning* of this freedom for her. If she does not want children, the reason—the only reason—is that she *cannot* want them. Because she can be a woman *only* as a female worker [*comme ouvrière*], and a worker only as the product of bourgeois extermination. In the empirical history of the worker, family strategies—Malthusian or anti-Malthusian, individual or collective—have played a major role in the constitution of a militant distance with respect to productive and reproductive fatality. But it is this distance that Sartre absolutely rejects when he makes Malthusianism the only bourgeois aggression against the worker body. In the realm of vulgar fatigue there is no place for vulgar freedom, the sort that is earned or lost or regained, that goes astray or loses itself in the intervals of exploitation—the freedom of male and female workers who decide that *they have the leisure* to think of something else while working; the time after work to learn; the possibility of writing literate prose or verse; the choice of having the children they

cannot have or of not having the children they *should* have; the obligation of organizing worker societies that they do not *have the right*
to create *or the time* to run: in short, the luxury that they *cannot treat
themselves to* as it is simply—and vulgarly—put by the philosopher-
friends of the people for the sake of "intellectuals pale as young
ladies."

For the philosopher of continuous creation, the intolerable
thing may not be what Merleau-Ponty thought it was: the interworld of blurred meanings. What he rejects above all are the elas-
tic intervals of autodidact freedom. The omnipotence that Sartre
now delegates to worked matter is the same as what he delegated
not long ago to the party: the freedom—his own—that would be
corrupted if it were refracted in the shattered time of worn-down
servitudes and saved-up leisures, in the uncertain light of demi-
knowledges and demi-cultures, in the disoriented space of path-
ways and dead ends where people searched not long ago for what
rebellious workers and dreamers called "emancipation"—the
self-transformation of the slave into a human being. The omnipotence delegated to worked matter is, first of all, the pledge that
freedom cannot come from there. It guarantees the right of the
only true freedom, that of the philosopher, which is conceivable
and operative only as the exact opposite of the impotence of serialized individuals. If the latter want to be free, they first will have
to renounce the freedom that they would claim to procure for
themselves in the calculus of their pleasures and their pains.

THE ABSOLUTE WEAPON

That is why, in the meantime, the philosopher has reappeared at
his window. This time not the window of his vacation dwelling,
which opens onto the originary scene of the gardener and the road
paver. This time it is the window of his study that opens onto the
décor of the city and its serial gyrations. Now without feigned
shame, a worker among workers, he observes people on the side-
walk waiting for a bus.

What, exactly, is he trying to do? Simply, he says, to help us
comprehend with the simplest example the elementary reality
in which the complex reality of class participates—the *collective*,
"the two-way relation between a material, inorganic, worked object and a multiplicity which finds its unity of exteriority in it."[21]
He then shows us that these isolated individuals waiting anony-

mously on line are already linked by countless bonds of interiority: not only the gaze of the observer but also the scarcity of seats on the bus, the distribution of tickets, schedules, work rhythms, and so forth. Once the notion is grasped with this simple example, Sartre can return to analyze the complex collective, the passive syntheses of the worker's class-being.

But a suspicion rises in our minds: the excessively academic pedagogy of these open windows might be a cover for another operation. By returning periodically to his window, the philosopher reassures himself of his power—the power the philosopher will have to lend to the collective of workers if it is to escape some day from the desperate situation in which he has placed it: the philosopher's power of synthesis that destroys the walls that he himself had built and that forges the supreme bond of the absence of bonds. The power of the lever commanding the whole ensemble is the absolute dialectical weapon which, since Hegel, has been called the *negation of the negation*. This power breaking down walls and chains is one that the workers remain forever incapable of forging in their relations to themselves or to things. He will then offer it to them in the form that is exactly appropriate in their case: *power as the self-negation of impotence.*

And so the reasoning process is laid out. Inscribed in worked matter, the impotence of all becomes *their collective* impotence. It is, in that, already opposed to their dispersion; it is already union, therefore force. The *unity of impotence* is the explosive identity of opposites in which the form-unity negates its content of impotence: "The object brings men together by imposing the violent, passive unity of a seal on their multiplicity. And in the very moment where this object is a threat . . . the *unity of impotence transforms itself into a violent contradiction*: in it *unity* opposes itself to the impotence that negates it . . . in the same moment [that] the *serial unity* of these oppositions posits itself as a contradiction of the same and of the Other demanding a unifying *praxis*."[22]

This power of impotence [*cette puissance de l'impuissance*] was, not long ago, the theater of the pure act of the party organizing in behalf of the masses the spectacle—effective by its impotence—of the power of the impotent [*de la puissance des impuissants*]. Now it is the pure act of the royal dialectician working at the heart of words, relaying the rhetorical power of images that evoke "the cement of impotence" through the continuous creation of adverbial locutions ("first," "at once," "at the same time," "at the very same moment"), and through the action of performative verbs conjugated in the reflexive form, in order to show us how the unity of impotence *is posited and transformed* in the power of its contradiction.

The philosopher alone now holds back the power of impotence *in actu*. But he cannot give it to the workers of *amor fati*. For them this power of the negation of the negation remains the Idea they cannot possibly catch up with. The most they can do is mimic it in the only negation of the negation they can manage, the confrontation with death. And so are woven into the text the words and images of the revolt in 1831 of the Lyons silk weavers ("to live working or die fighting") in a reversal of the impossibility of living colliding with the absolute master of the dialectic, Death: "The nerve of *practical unity* is freedom, appearing as the necessity of necessity—in other words, as its inexorable inversion. Indeed, in so far as the individuals of a given milieu are directly threatened, in practico-inert necessity, by the impossibility of life, their radical unity (in reappropriating this very impossibility for themselves as the possibility of dying humanly, or of the affirmation of man by his death) is the inflexible negation of this impossibility ('To live working or die fighting'); thus the group constitutes itself as the radical impossibility of the impossibility of living, which threatens serial multiplicity."[23]

The worker collective can only mimic this apocalypse which is the passage to the group, the negation of serial negation. The revolt of the silk weavers was an apocalypse without effect, a Fools Day on which the weavers of Lyons had offered a grandiose and theatrical demonstration of the impotence of the worker collective to ever be, by itself, a group.

The Sartrean King

To see the birth of the group, Sartre must then take a leap in shifting toward a more central and successful manifestation, the manifestation *par excellence* for revolutionary reminiscence—the storming of the Bastille. It is not the organized collectivity of mutualist weavers that can give birth to the group. It can be done only by the fortuitous gathering of the Parisian populace on 14 July 1789.

We should not see in that any privileging of spontaneity over organization. The privilege of the Parisian mob comes to it, on the contrary, from the fact that it is wholly constituted from the outside. What *makes* the group is the *Sovereign*, Louis XVI in this particular case. The *exis* of the Parisian gathering from which the united crowd will be born is the royal *praxis* that first constituted it. Or it may even be merely the imagination of this praxis, e.g. the current of rumors that day about the troops that the king assembled around Paris. True or false, they had in any case the effect that each individual was constituted as a "particle of a sealed materiality" within an encircled (or supposedly encircled) city. A serial relationship, then. But here the power, or the idea of it, will be redoubled and become the negation *in actu* of the negation: "the negative order of the massacre" that the king would have given to block the seriality that the positive order had sealed. The royal "order" constitutes the people in the synthetic unity of the object aimed at by extermination. There is no longer any way to defend lives menaced one by one except to arm oneself collectively against the king. Caught in the real or imagined crosshairs of the king's praxis, the Parisian gathering is surprised to find itself *existing as a group*. In fact, it is not just any gathering whatsoever. It is the people of the Faubourg Saint-Antoine, whose somber *exis* is the shadow of the Bastille, the sealed mark of royal praxis. And the Bastille is also the fortified place from which it will be attacked by the troop of royal slaughterers, or more exactly, from which it discovers that it "was exterminated in the future by the Prince of Lambesc."[24]

There is no point here in following the movement whereby each individual, on the road to the Bastille, is constituted as the *third* regulating the group. The essential is already given. The power of royal praxis through which the group comes to be is of the very same nature as the power of worked matter or the power of the pure communist act. But here it enjoys the advantage of being absolute. The counter-finality, dispersed in inert practice, is here concentrated in the praxis of the king (which in imagination surrounds and invests popular space), and in the edifice of the Bastille (which is its absolute visibility, its perfect materialization). The Lyons silk weavers lacked what the worker collectivity always will lack, this power of the Other that is absolutely constraining. The "order of the king" is the pure act that is absolutely pure. It removes from the Parisian gathering what the pure act of its "own" party will never manage to remove completely from the proletariat: its *passivity*. The "group" is the pure negation of the negation, besieged by absolute authority, by the One of sovereignty. The King is Descartes's God caught at the moment of creation. As with Hegel, the absolute rationality of the group is conceivable only from the point where it is identical with the absolute subjectivity of a sovereign individual.

Thus everything is given at the origin. The revolution is conceivable only as the negation of the counterrevolution. And the powers of the party will never be more than the powers of the reminiscence of the originary scene. The entirety of its becoming is prescribed in the myth of its origin; the sovereignty of this arbitrary power becomes all the more sovereign in that it may be imaginary. Evidently Stalin is included in advance in the necessity that gave birth to the group outside itself in the single gesture of the sovereign: the creation of a freedom that swooped down on it as the eagle did on Orestes. As the negation of the negation. As the Terror.

This fatality of the days following the party gives the second part of Sartre's *Critique* its tonality of gray on gray. We know in advance what to expect as we follow his overview which, leaping over worker history and Marxist history, leads us from 14 July 1789 and the Convention to the vicissitudes of an institutionalized group in which we recognize the silhouette of Stalin. In the shadow of the Sovereign we shall see repeated the games of serial flight and worked matter. The collectivity tried vainly to transcend itself and become group. The group will try vainly to transcend itself and become organism. Constantly threatened with the return to the nothingness of its dispersion, it will have to establish for its preservation the rule of a fraternal terror that does not derive from perverse wills or the heavy burdens of apparatus but merely from the "inert structure of common freedom."[25] Out of that will develop games of reciprocity and alterity, superimposing and counteracting their effects through the harsh exigencies of the real: organization; the necessary specialization of subgroups; the necessity of rescuing instruments of control from seriality; and the restoration of sovereign praxis to overcome the inertia of these instruments. From the king of France to the little Father of the Soviet peoples, the very logic of the royal act is to prevent the colloid from taking or blocking the flight of meaning through the barrier of the negation of the negation.

THE PHILOSOPHER AND THE TYRANT

Rather than those overly functional analyses we are taken with the gray upon gray of the tone, with the henceforth undecidable political modality of this discourse.

What exactly happened since Sartre wrote the angry certitudes of *The Communists and Peace*? Redistributed in the circles of the great dialectical wheel, the master figures have remained the same: the Malthusian bourgeoisie that continuously creates and exterminates the proletariat; the overtired servants of the machine; the ideologues of anarcho-syndicalism, who speak for the outmoded machine that brought them into being; the necessity of the pure bond that forms the absence of bond, and of the pure Act performed on the theater of the street; and the inflexible constraint of the confidence that sustains the creation of a group pulled back at every moment from nothingness.

But something has indeed changed, and that is the place of the philosopher. He no longer speaks *alongside the party*; now he speaks *from the interior of Marxism*. He has taken back the power he delegated to the party, now regarding it as a power that Marxism must integrate if it is to be *possible*. But this condition of possibility is turned immediately into a proof of impossibility. The reciprocal transformation of persons and things is a dead end if one does not back it up with the pure formal power of the negation of the negation. The party of the working class will always be a lie. It *cannot* be born of the working class. And the dictatorship of the proletariat is a contradiction in terms, a "bastard compromise between the active, sovereign group and passive seriality."[26] The class is condemned to being torn asunder among the sufferings of the collective, apocalyptic struggles, and institutions of representation. And one cannot see what sovereign, against the backdrop of what future, could make a totality out of them.

But what are we to conclude from this demonstration? The dictatorship of the proletariat, the heart of the Marxist dream in the twentieth century, is impossible. And it is precisely for that reason that Stalinism was necessary. The first moment of socialist society *could only be* "the indissoluble aggregation of bureaucracy, of Terror and of the cult of personality."[27] But could that "first moment" be precisely that without representing itself as the dictatorship of the proletariat? If the fatigue of the worker that serves as the call to revolution always deprives that class of the power of the group, and if only that power can some day liberate that class from its fatigue, then what remains except a Terror now rooted only in the sovereign's will? If History is explained in terms of its outcomes [*ses fins*], on what is its intelligibility to be grounded today other than the justification, after the fact, of what has been?

To be sure, the militant moralist can always disapprove of empirical communist action by comparing it to the aims [*aux fins*] of communism. But the philosopher, in regarding these same aims, has to establish the perfect dialectical rationality for what scandalizes him. If Stalin represented only the *social* positivity of the proletariat, one could distinguish his reasonable actions from his unreasonable ones, the good from the bad. But if he represents only the aims of humanity, then his action, whatever it may be, *has already been justified* in the human future. If Stalin the communist had been wrong, Stalin the tyrant would be right in having the habitual reason of tyrants: their good pleasure. But by the same token the philosopher would have nothing to do but pack his bags, carrying off with him the rationality of history and that of human hope. The philosopher is entirely trapped in his paradox. If Stalin is wrong, Stalin is right. And if Sartre is right, Sartre is wrong.

TANKS IN THE SNOW

This circle is illustrated nicely in Sartre's analysis of the Hungarian uprising. Sartre the *moralist* unequivocally condemned the Soviet intervention.[28] But Sartre the *dialectician* faces a different problem: if that condemnation is to make sense, it must be shown that the Soviet intervention *was not necessary*. So Sartre must shift his analysis and pose the question: did the political and social logic of the insurrection allow for a different outcome? But such a question is undecidable at the moment. Did the communist workers have the power to oppose with their own forces the petty bourgeois anticommunists? That is what practice should have unveiled. But this "translucent" practice does not unveil anything, except after the fact. It never has time for its own unveiling.

This, for example, is what came to light after the fact. From "trusted witnesses" Sartre obtained the following information. Among the insurgent workers there were also some petty bourgeois, those whom the Rákosi government had sent to the factories for reeducation. In the course of work at the factory, the workers could not recognize these petty bourgeois; in a factory, by definition, there are only workers. But in the praxis of insurrection, they needed inevitably to mark themselves off to reveal their petty bourgeois being, that of a desperate minority without a future. And, inevitably, their despair would impel them to radicalize the action of true workers, who, for their part, could neither deny the title of worker to their factory comrades nor expel from their group members united in representing the same goals and unified by the very force of their "despair." In vain did the insurrectional committees finally perceive the danger and seek to reorganize themselves to combat this distortion of their struggle: "there was not enough time, and the second intervention interrupted the reorganization when it began."[29]

It is obvious that the "trusted witnesses" can tell us only what we already knew in advance: the eternal dereliction of the petty bourgeois, eternally caught between the old ruling classes and the new proletarian forces, and eternally pushed to leftist exaggeration by the rage of their rightist despair. But this stale imagery of Stalinist discourse takes on for Sartre the tragic force of irrefutability. For he does not believe in precisely what sustains the Stalinist imagery of the "petty bourgeois," the working class positivity of the party as a *class group*. The passive characteristics of worker-being prohibit, in Sartre's view, the Hungarian working class from transforming itself into a group vis-à-vis the party that claims to be *its* party. The time lacking to the insurgent workers to reorganize is a time that will always be lacking to them, that they lack *by definition*. The insurrection did not leave the workers time to recognize the petty bourgeois because the factory does not give them the leisure to distinguish them, because their fatigue does not allow them to make their history. If, in Sartre's logic, they have been able to become a group in fusion, it is only because Geroe's royal order unleashed the apocalyptic movement of the petty bourgeois.[30] And the latter were able to cement the worker group because they were not true workers.

The loop determined by the absence of time closes in on itself. The first intervention anticipated the second insofar as the latter controlled it in the *future perfect*. The tanks of the dialectic make history because the workers of materialism do not have time to make it. The Soviet invaders respond to the petty bourgeois parasites because the history of groups is itself the ever-recurring parasitism of the serialities conducted by worked matter.

THE PARASITIC DIALECTIC

To put it another way, it is the dialectic itself that is continuous parasitism. And this parasitism is always doubled by its simulacrum. Ever since his forceful stroke of putting up a wall between the gardener and the road paver, the philosopher has rushed unceasingly from simulacrum to simulacrum: worked matter, which is a false synthesis; the practico-inert, which simulates the dialectic; the fiction of the royal order; the mirage of group unity, its revolving "quasi-sovereignty" . . . An intelligibility defined in terms of *ends* appropriated within things, and organizations that will always be a logic of *as if*. The dialectic of a liberating history will remain forever indistinguishable from its simulations.

So as to be no longer a parasitic traveling companion, the philosopher—explaining to his peers the reasonings of the party— decided to parasitize Marxism from within it: "I said that the Marxist dialectic does not establish its own intelligibility. In that sense my book was, first of all, a challenge. It said: 'Incorporate me into Marxism and you will have made a beginning in filling the original void of Marxism.' "[31]

But it was not for nothing that Doctor Marx had left a void here, neglecting to ground in praxis the unity of nature and history. By instinct rather than by cold calculation he rejected a world defined completely by practice, a world in which *everyone would be right*. Hence the voids in his work, the part reserved in history for buffoonery, the leap of the dialectic into nature. Waging war against the dialectic of nature and fighting for a history grounded completely in practical rationality, Sartre is imprisoned totally in the rigor of his enterprise. He fills the void with the dialectic of "as if." To refute Engels, he makes Stalin *theoretically irrefutable*.

Now the philosopher is no longer the victim of his political auxiliaries but of his own exigency, for if the world's matter is to bear the history of liberation, it must be traversed entirely by technique. But the universe of *ordinary* technique remains what it always was for Plato: the universe of splintered rationality belonging to those bastard beings—"amphibians," Sartre calls them—who are artisans. A world of undecidable ends, of fabrications that become imitations of themselves, of partial socialities—short circuits in which is lost the explosive force of the Nothing that engenders the All. A world immobilized by the very force of its overflowings and hemorrhages. For it to budge, a *great technique* must intervene to *block* it. Those amphibian liberties and bastard collectivities must be buried under the snows of eternal fatigue in order to preserve the rights of a freedom that is unconditioned technique, or a technique conditioned by the single absolute of the End.

Thus, freedom is *super-technique*, a continuous creation that puts up a barrier to stop the expansions of ordinary technique and freedom—those of the democratic and liberal city of Protagoras the Sophist. It is the rustic wall of the philosopher on campaign, the poured concrete and tempered steel of the Soviet *epos* that stop the little circuits of *technē* and *doxa* with the absolute of Exigency. It is the freedom of the Great Engineer endowed with the power of the conflagration of the Nothing and the All.

But the Great Engineer is indistinguishable from the Great Actor [*Comédien*]. The dialectic precisely resembles its simulation. And the philosopher is completely grounded by what he wanted to ground—the imitator of an imitation. The dialectic is exactly like magic, and the rationality suspended with regard to the most disadvantaged is nothing more than the reason of the reason of tyrants.

So the position of the "most disadvantaged" is tenable only if one refuses to make it a principle of historical intelligibility. It again becomes pure moral exigency. To be able to exercise his judgment again, the moralist either must renounce the philosophical postulate linking the possibility of the liberation of the proletariat with its absolute crushing by things, or else he must choose *philosophical* silence pure and simple. Sartre will choose the second course. To speak and act in favor of the most disadvantaged, he will now fall silent *as a philosopher*. From Russell's tribunal to the tribunal of Lens, he will speak only in the register and space of judgment.[32] As prosecutor or judge of the crimes of capitalism, he will have to refuse them the argument of necessity, affirming that those crimes could have been *not committed*. As investigator or witness in the midst of the masses, he will reduce the theatrical function of substitution to the more modest role of provoking free expression. As advocate of the Maoists, he will be very careful not to be their philosopher.

But this reasoned activism leaves open, and more unresolved than ever, the question of how we are to move from series to group without a takeover by force. The impossibility of answering that question reduces the idea of the group to the Kantian function of the regulative idea. But at that level the question is exposed in all its nakedness: why is it necessary to want the group? What, aside from the ethical choice and the generosity of the wager, prompts one exactly to give the figure of the "group" to the realm of ends?[33]

Is it simply nostalgia for the universal? Not any longer the "dream of death" of dialectical universality, but that universal of Kantian reason which, the friend of the people assures us, is the will of the masses? Or is it not, rather, the old prohibition of "nothing else" continuing in its course, maintaining philosophy in the new conditions of the technological world? Might the improbable dialectical humanism of the group be the response, first of all, to a fundamental aversion that finds expression in the image of the series and the refusal of the artisan's "petty" freedoms? The response to the menace that weighs down the very idea of philosophy with the old, indestructible phantasm, the figure— more-than-ever fascinating and disturbing—of the artisan-king?

THE LITTLE DYER

We can read this question in pages by Sartre that would seem far removed from such preoccupations, pages that he devotes to painting. They are privileged pages because they define the other side of the enchanted dialectic. Behind the paradox of politics (which is freedom-as-terror), Sartre pursues the insistent dream of another circuit of matter, of a trajectory of sense between persons and things that does not allow itself to be grasped in the universe of representation, in the enchanted world of reified meanings.[34] Thus, in the sixteenth century, when the mania of Spanish gold inaugurates the sorceries of capitalist history, painting represents the "sumptuous disenchantment" born of the "subsiding" of the mists of representation, when its divine warrant, returning to heaven, permits the painter at last to address the free "greeting of matter to matter."[35]

But this disenchantment is a thwarted revelation, affected by the plebeian prudence and technological artifice that mark the painter's belonging to the petty universe of the artisan. Sartre chooses an exemplary figure to depict this, the artisan-painter Jacopo Robusti, whom we know as Tintoretto ("The Little Dyer"). Sartre tells us that his canvases represent for the first time a mirror of the world freed from the parasites of representation: "His paintings contain everything, but *mean* nothing. They are as mute as the world."[36] This signifying muteness of the canvas is also the quality of the new disenchanted world, the work of an artist who is first of all a worker: "The artist was the supreme laborer, depleting and exhausting matter, in order to produce and sell his visions."[37]

Is it not the concept of the worker in general that Sartre has brought into play in the figure of this supreme worker who does not bow to the fatigue of matter but returns it blow for blow? A producer beside and beyond himself [en deçà et au-delà de lui-même] in the visionary's dream and the merchant's wheeling and dealing. It is not by chance that Sartre chose this painter of mute canvases, the social-climbing and virtuosic Little Dyer, who was also polite enough to leave hardly a trace of writing behind him. This extraordinary imagined dialogue—in which Sartre whispers to our mute artist thoughts that he then accuses Tintoretto of having disguised, or words that he then suspects the painter of having uttered in order to cheat his clients—is, however, an astonishing extension of Plato's reflection on the artisan and the sophist.[38] The Little Dyer is the Platonic archetype of the artisan: not the artisan put in his place by the royal guardian; not the unskilled worker kept in her place by the snows of fatigue; but the worrisome bastard who can do anything, driven by the force of tool-wielding folk that one never knows exactly how to label: routine labor or passion for profit, power of production or that of falsification. And so our painter-artisan, at the request of his clients, executes Veroneses and Pordenones better than nature, just as Hippias the Sophist indiscriminately fashioned shoes, rings, and discourses.

It is the myth of the artisan as the matrix figure of capitalism. For Sartre, the Little Dyer is the first to have remarked the absence of God in the new perspective space. In the same breath Sartre has him inventing in his shop the Weberian ethics of capitalism, taking note of God's retreat, and rationalizing the family unity of pictorial industry in order to seek new signs of divine blessing in social success. This anti-hero of nascent capitalism is also its Sancho Panza, the intellectual and aristocratic Michelangelo here playing the role of Don Quixote.

So a hero or anti-hero of manual labor. Tintoretto was the first to recognize the lie of Alberti's theatrical cube, that ersatz of Platonic heaven, that ridiculous perspective enslaved to the staging of political hierarchies. And he pricks that lie because he knows himself what he is—a worker, a small proprietor, a manual laborer surrounded by manual laborers, for whom flights to the seraphic heaven of contemplation can be counted as so many hours of work: "The painter is an entrepreneur surrounded by workers, who executes with his crew physically exhausting works.

He is on ladders more often than he is at his easel. He bends over in two, stands on one leg, lies on his back to reach the ceiling. He moves his brush on surfaces that amount to square miles at the end of a month. In other words, he sweats, does contortions, comes home bathed in perspiration and falls asleep only to wake up with aching bones the next morning. He doesn't get by three months without pulling a muscle, or a year without nearly breaking his neck."[39]

A perfect picture of proletarian life. Even on-the-job accidents are included. On his canvas Tintoretto will project these experiences with space, this weight of fatigue, these risks with the scaffolding. He will have his thaumaturgic saints fall from heaven like aerolites, swing their bodies to the front of the picture, or turn into a mountain the steps that the young Virgin Mary must climb to be presented at the temple. This perspectival space, unbalanced by the weight of gravity and devoured by the savage force that "simultaneously gnaws away at the work and the worker," is something that our supreme worker will turn into a supreme challenge to his client, who will be obliged to feel the weight of these tumbling bodies on his own shoulders and to offer not only his gaze but his whole body—in short, to work himself in order to regain the balance.

THE KING WITHOUT A SHADOW

Good hard work, then. To be sure, though, nothing but work: the practice and philosophy of scaffolding common to the Little Dyer and the worker-philosopher Pierre Proudhon. What for Marx was bricolage is, for Sartre, cheating. It is a way of filling in with tricks of imitation to smooth over the new disturbances introduced by the new world of production—of artistically plugging the holes through which nothingness comes into being. Citizen of a Queen of the Seas in decline, Tintoretto had, or is said to have had, a vision of the world deserted by divinity, of Being eaten away by Nothingness. Acrobat and painter, he sensed, or is said to have sensed, the perpetual resistance of three-dimensional space to being brought down to the "knife-blade" that is the painter's canvas.

Unhealthy visions. But we know, ever since Plato, that artisans are healthy men with no time for nausea. The Little Dyer has "the horrifying moral wholesomeness of the ambitious."[40] He cannot treat himself to the luxury of nothingness. He has to earn his living, keep the family workshop going, satisfy his client. Our painter-artisan also loves his trade, and he is only too skillful at it. The vertigo of the Infinite that inhabits the representation of the third dimension could have stopped his hand. Instead it will stimulate him as a technical challenge to be met, an artisanal masterpiece to be realized. So he will indulge in optical trickery. He will push some bodies forward, pull some others back. He will make some tumble on the one side, straighten some out on the other. He will not show the third dimension; he will hide its absence. Through artifice he will stop the flight of this perspective as enchanted as Spanish gold. He will hold in balance the world that seesaws under his brush: "He lacks the courage and the words to translate into Italian the opinion of his palette and his brush."[41]

What else could he do in those days, after all? It would take four centuries—four centuries in the development of capitalist "ethics" and bourgeois society—for the representational presuppositions of painting to be called into question, for the vibrations of matter to replace on canvas the parlor games of resemblance. The artisan-king can reverse the servile perspective of gradations rising toward the royal gaze, or of cloud-elevators gently lifting the soul towards the heights. He can affect God and the saints with gravity, or hold them suspended on the edge of the abyss, but he cannot incarnate the pure presence of the world in their place: "Courage will come later."

But as we also know very well, such courage—the confrontation with non-being—will never be the Dyer's virtue. He plays tricks with the "impossibility of the impossible." He shuts up the vertigo of the Infinite in the social-climbing frenzy of production. An anarcho-syndicalist in his own way, he transforms his workshop into Idea and projects the scaffoldings of his trade into the heaven of his canvases. At that price he succeeds in his attempt the way artisan-workers do: with technical ruses and an artisan prudence that short-circuit the free unveiling of the world's matter. The artisan-king makes a universe in his own image, an amphibian world in which are lost at once the sharp edge of pure negation and the vertigo of pure presence. In it sumptuous disenchantment is corrupted by technological prestidigitation, production by imitation, and the justice of the profane world by the over-healthiness of the worker's social-climbing.

For the philosopher it is a world at once fascinating and intolerable. The dreadful hardiness of the Little Dyer—like that of Good Soldier Schweik in Brecht's meditation[42]—dismisses persistent mystifications of intellectual Platonism and rejects in advance lies about the death of dialectical universality. But it proposes to us a universe in which the edge of justice is blunted. One need only see the two canvases at the analysis of which Sartre's manuscript symbolically breaks off: Tintoretto's excessively calm *Massacre of the Innocents*, and his *Last Judgment* without heavenly bliss or hellish tortures. A scandal for religious tradition, but also, perhaps, for the philosopher of negation. In the *Massacre of the Innocents* the flesh and blood of the little boys and the sadism of the soldiers are absent, replaced by women in panic—a panic without revolt, a seriality without royal alterity that might introduce it to its impossible. A July 14th without the storming of the Bastille. King Herod casts no shadow where the project of the massacre might be reversed and turned into a project of Humanity. And in Tintoretto's *Last Judgment* the elect, for all their bliss, have only vertigo at the edge of the abyss at the bottom of which circulate without suffering the mob of amphibians: "The indefinite perpetuation of a crawling swarm. Toads and toad nest. . . . Ankylosis of the individual by the mass."[43]

THE EXPLOSION ON CANVAS

That is what Sartre rejects: the ankylosized universe of too hardy and skillful artisans. Even at the price of burying the amphibians under the eternal snows of factory fatigue. Even at the price of obliging them to play out their improbable liberation on the grand wheel of History and within dialectical universality's dream of death. Even at the price of refusing himself the honest *prudence* of intellectuals born of the common people: the departures and returns of poor white Algerian Camus or of peasant-philosopher Parain between the convention of words and the weight of things.[44] According to Sartre, assuming this risk is also the only way to preserve the chance of another universality, one formed in the authentic encounter of persons and things. An aesthetic universality in the Kantian style, unfolding before mirages of representation and prestidigitations of reified dialectic.

For Sartre, the aesthetic utopia of the Kantian *sensus communis*, which anticipates the promises of equality of the reign of ends, presupposes people who move beyond technology's fleeting successes, the closed socialities of "reciprocity," and the specular recognitions of resemblance. It calls for the abandonment of the to and fro [chassé-croisé] of resemblance, such as when the philosopher Diderot dreamed of a painting that would capture the gesture of the artisan and criticized his cutler father's vanity for letting himself be painted in his bourgeois Sunday Best. Worker, philosopher, and artist will be united there only by a completely new work [travail] of the hand, eye, and body in movement—there, where the painter will no longer be a prestidigitator but a medium, a transcriber of the becoming-world [du devenir-monde] of matter; there, where the work [l'oeuvre] will address a worker and a philosopher who will no longer be technicians but virtually, already, subjects of the group.

Over against the Massacre of the Innocents rigged up by the artisan, Sartre will set Les Foules [The Crowds] by the "painter without privileges" Lapoujade. In the "abstract" canvases devoted to the anticolonialist demonstrations of 17 October 1961, "Lapoujade gives the crowds a matter in motion but unified in the midst of its dispersion. The unification of disintegrated particles realizes a beyond: the explosive unity of the masses."[45] The movement of the brush on the canvas in fusion is thus exactly equal to the movement of the masses who become a group in the street. To the presence rigged up by the prestidigitators of resemblance, Sartre opposes Lapoujade's "true, indecomposable presence," a unity "of the labor of the painter and of the labor of those who recognize themselves in it." A man of the crowds, united with those he "paints" by common practice, the painter evokes in his demiurgic labor a presence that is "recognizable" as the material explosion of the group in fusion. The trajectory of meaning is doubly required in the conjunction between "the shudders of matter in the process of organizing itself" and the "urgencies common to the one who makes the canvas and those who look at it."[46]

An exemplary conjunction, indeed too exemplary. The workers of the demonstration (who are no longer workers) will be able to recognize themselves on the canvas of the painter (who is no longer an "artist") only at the price of not recognizing themselves in it. It is only on those holidays when they repeat their great Founding Day that they can coincide with the new "subject" of liberated painting: the free organization of matter purified of metaphors of identification and delivered to the Dionysian freedom of swellings, erections, cave-ins, flowings, and swirlings that hollow out "the very stuff of being."[47] It is only this street theater that permits them sometimes to be at the "crossroads of uncertainties" where the "enjambments, inert gushings, transparent opacities, metamorphoses" manifest a freedom that identifies itself with the autonomous productivity of matter.

But this conjunction exists only for the painter. He alone is at all the crossroads of meaning. He alone realizes the totality of this *explosion* won over the political circuit of representation. He was at the crossroads of the workers' manifestation. Will they be at the crossroads of his? For this pictorial revolution that has made the painter capable of translating "the explosive unity of the masses" is a revolution that has made painting into a "language" no longer understood by the masses.

A WORLD WITHOUT WORKERS?

Behind the contradiction there is clearly a more crucial slippage. The conjunction of crowds and "their" painter recalled, under a new form, the Kantian theme of aesthetic reconciliation, of the idea of the Beautiful as a promise of equality. That same idea inspired Sartre in *What Is Literature?* But in pursuing the misadventures of the dialectic, the Sartrean idea of the Beautiful seems to have slipped from the first to the second part of Kant's *Critique of Judgment*—from the "democratic" valorization of aesthetic *sensus communis* to a fascination with the kind of self-organization in which matter tends to be identified with its own idea. Calder's exemplary mobiles, which are "not quite mechanical, and not quite alive," already evoked "that great vague Nature squandering pollen and brusquely producing the flight of countless butterflies without our ever knowing whether it is the blind linking of causes and effects or the timid, continually retarded, upset, thwarted development of an Idea."[48]

Another figure of *as if* just as distant from dialectical snares and artisan tricks. Worker finality is here annulled and identified with the dream of matter that would be disordered by the noises of technology and confused by games of *doxa*. "To be matter": the last temptation of Flaubert's Saint Anthony. If Sartre lays stress on the "rock slides," "swellings," or "hissing of vipers" through which matter explodes on the liberated canvas, is it not to put the greatest possible distance between himself and the dream of *rentier* Flaubert: the immobile work, a sea without shores, a desert without limits that, like nature, means nothing and only induces dreaming?

The Spinozist dream of a universe that can imitate finality only on the condition of not having any and of imitating nothing. Is this a bourgeois dream of death that the philosopher friend of the people would have to put as far away as possible so as not to have to accuse himself of something like a secret quietism doubling for his passion for justice? Or the dream of a world without workers through the inherent significance and self-organization of matter? A world as calm as the sea, empty as the oriental desert in the mind of the hateful bourgeois writer of Croisset?[49] Stocked with the machines, circuits, explosions, swirlings, and swellings of disturbed tranquility in the minds of the philosopher-friends of equality?

A double truth, rather, where the philosophical passion for Justice is torn apart against the backdrop of the Marxist horizon. It finds itself trapped between the initial rejection of positive necessities and the disgust, felt sooner or later, for the fraudulence of ends; between the sharpness of the cut of an unjust world and the ambiguous sense of games of *technē* and *doxa*; between fascination for the machines of all productions and perplexity before the artisan's disturbing hardiness.

From which derives the singular vibration of these philosophical machines that sometimes march to the rhythm of worker hope and sometimes slide toward the dream of matter working by itself before the prestidigitations of technique can begin—before, that is, the objective deceptions of the Marxist horizon. Perhaps it begins with the much disparaged idea of Engels's dialectic of nature, a precaution taken against the intelligibility of "practice" alone. But beyond the marvels of the historical dialectic, doesn't Sartre return to the starting point? The Spinozist denunciation of representation, the fascination with the free movement of a matter that subjects of history would not have to modify with their parlor games: perhaps this is the necessary philosophical double of the Marxism horizon.

9 :: The Sociologist King

IT IS POSSIBLE to conclude more simply, of course: the philosopher's contorted relations with the men of iron reflect his inability to think his own place, the necessary forgetting of the myth that wagered his destiny's gold on the rule imposed upon shoemakers to do nothing else than make shoes. Philosophy is too concerned with its "own business" ever to rethink the extent of the arbitrariness linking the distinctions of the order of discourse to the hierarchy of the "businesses" assigned to each class. The technological passion that seized the philosopher in the modern age is the most elegant and devious attempt to circumvent this founding myth, this *lie imitating the truth* with which, however, it constantly plays "hunt the thimble [*cache-tampon*]." Is it not, indeed, his own portrait that the philosopher of freedom sketches when he writes that "the whole man as defined by the aristocracy is the sum of opportunities taken away from everyone; it is he who knows what others do not know, who appreciates what they cannot appreciate, who does what they cannot do"—is he not, in short, the other side of the "nothing else" that puts the men of iron in their place?[1]

THE MUSICIAN, THE CHIEF, AND THE DYER

Such is the question that the sociologist lodges in the words of the philosopher. When indeed one reads the analyses of reproduction and distinction that Pierre Bourdieu develops—against philosophy—one is struck by the original commonality of the problematic. The logic of these analyses, their persistent ironic reference to the Platonic myth of the "free choice" of souls, makes it an interminable refutation of Sartrean freedom. Bourdieu's *Distinction*, however, could easily be summarized by these words of Sartre: "Wherever an élite functions, an aristocracy of the aristocracy outlining for aristocrats the shape of the whole man, new values and works of art, far from enriching the oppressed man, increase his absolute impoverishment. The productions of the élite are, for the majority of people, rejection, want and boundaries. The taste of our 'art lovers' forcibly defines the bad taste or lack of taste of the working classes, and as soon as refined minds consecrate a work, there is one more 'treasure' in the world which the worker will never possess, one more thing of beauty that he is unable to appreciate or understand."[2]

So where is the difference? The context will help us understand. Sartre is pondering the rejection of dodecaphonic music in the Soviet Union and interprets it through the contradiction inherent to modern art, which freed itself from its "bourgeois" servitude only at the price of cutting itself off radically from popular taste. The official Soviet attitude can then be understood as refusing aesthetic pleasures that would be reserved, by their very nature, for the bureaucratic élite and would cut them off still further from the masses.

An explanation in terms of strategy. But Sartre is forgetting precisely what every philosopher should have learned from Plato, that the art of the strategist does not fall within the purview of the science of ends but within that of *right opinion*—this instinctive, unreflective knowledge of encountered situations and adequate responses. When he is censoring Schönberg in the name of Tchaikovsky, Stalin is not furthering any program to combat élitism. He simply privileges his own taste as a parvenu peasant, governing with an aristocracy of petty bourgeois a "workers' state" massively populated with peasants. The norm he is imposing on the revolution is that of his ethos, which was produced by the conditions that produced this revolution: a musical taste susceptible of working for the revolution for the same reasons that the revolution worked for Joseph Stalin. The general's strategy is the dye of the dyer.

The philosopher has thus forgotten this lesson from another master of his art, Leibniz: "We are automatons in three-quarters of what we do."[3] In bourgeois distinction or "proletarian" academicism, he can see only strategies consciously ordered according to their class purposes. A way of preserving his own freedom, of not having to ponder whether it is not simply *his* right opinion, his *orthodoxy*: the craftsman's dye holding him in his place like a common dyer.

THE SCIENCE OF RIGHT OPINION

Such is the lesson that the sociologist wants to administer to the philosopher: he does not know the reason of what he says. He is unable to think the virtue by which each of them, beginning with himself, does "his own business"—right opinion, this knowledge adapted to its object but unconscious of itself, which in Plato characterizes the gift of the inspired man (Ion the rhapsodist or Pericles the strategist) as well as the successful training of a student of the philosopher. The sociology that Pierre Bourdieu proposes is therefore a challenge to philosophy on its own ground, the scientific exploitation of the Platonic theory of right opinion.

This supposes a democratization of the virtue in question. If, for once in his life, Socrates bothers to adduce the mind of a slave, the main object of the education of the philosopher-king-dyer is the warrior. His important task is to imprint onto the soul of the warrior the right opinion about what is to be feared and not to be feared. For shoemakers, on the other hand, there is no education. To do nothing else than make shoes, they need neither inspiration nor dye. Their virtue is only ranking [classement].

The sociologist, on the contrary, pledges also to think the dye of the shoemakers. All in all, since workers have become soldiers of production and philosophers militants, it is legitimate to generalize the model of military education. The setting of ranks [rangs] has to be thought of as the unity of the guardians' education and the shoemakers' non-education. In place of the doxa, there will be a science of rankings setting individuals in their proper places and reproduced in their judgments. Within this schema, it will be legitimate also to include that form of ranking and elevating [classante et classée] activity that constitutes philosophy.[4]

This scientific project presents a classic figure: the young science wresting from the old metaphysical empire one or another of its provinces in order to make it the domain of a rigorous practice armed with the instruments and methods suitable for transforming the impotent dream of speculation into positive knowledge.

Yet in the case of social science, this "emancipation" is singularly ambiguous. Isn't the territory that it claims to wrest from philosophy also the circle where philosophy imprisoned it, the territory of the poor where philosophy gave sociology the leisure to inform philosophy of the social causes of optical illusions? The work of an auxiliary, a purveyor of useful "empirical materials" guilty only of wanting to exploit them itself: this is, for example, how Sartre in the *Critique of Dialectical Reason* judges sociology's contribution.

And there is above all the dirty trick played by the philosopher

Marx who, in creating his science of historical materialism, took sociology backward. He placed the truth of its phenomena outside itself in this "anatomy" of civil society established by the relations of production and productive forces. Among the truth of productive structure, the simulacra of ideology, and the transformative action of politics, he bequeathed sociology only the leftovers.

Besides, it seems to be sociology's destiny to be outstripped every time. Already by the time of Saint-Simon's death, Auguste Comte let himself be overtaken by Enfantin's and Bazard's militant enthusiasm.[5] And his science then became outflanked by the Marxian operation that sought to locate in the relations of production the truth of the beings of *doxa*. This would be a way of assigning it as an "object" the only parlor game through which this truth lets itself be misrecognized, and a way of assigning it as a task the production of a *doxa* about *doxa*. From whence, perhaps, the curious evolution which soon transformed the young, optimistic militant science of the new social bond into the disabused knowledge of the great inertia of collective thinking. Caught between the pincers of economy and philosophy, sociology responded by hollowing out the space of *doxa* to reverse the game—to reinscribe the particularity of historical materialism into the generality of the disenchantment of the bourgeois world; to make the economy of production a particular case of the economy of symbolic practices.

THE SCISSORS AND THE KETTLE

A difficult game since the dice truly seem to be loaded. The sociologist's weapons are those of his adversary. To construct his science, he has two essential instruments: statistical tables and opinion polls. But from the start he immediately can see the truth of his object slipping away. Before him, for example, the statistician demonstrated that school eliminated the majority of the workers' children and promoted the majority of the sons of the bourgeoisie. Before him, too, the economist provided figures confirming that each class consumes whatever its revenue allows it to. One might argue that these figures need still to be interpreted. But they possess, precisely, the formidable property of already putting forward their explanation themselves. When we read consumption statistics, for example, "the theory which makes consumption a simple function of income has all the appearances to support it."[6]

We know what this "appearance" is: the great law of the social machine, the law of exploitation and domination which, in advance, renders detailed explanations futile and virtually assigns to sociology the single task of putting off to the last instance of the relations of production the *doxa* effects that they mint as their small change. The justice of statistics continuously dissolves the sociological object, producing in short its own *doxa*—*demystification*, which returns pure ideas to the impure inertia of domination. Wherever it goes, sociology finds itself preceded by its shadow or its simulacrum: the approximation of its conclusions, which are supported by the statistics of its domain. For example, if school eliminates proletarians, it is because it is a grade school [*une école de classe*] functioning in the service of bourgeois domination.

This is a production of evidence that sociology finds difficult to combat with its other weapon, the opinion poll—a game that *doxa* plays with itself. How could it grasp the truth of right opinion? This is the lesson of those simulated surveys with which Plato, twenty-four centuries ago, exhausted the genre: *right opinion always misses itself* [*répond toujours à coté d'elle-même*]. It is the art of responding to situations, not questions. To the survey taker, it will reflect only *clichés*. What, then, if the constraints of his science oblige the survey taker himself to propose these clichés to his interlocutor: a prefabricated *doxa* awaiting its subject without surprise—whether intellectual ("All music of quality interests me") or popular ("Classical music isn't for people like us")—and closing off to the latter any other choice than "his own" through the trick-response that drops into "allodoxia" his vague anomie ("I like classical music, Strauss waltzes for example")?[7]

Of course, these types of answer are not the result of the sociologist's arbitrariness. If he retained them, it is because they roam the streets. But what is a guarantee for opinion is also a curse for science. Roaming the streets with opinions on a leash when they roam there already on their own, the sociologist always falls behind his own caricature, trapped in the circle of these verisimilitudes that impose themselves only as they distance themselves from the truth they resemble in every detail except the critical one: truth, by definition, does not roam the streets.

In this circle, the sociologist would like to see only the insincerity of an opponent who employs kettle logic. How can he be reproached for "saying things that are simultaneously banal and untrue"?[8] But he must not be fooled by this rhetorical argument. With his philosopher colleagues he learned Bachelard's lesson that the rotation of the sun around the earth was, before Copernicus, as false as it was banal. And it continues to be as banal as it is false. It is the ABC of epistemology: the scientist must think "against evidence" because "there is no science but the science of the hidden." Here lies the problem, for where are we to find the hidden in this scissoring of statistics and opinion, this immense chattering of demystification where truth cannot be distinguished from its imitation? "The particular difficulty of sociology comes from the fact that it teaches things that everybody knows in a way, but which they don't want to know or cannot know because the law of the system is to hide those things from them."[9]

Because . . . The conjunction wakes us up with a start; without our noticing it, something has happened. This sentence which started out as the statement of a problem has, along the way, become its solution. We thought that the difficulty of science came from the fact that *everybody* more or less knew the secret that it was to reveal, and now a slight displacement of the impersonal shows it to us as threatened because *they* do not want to know it. We were wondering what the *this* was which was hidden, and an imperceptible slippage of the demonstrative pronoun explains to us now why the *that* is hidden—because the law of the system hides things from us. But what, then, is hidden within this secret that everybody knows? The answer is blindingly obvious: *its dissimulation*. The truth everybody knows is a truth that hides the fact that it is concealed. The evidence roams the streets to dissimulate its own secret.

It must not be thought that the sociologist goes around in circles; on the contrary, he has done the only thing he could do. Condemned to remain within the apparent movement of *doxa*, prevented from returning it to a real movement that would no longer be a part of his domain, *he divided the apparent movement into two.* He hollowed out a dimension of paradox in the platitude of the *doxa*: it is because everybody knows that nobody can know. If the social machine captures us, it is because we do not know how it captures us. And if we do not know how it captures us even though it is right before our eyes, it is because we do not want to know it. All recognition is a misrecognition, all unveiling a veiling. If the educational machine eliminates proletarian students, it is because we do not know how it eliminates them—because it dissimulates the way that it eliminates them in dissimulating the way that it dissimulates.

Such is the logic propelling the works of Pierre Bourdieu and Jean-Claude Passeron on the educational apparatus, *The Inheritors* and *Reproduction*. At the beginning of their analysis they note the brutality of the statistics and their effect on opinion: the chances of entering higher education are 0.89 percent for the son of a farm worker, and 58.9 percent for the son of a senior executive. From this point on, two explanations oppose one another. The traditional republican explanation, taken up by the worker parties, is simple. It is not school itself that excludes the children of the common people. It is their parents who do not have the means to let them keep up with it or faith in its effects of promotion. School eliminates only those who do not attend. It need only give everyone the means to go to school and the conviction of its usefulness.

Conversely, libertarian pedagogism incriminates the educational structure itself. School crushes the children of the common people because its authoritarian structure reproduces the hierarchical structure of society in forming the disciplinary spirit of its future officers and their troops. At the time when Bourdieu and Passeron are writing *The Inheritors*, this is the position of the Young Turks of the Student Union. To the lectures attended by a passive mass of solitary students, they want to oppose the revolutionary virtue of work groups in which students educate themselves. No one will be surprised by this: these Young Turks who oppose the economism of the Communist Party and critique the authoritarianism of the professors—including professors of sociology—are often students of philosophy.

Always the same pincers of economy and ideology. But the sociologist has taken its measure. In the gap between the two branches, he comes to assert its hidden truth: it is school that really eliminates proletarians. But it does not do this through its elimination procedures. It does not act through what it does, but through what it does not do, or does beside itself. Through *what it makes people believe*. School eliminates by *making people believe that it does not eliminate*, by obliging those for whom school has not been created to eliminate themselves spontaneously—to judge by themselves that they are not *gifted* since they are unable to profit from the course of studies offered them. It is the idea of *gift*—and of its absence—that produces self-eliminating behavior. In Platonic terms, the paradox of right opinion shall be expressed as follows: *it is the illusion of inspiration that produces the dye of the shoemakers* in producing the dye of the general and the philosopher.

School therefore eliminates by dissimulating that it eliminates. Which of course implies another trick. In order to perfect the system, it must eliminate in order to dissimulate the fact that it eliminates while pretending not to eliminate. Such is the function of the examination in this logic. It eliminates fundamentally those who do not take it, those who stop a few years before they reach it. It is the myth that allows those who do not go as far as applying its norm to themselves to recognize the destiny they deserve in the destiny of those it eliminates. But this is still not all: this function of incitement to elimination by way of its simulacrum presupposes that the examination dissimulates, in its simulation, the continuing elimination that dissimulates itself in this school that pretends not to eliminate: "Only when the examination is seen to have the function of concealing the elimination which takes place without examination, can it be fully understood why so many features of its operation as an overt selecting procedure still obey the logic governing the elimination which it conceals. . . . Class bias is strongest in those tests which throw the examiner onto the implicit, diffuse criteria of the traditional art of grading, such as the dissertation or the oral, an occasion for passing total judgments, armed with the unconscious criteria of social perception on total persons, whose moral and intellectual qualities are grasped through the infinitesimals of style or manners, accent or elocution, posture or mimicry, even clothing and cosmetics."[10]

Images from a jury of the École Nationale d'Administration [ENA], howlers from *agrégation* reports . . . A strange colored prism through which the sociologists of reproduction observe the educational apparatus, as if it all were prescribed by the *telos* of these initiating ceremonies or ritual discourses. A series of slippages comes into play whereby the end explains the beginning: the nostalgic comments of the writer of the *agrégation* report become the reality of its practice, which then is followed by the daily experience of the *baccalauréat* examiner, the supposedly inspired atmosphere of *lycée* literature classes, and finally the feeling of shame driving the proletarian child to exclude himself as unworthy of the enchanted universe of *charisma*.

This, then, is how the case could be summarized: school makes the children of the common people believe that it welcomes them and their others with equal opportunities, that success and failure depend on personal *gifts* independent of social conditions. This dissimulation is simulated in the games of cultural charisma in which the teacher pretends to exercise his students in an aesthetic vision transcending the routine of school exercise. He thus obliges them to expatiate on "the *je ne sais quoi* and litotes of classical passion or the infinite, infinitesimal nuances of good taste."[11] In doing so, of course, he attributes the charisma of gifts to those for whom culture has an existence beyond the walls of the school: those who own it by birthright and who are able to bring to the perception of the *je ne sais quoi* the ease that characterizes their manners or their clothing.

Which was to be demonstrated. And which does not let itself be refuted. The major and minor premises of the argument still perplex us, however. Did the great mystifications of equal opportunity and the inequality of gifts ever really exist anywhere else than in the cutting words of the demystifiers? The founders of the public school never designed it for social equality, only for political equality. Its powers of social redistribution were never conceived in any other way than the one in which they were exercised: *marginally*. In the manner, that is, of the Platonic selector promoting the more gifted children of the common people and demoting the more obtuse children of the elite. And, in practice, the ideology of "gifts" has served less to distinguish those who were chosen from birth than to recognize the children of the common people who could compete with them. It is the arbitrariness of the concept of *charisma* that makes the teacher's judgment informed by his own experience comparable to the exquisite charm of Racinian litotes. In the same way the French literature class is compared to the self-consciousness of an *ENA* jury, the native universe of bourgeois inheritors to a hothouse of celebrated witticisms and cultured allusions, and the reasonable forecasts of students concerning topics to expect from their lazy examiners to the fetishism of church candles imploring divine protection.

But the sociologist is armed against these commonsense objections. It will be objected in vain against him that ordinary educational practice or bourgeois conversation is scarcely made of Racinian litotes and that according to his own statistics, the knowledge of these litotes is what least separates bourgeois students from those of popular origin. This would be forgetting indeed that the system operates by doing—that is, both by making believe and doing—the opposite of what it seems to do. It is very true that ordinary pedagogic practice is modestly charismatic. But charisma, precisely, is never better produced than through its absence: "The most routine teacher, who, contrary to his intentions, provokes his students to espouse an 'anti-culture' that they see as more vital and authentic, is still, despite himself, fulfilling his objective function—persuading the neophytes to worship culture and not the university, whose rôle is merely to organize the cult of culture."[12]

The Denouncer Denounced

Such is the paradox closing in around the apprentice philosophers who contested the overly pedantic methods of the sociologist, and who opposed the free work of the student collective to professorial authority. It is precisely by "denouncing" the institution that they express its truth despite themselves. In denouncing the authoritarianism of the pedagogues, they claim in dissimulating it the real law of the institution of which they are the quintessential representatives: the law of *laissez-faire* for which the inheritor's incorporated knowledges are uniquely profitable. They refuse the constraints of a rational pedagogy that coins in the form of democratic learning the "total and infrangible gifts of the charisma ideology."[13]

Young Clinias has therefore learned at his own expense what it meant "to not want to know" what everyone knew. His denunciation was the system's incarnate misrecognition. And, conversely, the knowledge [*connaissance*] of the system is identified with the knowledge of its misrecognition [*méconnaissance*]. Concretely, the micro-sociology of the philosophy students provides the reason for the exclusion shown by statistics, for these reveal to us massive social inequality in the process of selection. The latter points us to *leisure*, the aristocratic virtue of those selected: if students—and more particularly philosophy students—insist on their inability to organize their use of time [*emploi du temps*], is this not telling us that they have the time to do without the time they have [*qu'ils ont le temps qui permet de se passer d'emploi*]?[14] We can then conclude directly that school makes its selection through the virtue accorded the aristocratic values of dilettantism. In the freedom claimed by these aristocratic denouncers can be read the common essence of school exercise and bourgeois nature, the virtue (both apparent and hidden) of the gift and inspiration: leisure, this *scholē* which gives school its name and its *raison d'être*— the reproduction, through misrecognized imitation, of the freedom of the dominant: "The school, a place of *scholē*, leisure . . . is the place *par excellence* of what are called gratuitous exercises, where one acquires a distant, neutralizing disposition toward the social world, the very same one implied in the bourgeois relationship to art, language and the body."[15]

It is useless to oppose to this improbable phenomenology the experience of the schoolchild to whom classes and bells, lessons and homework, rewards and punishments do not precisely call to mind free and disinterested exercise. Sociological description is first and foremost a mythical tale. This is why the sociologist, while talking to *lycée* teachers, can present them with the representation of his auditorium as the essence of their class.[16] The description of this unobtainable school is the tale imitating the essence of School. A myth of leisure that recalls the Platonic argument concerning the absence of time. The binding of each worker to his place dissimulated itself in the absence of time and hid itself in the final myth of *The Republic*, the myth of the free choice of souls. Behind the illusion of free choice must be shown the law of Leisure. School time must be restored to this empty time which is necessary simply so that Leisure can recognize its children and be recognized by those who do not possess it. From which proceeds, according to this logic, the very natural explanation for the extension of compulsory education: keeping the children in school who eliminated themselves from it is the best way of eliminating them through the dissimulation of their elimination.

Thus the scientific explanation is rather the myth of science. An anti-Platonic myth of the separation of souls. But in what, really, does its anti-Platonism consist? For one cannot see what possibility of doing *something else* than their "own business" was won there by the artisans. The denunciation of the *scholē* also denounces the parvenu who arrogates to himself the leisure to study that he *does not have*. A particular case falling under the rubric of accidental causes: if he thinks he can study, it is because he belongs to a social circle in which people already have done so; if he deludes himself about his "gifts," it is because of his "exceptional abilities."[17] Behind the tautology emerges the verdict that one escapes the impossibility of the principle only through the betrayal of its principles. The "parvenu" of education appears doubly as a traitor to his class: individually, in forcing himself to acquire the "dispositions" that allow the privileged classes to assimilate legitimate culture; and collectively, in masking with his own success the global effect of elimination.

To this individual betrayal seems at first to be opposed the collective chance of a "rational pedagogy" transforming the implicit knowledge of inherited culture into elements of an egalitarian apprenticeship. But the question immediately bounces back: isn't the rationalization of the apprenticeship of legitimate culture a reinforcement of the arbitrariness of legitimacy in general? Even so, a privilege distributed to everyone is a contradiction in terms. Rational pedagogy can function, like all pedagogy, only marginally in optimizing the chances for success of the better situated members of the dominated class—"the controlled mobility of a limited number of individuals" serving "to perpetuate the structure of class relations."[18] From *The Inheritors* to *Reproduction*, this has become as illusory a utopia as libertarian pedagogy.

EPIMENIDES THE CRETAN AND
PARMENIDES THE MARXIST

The sociologist, therefore, can always show his solidarity with the laboring classes by denouncing the law of *laissez-faire* perpetuating the system. But he cannot find anything to oppose the infinite logic through which the pelican hatches from the egg laid by Jonathan's pelican.[19] Or rather, he must not oppose anything to it. For rational pedagogy certainly would entail the regrettable inconvenience of ruining the solidarity of the working class. Above all, however, it would entail the repudiation of sociology as a science.

For as we know, there is no science but the science of the hidden. But the only hidden that can return as such to sociology is *misrecognition*. Yet this remains to be understood. The term "misrecognition" presupposes generally an object hidden behind the veil of the misrecognition: in this case, the force of the relations of production, which escapes the legislation of sociology. To remain master of its field, the sociology of reproduction will assert as a principle of the pedagogic apparatus a misrecognition that should not be the misrecognition of a hidden content but merely of itself.

The first axiom of *Reproduction* thus explains the necessary requisite of sociology, the efficacity of a symbolic violence added to the simple violence of the relations of power. But the science of this "added" is a menaced auxiliary. If rational pedagogy could tell the truth about pedagogic authority, the "hidden" of science would vanish. This violence therefore must be even more irremediable than that of domination; it must be the irreducibility of the law that leaves the agents producing it or subjected to it no means to recognize it.

Everything can be summed up in one concept: *the arbitrary.* Pedagogic action in general (prior to any school system) is arbitrary *in a double sense,* not only because it reproduces a determined cultural arbitrariness, the culture of a class whose power it thus confirms, but also because its simple existence introduces into the field of possibilities a division that never bears its necessity within itself.

From this point on, everything has been said. The arbitrary, in the first sense, could always be recalled to its necessity. But in the second sense, it is irreducible. For pedagogic action can speak only in the mode of legitimate enunciation. The arbitrary cannot proclaim itself as arbitrary in the act that produces it, unless it cuts itself off from the right to be heard. This is the meaning of Epimenides' paradox. If the Cretan Epimenides says that all Cretans are liars, nothing can be concluded from this. The arbitrary thus must proclaim itself as necessary. All pedagogic action is carried out by the power of a pedagogic authority that asserts itself and asserts this act as legitimate. Pedagogic authority is arbitrariness *necessarily misrecognized* and, for this reason, *objectively recognized as legitimate* authority.[20]

The arbitrary is then out of reach. It is no longer only the demonstrable efficacy of domination but the non-necessity of the necessity the pedagogue will never have pronounced. The contradiction has been raised to Parmenidian heights. One can never force non-being to be. Never can the arbitrary be necessary. And the language of the necessary can never proclaim the arbitrary. Pedagogic action justifies pedagogic authority which legitimates it in turn—an unvicious circle authorizing pedagogic work without failure: "Pedagogic work produces the legitimacy of the product and, inseparably from this, legitimate need in producing the legitimate consumer."[21] The reproduction of the legitimate word [*parole*] cannot disturb itself nor be disturbed by some prophetic word: "The religious or political prophet always preaches to the converted."²² In prosaic terms, Jesus or Mohammed is produced by "social demand." Hence the identity between the great law of the symbolic and marketable banality, which ensures that the habitus is perpetually produced and reproduced so that everyone does "his own business": stitch shoes or mount the Cross.

His own business is, first of all, the business of the sociologist. For the social machine thus regulated is ever only the developed form of the axiom allowing sociology to exist as a science, ensuring that its object will never teach itself.

His critique of Platonism then takes a most singular form. In a sense, *The Inheritors* and *Reproduction* are Plato's *Republic* explained the first time with images, the second with axioms. But in this *Republic*, the authors have made a highly determined choice in starting with the end—the myth of Er, the myth of the free choice of souls that closes the last book. They have left to the side, however, what should have interested them in the first place, the "pedagogic" myth of the three metals.

The reason for that can easily be understood. The myth of the three metals presents an inadmissible singularity for the sociologist in pretending *to tell the truth about the lie*. One might say that it takes very exactly the place of the axiom *the place of the sociologist*. The latter therefore chooses to attack philosophy not at its beginning (the declaration of arbitrariness) but at its end (the myth of the free choice of the souls). The latter is the "good" myth, the myth that does not tell us it is lying. One can then make it the allegory of symbolic power; one can make of its denunciation the science that criticizes the philosophical illusion—always reproduced, always to be unmasked—of freedom of choice. The sociologist is thus a winner every time. But he is also strictly subjected, in the conclusion of his scientific work, to the philosophical interdiction. He will reach *the same result* going the opposite way. Instead of moving from the third to the sixth book of the *Republic*, he will go from the tenth to the sixth. Instead of starting with the myth of the three metals to end up with the condemnation of the autodidact, he will begin with the myth of Er to reach the same conclusion. At the meeting point, this alone will have changed: the philosopher-king will have become the sociologist-king.

"To the great despair of the philosopher-king" who assigned to the lowly ranked [*aux mal-classés*] the essence that condemned them to their place, the sociologist has taken the side of these "lowly ranked" who reject "the principle of ranking [*de classement*] which gives them the worst place."²³ Only this "taking sides" consists in explaining backward *the same thing* as the philosopher. But this reversed order is not indifferent. The philosopher started from the arbitrary in order to reach necessity. The sociologist reaches necessity starting from the illusion of freedom. He proclaims that it is the illusion of their freedom that binds artisans to their places. The declared arbitrariness thus becomes a scientific necessity, and the redistribution of cards an absolute illusion. The guilty verdict is then pronounced, more implacable than ever: "The established order, and the distribution of capital which is its basis, contribute to their own perpetuation through their very existence, through the symbolic effect that they exert as soon as they are publicly and officially declared and are thereby misrecognized and recognized."²⁴

"Thereby": the pivot at which Parmenidian necessity communicates with the "at the same time" of dialectical liberation. It is impossible that an order, as long as it still exists, will ever cease to work "through its very existence" towards its own perpetuation. It is impossible, then, not to always recognize (hence misrecognize) and misrecognize (hence recognize) the empire of the arbitrary.

To ensure his kingship, the sociologist for good measure rationalized, absolutized the arbitrary. To philosophy, he opposed a dullness of social domination reinforced by the logical rigor of the principle of non-contradiction. He doubled Marxist necessity with the Parmenidian necessity of its eternity. He combined the old interdiction with the new one. "Let each remain in his place," the old one would say. "Do not forget the class struggle," proclaimed the new. The combination of the two provides the novel image of a Parmenidian Marxism recovered from proletarian terror to become the disenchanted banality of a bourgeois world that cries out, at every street corner, the great secret everyone ignores: class struggle has become an eternal truth possessing the double credit of no longer killing anyone, but also of lending to science the eternal denunciation of its eternal forgetting.

THE PHYSICIAN AND HIS PATIENTS

There remain the lowly ranked. We now know that they can expect nothing from emancipatory pedagogy. As for the prophetic word which, through its *misunderstandings*, sometimes allows them to leave their places, they soon will recognize—misrecognize—in it the legitimacy of the new pretenders to the "monopoly over the power to judge and to rank."[25] For the lowly ranked, sociology can do no more than explain why philosophers misrecognize the true reasons keeping them in their places. A somewhat depressing conclusion. But as we know, the moral of science is austere. Like the philosopher, the sociologist never promised anyone happiness. Or rather, he had to make a choice. There is no sociological science without the sacrifice of this rational pedagogy promised imprudently for the emancipation of the lowly ranked. Who would blame the sociologist for having judged in good faith that in the long term, his science would be more useful to the lowly ranked than his pedagogy? After all, what liberates is not pedagogy but science.

Only this science has such particular properties. Others generally impose the recognition of their *necessity* by promising to put it in the service of some liberation. But this one proposes to us as its object a misrecognition without recourse. What can one do with a science of the school that says pedagogy is impossible? With a science of relations of power that says these are infrangible? Once the positions of the pedagogue and the politician are annihilated, there remains only the position of the psychoanalyst. The sociologist would be, generally, the scientist [*savant*] and physician of self-denial. By not changing the ranking of the lowly ranked, he would give them "the *possibility* of taking on their habitus without guilt or suffering."[26]

The program is not absolutely enthralling. This may reflect the honor of science, but the latter complicates itself with a new paradox, for if the sociologist is a psychoanalyst, he deals only, like his colleague, with rich patients: "The sociologist's misfortune is that most of the time, the people who have the technical means to appropriate what he says have no wish to appropriate it, . . . whereas those who would have an interest in appropriating it do no not have the instruments for appropriation (theoretical culture, etc.)."[27]

The matter is a little more complicated. Whatever the sociologist may say, the desire to appropriate his science is hardly absent from people who have at their disposal the "technical means" to do so. Many art lovers have understood the advantage of being art lovers capable of explaining, at any place and time, in any variety of print and on any wavelength, that the love of art is a privilege of the inheritors. And the critique of élitism has soon become the new justification of hierarchy. The university professor analyzes the élitist methods of the suburban schoolteacher. The professor from the École des Hautes Études demystifies the élitist ideology of the university subaltern, and the national minister of Education courageously undertakes reforms aimed at suppressing the élitism of his subordinates as a whole. Thus is spread in the higher spheres the possibility of assuming the habitus of the others "without guilt or suffering."

One cannot see very well, though, what the lowly ranked could get from this hygiene. What does it mean exactly to appropriate the science of one's dispossession? The love of art is a privilege of the inheritors; what consequence will a non-inheritor draw from the appropriation of this knowledge? Could he claim the right that the inheritors reserve for themselves? But is this not falling into the charismatic ideology that justifies their inheritance? Would he renounce pleasures that in order to be tasted presuppose the habitus of distinguished people? But is this not what necessity already teaches? Could he liberate himself from this "misery" that "often comes from a dispossession that cannot be assumed"?[28] Should he therefore assume this dispossession? This advice is "good" only for the ones suffering from it—for the ones who try to change something in the destiny of those who have "nothing else" to do than assume their destiny. This would mean, in sum, closing another door before them.

This would mean . . . *if* this discourse reached them. Those whom it reaches instead are the "inheritors" in charge of educating them and the politicians in charge of reeducating the educators. In post-Marxist Marxism, the science of the sociologist has become in a way the imaginary of the Sartrean communist party. Besides the fortunate classes it represents those unfortunates who lack the sociability of distinction to represent themselves. The lowly ranked person is the hostage of science—the guardian-machinist who, with his massive silence, blocks the indefinite flight of *doxa*. With his mute support, he offers science the position of legitimate enunciation that isolates it from the games of cultural relativism where it seeks to confine the others.

But it does not take long for this science to be doubled by *doxa*, and it does not take long for this militantism to become ordinary order. Denunciation for the sake of an absent class becomes the daily fare of semi-learned opinion, and the struggle against élitist reproduction the common program for ministers of every trend. With scholarly disenchantment reinforcing the usual lack of cultivation, these politicians obtain, all in all, satisfying results. The children of the élite have left at last the hothouse of Racinian litotes. To know what the children of the common people gained from it is another story.

This is no longer the affair of the sociologist-king. Indeed, he warns us himself against the extension of the pattern of reproduction. The latter is truly appropriate only for institutions whose functioning is homothetic to their conditions of reproduction—a limit case represented by the old university, ordained for the reproduction of university scholars. To conceive more broadly the modes of symbolic violence that lead each to do his "own business," we need to turn away from the great reproductive machine and look at these small machines whose movements, free within the space of their own necessity, espouse and retrace the configuration of the social field. We need to consider the forms of habitus through which social agents enabled the incorporated past to serve the anticipation of possible futures. For the fatalist image of the machine we need to substitute that of the market where free choices contribute to setting the price of products, but also where subjects who delude themselves about their freedom to sell or buy anything at any price are soon acquainted with the limits of this freedom.

Even better, one has to conceive of social practices within the category of the game, where the science of the moves transcends knowledge of the rules. At this price, one can exit the morose science of *misrecognition* to enter the ludic universe of the *illusio* understood in its etymological sense—not as false perception but as interest *at stake*, the very stake of the match: "Produced by experience of the game, and therefore of the objective structures within which it is played out, the 'feel for the game' is what gives the game a subjective sense—a meaning and a *raison d'être*, but also a direction, an orientation, an impending outcome, for those who take part and therefore acknowledge what is at stake (this is *illusio* in the sense of *investment* in the game and the stakes, *interest* in the game, commitment to the presuppositions—*doxa*—of the game)."[29]

Thus is drawn up the space of a sociology that would be at last the *science of practices*, not a dictionary of regulations or collection of locker room opinions. A total science of the game, including, with its rules and moves, the opinions of the players, the ethnological objectivation of the game, and the objectivation of the ethnologist's objectivation procedures. A virtuoso science opening, between the evidences of law and those of opinion, the same breach that the inspired striker opens through the wall of opposing players. But this is also a science made useful again for the lowly ranked. To them, or at least to their defenders, it could teach the non-written rules of the social game, the strategies of domination and the moves that can be played effectively between the wall of the impossible and the lures of utopia.

The game, however, soon becomes restricted for the philosopher and even more so for the lowly ranked. The Kabyle villagers, within the subtle temporality of gifts and counter-gifts, can doubtlessly refute the objectivist reduction of ethnologists who reduce the game to the immediate reciprocity of a rational economic exchange.[30] But they can *cheat* the observer only insofar as they conceal from themselves the truth of their practice. In short, the game is always fundamentally dissimulation.

What the Kabyle villagers dissimulate (from themselves) in the game of symbolic exchanges may be the state of the productive forces, the weak productivity of agricultural labor. But what regulates the apparent global reciprocity of prestations are above all relations of domination. In order not to trace this "truth" of the game to the efficacity of the relations of production behind ideology, one has to think of domination as the intrication of two economies, those of economic and symbolic capital. The "dissimulation" is the *reconversion* of economic into symbolic capital. But obviously, one can reconvert only what one possesses already. One can play only if one has something to put at risk. The more the law of economic capital imposes itself, the more does this truth as well: the symbolic game is reserved for the rich and is merely the *euphemizing* of domination. As for the poor, they do not play. Indeed, their habitus discloses to them only the semblance of a game where the anticipated future is not what is possible but simply the impossible: "a social environment" with "its 'closed doors,' 'dead ends' and 'limited prospects'" where "the 'art of assessing likelihoods'" cannot euphemize the virtue of necessity.[31] Only those who are chosen have the possibility of choosing.

The open space of the game and the market was to have delivered us from the closed logic of reproduction and leisure, to show us social *stakes* and *values* as the products of a struggle, transformable by other struggles, and helped by the sociological explanation of the rule and state of the game. But the opening quickly closes up again. The only point at which the sociologist has grasped a habitus that is neither *free* nor *mechanical* is the "knowledge effect [l'*effet de connaissance*]" that makes it function differentially.[32] But if this knowledge were adequate, it would lead us back either to the freedom of the rational actor—a Sartrean philosopher or neoclassical economist—or to the implacable necessity of the relations of production and domination. This "knowledge effect" is therefore always an effect of misrecognition. But if the latter is simply the madness of the sublunary world or the cunning of reason, the economist—Marxist or neoclassical—triumphs once more: the capitalist is only Capital's puppet or, conversely, the proletarian is a little capitalist, a liberal entrepreneur managing his "human capital."

To escape this dilemma, the sociologist will employ the simplest solution by combining the two economies. As a good host, he will give to each the share that suits: capital to the neoclassicists and labor to the Marxists, but also struggle to the bourgeoisie and preservation to the proletariat. The symbolic universe will be organized on the basis of the world's division [*partage*] into two: those who have capital to place on the symbolic market and those who have only their labor power to reproduce; those whose necessity becomes identified with illusory games of free will; those whose freedom is reduced to internalizing necessity as *amor fati*, love of fate.

THE PIANIST, PEASANTS, AND
THE SOCIOLOGIST

Such is the image presented to us by *Distinction*, a *social* critique of judgment—a refutation, therefore, of Kant's *Critique of Judgment*, its philosophical homonym. Pierre Bourdieu wants to show that the social reality of exercising the judgment of taste is the exact opposite of the Kantian theory, which he sees as the quintessence of philosophical discourse. He thus will apply himself to show that taste is *one* where Kant divides it and, conversely, that it is divided in two where Kant makes it common to all. Kant contrasts the aesthetic pleasure that results from the judgment of the Beautiful with the pleasure of the senses that appreciate Canary Islands wine. Bourdieu will show, on the contrary, that the same taste judges works of art, wines, or table manners. Kant affirms the formal universality of the judgment of taste. Bourdieu's critique will show that taste is always the reverse of distaste, referring in so doing to the opposition between the "taste of freedom" specific to persons of leisure and the "taste of necessity" specific to workers of reproduction. And through the exemplary misrecognition of the archetypal philosopher, Bourdieu will disclose the three-way game that constitutes the social matrix of judgments of taste, the conjunction of two great oppositions. The first opposes the dominant and the dominated, those with or without capital to put at stake in the symbolic market. The second opposes the dominant fractions of the dominant class, characterized by the predominance of economic capital, and its dominated fractions, characterized by the predominance of cultural capital.

The problem with the demonstration starts with the sociologist's first object, which is also the last entrenched position of his enemy: the music-queen of the philosopher-king. For someone who truly wants to know whether different social classes are more or less sensitive to classical music, a method springs naturally to mind, which is that of playing it to their members. Thus sometimes a "bourgeois" artist, in love with the people and anxious to communicate to them the treasures of his art, undertakes the crucial experiment. Thus did Miguel-Angel Estrella, without letting his fame precede him, transport his piano to a village on the Andean plateau and proceed with the old experimental method of trial and error. An error: Debussy, who keeps the villagers at a respectful distance from his art. A success: Mozart, who makes them slowly approach the instrumentalist. A triumph, a priori unpredictable: Bach, the "elevating" [classante] musician par excellence, adopted as the son of the people by the village community.

This sort of practice for the science of the sociologist comes under the heading of a very precise illusion, that of "cultural communism," which is the illusion of making those who do not have the habitus required to appreciate legitimate works believe that they can appreciate them. The formidable perversity of this illusion is obviously that it does everything as if it were not an illusion. It works [elle marche]. It does not waste its time training anti-sociologists charged with explaining to peasants that they can appreciate music that was not made for them. It makes them appreciate it. Directly. Fraudulently.

Such is the fraud of music. It dissimulates what it is. Already in Kant's time, Emmanuel Schikaneder, the king of wheeler-dealers, was passing off a Mozart opera under the guise of mass entertainment to his suburban audience who very likely did not have any interest in classical music. Since that time the genres have separated, but never enough to prevent "allodoxia" from functioning and arrangers from insidiously offering Mozart to their clientele under the mask of a disco tune, a movie soundtrack, or in the background of a commercial.

The illusion, the "communist" fraud of music, is due to the vice that in Plato was the characteristic of writing: its *silence*, its ability to do without comments and indeed to resist commentary. On the one hand, like the "mute discourse" of the *Phaedrus*, it would gladly roll right and left in forgetting to signal for which habitus it is suitable and for which it is not. On the other, music is the art that resists most resolutely the empire of commentary, the banalization through which the professionals of demystification are eager to establish the social banality of the aesthetic ideal.

One can evidently conclude from these two properties that music is par excellence the art of the "denegation of the social world":[33] the art that ranks by remaining silent, by functioning as if it did not rank and occasionally managing to do so. Religious art that persists in imposing its silence on the chatter of desacralization. Through puns on "the soul of music" and "the music of the soul" that evoke the author of *Nausea*, as through the casual texts that Bourdieu devotes to the trances of Saint Thérèse d'Avila, the *aggorniamento* of the Church, or the social demand that created the prophets Jesus or Mohammed, one can sense a more fundamental annoyance toward the common property of music and religion: the unforeseen affecting the choice of the elect; fraud or theft coming to disturb the scientific mechanism of "incorporation" through which "property appropriates its owner."[34] As with the Son of Man, the musician-friend of the people enters like a thief. And *there are no thieves in the city of the sociologist-king, only the possessors and the dispossessed.*

The sociologist, therefore, will not allow this theft to happen, the theft that dissimulates legitimate cultural property. He will indicate, in the conditional tense, the "properly interminable" task that the analysis of the differential social customs of musical works would constitute. But he will not give his consent to fraud. He will judge musical tastes *without having anyone hear music*. This is a matter of method: the sociologist is not a well-meaning pianist who runs from village to village to find non-representative samples of people, polled in the non-scientific manner of the Son of Man. He will give representative samples of each socio-professional category a questionnaire to fill out that includes three music questions: opinions to choose among (for example, "classical music is not for people like us," which is what Estrella's peasants probably would have answered if they had known what classical music was); a test of knowledge concentrating on four-teen musical works; a choice of three of these works. No sur-prise, the workers answer *en masse* that classical music is not for people like them, show only limited knowledge, and select *The Blue Danube*, whereas distinguished people claim that "all music of quality" interests them, know all of the titles, and choose *The Well-Tempered Clavier*.

To no effect, of course. It was all about refuting Kant, and science has removed from itself in advance the very means of doing so. In aesthetic judgment, Kant affirms the exercise of a capacity different from that of knowledge, whether erudite or mundane. In transforming the test of musical taste into a test of knowledge, the sociologist has solved the problem without even tackling it. He has tested the ability to answer a test on the history of music, which is, in the last instance, the ability to judge the meaning of the inquiry and to answer accordingly. A typical exam-ination situation where, of course, students from the university obtain the best grades. Neither according to their musical taste, nor even to their knowledge. According, rather, to the one quality which is the queen of examinations, the art of knowing only what it is necessary to know—in this case not *The Well-Tempered Clavier*, but the fact that it is the most "elevating" of the proposed works.

The interviewer thus could not retain judgments about music where "the choice of the most legitimate judgment" imposed itself too obviously.[35] But this particular defect leads us to a general problem: "Bourgeois respondents distinguish themselves spe-cially by their ability to control the survey situation."[36] Not, as the interviewer suggests, by their art of "skimming, sliding, and masking," but more simply because his questions designate in advance what the better rankings are. They essentially separate those who know from those who do not know the rules of the game sufficiently to choose the role they want to play in it. For the test that is to refute the illusions of philosophical freedom, there is a winner every time: the Sartrean subject who can freely make himself a philosopher or a waiter.

What should be done, then, in conformity with the project of an *economy of practices*, is to shift the perspective from judgments concerning legitimacy toward forms of legitimation *in actu*; to grasp in their positivity the perceptions that constitute the aesthetics of the dominant, of the dominant-dominated, and of the dominated. From which arises the importance of research on the minor arts or media like photography that are in the process of gaining artistic recognition. In order to identify the work's differential aesthetic dispositions, Kant again will be asked to provide the criterion *a contrario*. For him, pure taste bears on the form of the object, abstracting from its function. The sociologist will show that this "pure" taste is simply bourgeois taste. Popular taste, conversely, expresses itself through its "realism," refusing to separate the image from its content and its function. In this it corresponds quite exactly to the Kantian definition of "barbaric taste."

The photograph of an old woman's hands thus should allow us to perceive, *in actu*, the bourgeois gaze neutralizing the content and the popular gaze evacuating the form. But the interviewer does well to announce the result in advance. For among the manual worker for whom "grandma must've worked hard," the engineer who sees "the hands of someone who worked too much," and the teacher to whom these hands "unquestionably evoke a poor and unhappy old age," the reader has a hard time discerning anything other than the euphemization of language. And the clerical worker for whom "it's as if it was a painting that had been photographed," or the technician who evokes a Spanish painting, are as engaged aesthetically as the engineer who sees in it the character Félicité's hands from Flaubert's *Trois Contes*.[37]

Irremediable trouble induced by the "mute discourse" of the object, which is always too silent or too garrulous. Music remained silent about its legitimacy. The image here imposes its reading. In order to demonstrate the *distanciation* specific to the taste of the aesthete, the sociologist will have to produce the distance himself. To make inquiries not about images, but about the intentions of images. To propose subjects to the people surveyed, asking them which ones would make beautiful photographs. A conclusive test. One will recognize from it that popular taste privileges the functional image of the first communion and refuses the insignificant images of bark or cabbages. Conversely, the aesthete will despise the family photograph and affirm his choice by valorizing cabbages or bark.

The answer is conclusive, but at the price of concluding that the question itself is in vain. The sociologist himself acknowledged as much in a previous work: "The problematic situation of the interviewer and the survey situation itself throw up a question which is artificial and fictitious for the working classes, that of the aesthetic value of photography."[38] Indeed, the person polled who privileges the first communion does not claim any "functionalist" aesthetics. He claims no aesthetics at all—for the simple reason that photography, for him, *is not* art and hence should not be judged according to the criteria of art.

In other words, the interviewer has done here what he later reproaches political scientists for doing: he has pretended to address a subject, mastering the meaning of the question, only to conclude that he lacks the disposition that gives meaning to the question. He feigned competence to prove its absence. The survey reveals only what the sociologist already "knew" in elaborating the question: "popular aesthetics" is simply the absence of aesthetics. Or, conversely, aesthetic judgment is pure distance taken in relation to the popular *ethos*.

One might as well say that the "success" or "failure" of each experiment amounts to the same thing. The sociologist needs only to show each time the sufficient reason organizing the universe of judgments—simple distinction. He needs only to widen the distance. Questions about music without music, fictitious questions of aesthetics about photographs that are not perceived as aesthetic, all these produce inevitably what is required by the sociologist: the suppression of intermediaries, of points of meeting and exchange between the people of reproduction and the élite of distinction. Everything happens as if the science of the sociologist-king had the same requirement as the city of the philosopher-king. There must be no mixing, no imitation. The subjects of this science, like the warriors of *The Republic*, must be unable to "imitate" anything else than their own dye. Everything must work according to *right opinion*. Artistic fraud must be excluded from it. To this end, one has only to bring aesthetic passion back to the company of legitimate works that double the "bourgeois distance from the world." Thus an extraordinary pirouette around a phrase by Virginia Woolf lets us understand that the novelist, faced with the "militant" literature of Arnold Bennett, expresses a refusal to "invest too much passion in the things of the mind [l'esprit]."[39] Thus the terrorism through which, in the 1960s, poor students among the militant cinephiles took revenge on professors who had given them bad grades by forcing them to admire, without knowing why, the melodramas of Douglas Sirk or the westerns of Anthony Mann—this becomes a pure manifestation of the "detachment" of the aesthete who appreciates form "relationally" where popular audiences immerse themselves in content. Thus when fanatical music lovers spend their nights lining up at the opera to attend the "vulgar" works of Verdi, Puccini, or Bizet, the sociologist can assure us that the concert programs "are testimony" to the scientifically irrefutable displacement of "the most knowledgeable" audience toward "the most modern music"[40]—which is, of course, more and more "distant."

Such is, indeed, the indefinitely reproducible logic of the analysis. In the aesthetic universe, *there must only be distance*. The world of being must be separated absolutely from the world of appearance. The always suspicious presence of the *aesthetic thing* must be brought back entirely into the *doxa*'s circle of empty words. No more charismatic reverence for the "artwork [l'oeuvre]" claims the scientist. There only are "fields," only struggles that paint in glowing colors one stake or another as a privileged manifestation of the state of the game. Thus his preferred domain will be that of the disappearing artwork become a pure support, or better a pure absence, engendering cross-plays [*jeux croisés*] of commentary or tautologies of auto-designation: e.g., rituals of the *Figaro*'s theater critics who produce a discourse about the boulevard play (the reproduction of a stereotyped reproduction of bourgeois life) that is simply the anticipated refutation of the predictable discourse of his colleague from the *Nouvel Observateur*;[41] or provocations of art forms reduced to the derision of their designation—piles of coal, pieces of cardboard, or blank paintings bearing only the word "painting" with the dimensions of the thing.[42] Procedures for the rehabilitation of minor cultures and the desacralisation of high culture, which constitute the daily fare of left-wing culture, the bustling commotion of the *doxa* in which the resisting presence of the artwork vanishes. The science effect produced by the sociologist is linked with this commotion, which results in the expulsion of everything not reducible to an effect of distinction. What testifies to this are his montages, photographs, balloons, graffiti, and marginal notes that exacerbate the daily fare of "demystificating" *doxa*, radicalizing the operation of the withdrawal of appearances. The limit-point of this demystification is the passage taken from the preparatory notes to Flaubert's *l'Éducation sentimentale* and annotated with the revengeful graffiti "before euphemization," which lets us see that the long narrative of the onanistic state of the souls of the two heroes could be reduced, after all, to quick answers to two questions. Do they make love or not? Does it work out or not?[43]

The expulsion of art is then the particular case of a general mechanism for the production of a void wherever the popular *gestus* could, by accident or fraud, meet up with the bourgeois *gestus*. The principle that commanded the "fictitious" interrogation of aesthetic practices also determines the tautological analysis of sports practices. Particularly significant is the case of sociologically mixed sports, soccer or rugby for example, that went from popular exercise to aristocratic schools before resuming a "popularity" that does not prevent the bourgeoisie from enjoying their practice or their spectacle. Intent on producing, here as everywhere, the radical difference of habitus, Pierre Bourdieu assures us that these sports "accumulate all the reasons" to repel members of the dominant classes with the qualities they demand: "strength, resistance to pain, a disposition toward violence, spirit of 'sacrifice,' docility and submission to collective discipline, a perfect antithesis to the 'role distance' implied in bourgeois roles, exaltation of competition."[44]

This "accumulation" of reasons leaves us perplexed. Could competition, resistance to pain, the spirit of sacrifice, and the submission to collective discipline be qualities so unknown in the schools, churches, publications, and armies of bourgeois domination? Were these sports not imported precisely after the defeat of a "weakened" France by robust Prussia in order to inculcate these qualities in soldiers and especially the officers of the nation? The improbability of these "accumulated" reasons refers then to the single (and always identical) sufficient reason: the repulsion felt by the distinguished for the vulgar; the bourgeois turn away from rugby when it becomes popular. A short-circuit in the analysis prevents us from posing the question backward, from interrogating the popular passion for a sport in which the astuteness of the little halfbacks in transmitting the fruit of the scrum's obscure labor to the spirited, thoroughbred three-quarters makes the most implacable social statements.[45] Which would be a way of returning this ambiguous practice to the side of the pure asymbolic exhibition of popular physical qualities, of producing the void between a popular ethos of reproduction and a bourgeois ethos of distinction—which is to say, of leisure.

This is the circle of the sociologist-king. He gets irritated easily with critics who drop the concrete contents of his survey polls, tables and diagrams, who show themselves incapable of thinking relationally the universe in motion he describes to them. But this blind reading is the strict counterpart of the operation that always refers to the same sufficient reason—leisure—and leaves room, through all translations of social space, for only one conflict in which are opposed the two modes of the existence of leisure: the incorporated leisure of the dominant, for whom aesthetic practices are material for the partial and passionless reconversion of the economic and symbolic capital acquired; and the militant intention of distinction of the dominant-dominated, who seek to compensate for their economic and political inferiority by putting pressure on cultural competition and on the imperialism of aesthetic intention that takes hold of every object: "The struggles to win everything which, in the social world, is of the order of belief, credit and discredit, perception and appreciation, knowledge and recognition . . . always concern the 'distinguished' possessors and the 'pretentious' challengers."[46]

The empire of tautology; the empire of leisure. It alone creates bourgeois distance from the world, the "disinterested" exercise of school, feminine investment in home decorating, and the half-idle, half-revolted aestheticism of the inheritor spoiled by his mother's idleness: "It is not surprising that bourgeois adolescents, who are both economically privileged and (temporarily) excluded from the reality of economic power, sometimes express their distance from the bourgeois world which they cannot really appropriate by a refusal of complicity whose most refined expression is a propensity toward aesthetics and aestheticism. In this respect, they share common ground with the women of the bourgeoisie, who, being partially excluded from economic activity, find fulfillment in stage managing the décor of bourgeois existence, when they are not seeking refuge or revenge in aesthetics."[47]

Thus the field of symbolic conflicts restricts itself again. The struggle of the pretentious challengers against the distinguished possessors is basically only a family affair, a quarrel between generations. The games of the symbolic are the years of apprenticeship or popular rites of bourgeois maturation. The aesthete, like the rebellious student from The Inheritors, is only the prodigal child of bourgeois leisure. Like the democratic man in Plato, the adolescent smitten with the blending of colors and the wanderings of insatiable leisure was the son of the industrious oligarch. The sociologist of Distinction only hints at his skeptical thought, that there may be no other struggles than conflicts between generations. Since The Inheritors, he continues his settling of scores with the same character: the inheritor who in 1964 revealed in his critique of the institution the essence of school leisure; the rebellious student who in 1970 imagined he had "unveiled" the system while it fell to the sociologist to display its new veils. In Distinction, the mocking eye of the master finds him again, older and stale, déclassé and aspiring to reranking [reclassement] through his feats in the great simile industry of the new petty bourgeoisie: the manufacture of junk jewelry or sale of symbolic services; the commerce of youth leaders, marriage counselors, sex therapists, advertising executives, or dietitians determined to create within people the symbolic needs necessary for the enlargement of their market, hence for the reconquest of their inheritance.[48] Prophets who deliver their marketable truth in "the exemplary story of all those who started by professing a faith and ended up making it a profession."[49] Forgers with regard to the illusion they provide to their traveling companions from the petty bourgeois interworld, making them believe in a common ascent where there is only the return to the fold of the prodigal children of leisure.

A theory of the social game as a family affair—such is the strange relationship that institutes itself between the procedures of science and its philosophy. Beyond economic necessity, sociological science required a space of symbolic practices whose agents were not the rational actors of the liberal market but the bearers and vectors of the properties of an interaction of specific fields. But the agents that the survey valorizes are always rational actors whose desire for distinction is simply limited by the volume of capital to be placed on the symbolic market. The fields whose interactions should define the thousand games of social mobility are ever only redoubled mirrors where the simple law of distinction gets pulverized in a thousand reflections—ever only the false struggle that is a real complicity between "distinguished possessors" and "pretentious challengers" who divide themselves in two: hopeless candidates condemned to the mere appearances of distinction, and disguised inheritors investing their appearance of struggle in the sale of appearances. The positivity of classes or the fields of social space ultimately become the developed myth of a metaphysics of vanity. The world of rational actors from the vital and optimistic American-style economy finds itself euphemized by the pessimistic and distinguished aura of the old national and European culture. We are just puppets, claims the scientist, to whom only the rattles of power give the appearance of sufficient reason. And this alone may be the only reason why there are social classes: "through a kind of curse, because of the essentially diacritical, differential, and distinctive nature of symbolic power, the rise of the distinguished class to Being has, as an inevitable counterpart, the slide of the complementary class into Nothingness or the lowest Being."[50]

We must not be taken in by the disabused nonchalance of this confidence where, against a background of Sartrean angst, the Pascalian intonation affecting the scientific rigor of adjectives, and the Parmenidian elevation of substantives euphemize the sad truth of human vanity. By confessing the fundamental inconsistency of his object, the sociologist-king only better ensures himself of his power. For the relationship established here between being and non-being allows him to kill two birds with one stone. On the one hand, he takes the place of the philosopher as the author of the tale about the arbitrariness of the social game. But this arbitrariness will soon turn itself into necessity as the "complementary class" becomes the motor that gives the puppet show its rigor as a scientific object. And the fall into non-being will be the descent into Hell of the popular positivity denouncing the illusion of philosophical Heaven. Hence, philosophy will be driven away twice and, thanks to a mute people, the sociologist-king will be left without rivals.

On one condition, of course: that these people remain in their place, which is that of the first immobile engine setting in motion the antagonistic and collusive games of the distinguished possessors and pretentious challengers. For what distinguishes the universe of the sociologist-king from the platitudes of neoliberal economy is the superimposition of two economies: Bentham for the rich and Marx for the poor. The symbolic struggles of the distinguished élite escape the non-sense of pure competition because they define themselves as separate from the primary economy of a people affected solely by the movement upon itself of Parmenidian Marxism, by the eternal reproduction of the relations of production. An infra-world of the pure adhesion of the popular body to itself, with no other possible judgment than a love of fate which resembles fate, and with no other thinkable symbolic than marks of virility—that is to say, of reproduction.

What distinguishes this generalized capitalism is therefore its Marxist unconscious: a "class struggle" functioning only at the price of not leaving to the classes a point where they could ever meet. What transforms the too predictable strategies of the possessors and challengers into the objects of a "science of the hidden" is the bar of repression: one must read, in these tastes, expressions of disgust perpetually haunted by the fascinated horror of a swarming and boisterous popular body covered with marks of adhesion and fed with the ragouts of mixture. A popular unconscious that would force the flight of the refined actors into the infinite vertigo of denegation. A sticky source of bourgeois civility that would be the true basis for the free philosopher's nausea and the secret reason for the games of refinement that he plays with his waiter.

The theoretical, political, and medical act of the sociologist might therefore be the forcing of the bar of repression to show us this people with whom he took such care to prevent us from having any other contact:

> It is not possible to advance the science of the social world, and to make it known, except by forcing the return of the repressed, by neutralizing neutralization, denying denial in all its forms, not the least of which is the de-realization through hyperbolic radicalization performed by some revolutionary discourse. Neither true nor false, neither verifiable nor falsifiable, neither theoretical nor empirical, such discourse—like Racine, who never referred to "cows" but only to "heifers"—cannot talk of the SMIC (statutory minimum wage) and the undershirts of working-class men but only of the mode of production and the proletariat or of the roles and attitudes of the "lower middle class." To break with this genteel abstraction, it is not sufficient to demonstrate: one has to show—but not denounce—things

and even people, make them palpable, and take into a working-class café, onto a rugby pitch or a golf course, or into a private club, people who are so used to saying what they think that they no longer know how to think what they say.[51]

But is it really necessary, to "liberate free-floating intellectuals"[52] from their Racinian litotes and revolutionary hyperbole, to reduce heifers to the rank of disavowed cows and transform industrial Billancourt into a rural village in Béarn? The working-class café where the sociologist forces us to accompany him is, in spite of everything, of a slightly nostalgic kind. No Skai leatherette, pinball games, or juke-boxes; no consumers of strawberry milkshakes or young people with loud clothing; no calculations or dreams placed on horse races or lottery numbers. An image of a popular world totally foreign "to the Benthamite calculation of pleasures and pains,"[53] foreign to games of the symbolic, to calculations on the future and risks of anomie; where logically one should find no more poets than players or *arrivistes*, money savers, apostles, or delinquents. Such at least is the image aroused by these evocations of proletarian adepts of an "outspokenness [*franc-parler*]" that disregards the stakes of the "linguistic market," and of an "appetitiveness [*franc-manger*]" that feeds them "foods that stick to the ribs" without any fuss; by these performative tautologies on the "prolificness of the proletarian reproducing himself as such and in great numbers"[54] through which the statistical gap of half a child widens into the Platonic difference between the One and the Many; by these paradigmatic photographs of bean eaters appropriated by their plates, of working-class interiors where piled-up boxes assure us that the art of tidying up is an unknown frivolity among the common people, or old couples so close to their asymbolic ethos that one cannot imagine their ever being able to bear the marks of youth or displays of seduction. A working-class world more sunk in nature than the "primitive" universe of the ethnologists since objects there have only the value of utility and foods only the function of filling oneself up—since one is reproduced there "as such" without rites of seduction, education, or passage. Besides, adolescence—the age group surcharged with the marks of distinction and that accumulates both the emblems of the group and the emblems of the group's refusals—does not exist there. Adolescents remain absent from the optic that returns the repressed, just as absent as the

Portuguese, Yugoslav, North African, or black workers who form the core of our proletariat. An ineligible, unsurveyable, unphotographed population, represented here beside itself by this sixty-something communist carpenter whose working-class and Thorezian nostalgia (the counterpart to the sociologist's peasant and Bakhtinian nostalgia) laments that the working class is not similar enough to itself, "not miserable enough."[55]

Suppression of everything that could color or tattoo the simple face of working-class identity. Militant medicine of a habitus "without guilt or pain" applied to preserve the simplicity of this ethos from all the swellings triggered by the demand—voluntary or market—for bourgeois symbolic goods (*The Well-Tempered Clavier*, marriage counseling, or Skai sofas); from all the "malapropisms" identifying workers who with borrowed words wish to give "their" opinion on the "wage bill" or the "underprivileged strata."[56] No double meaning must "break down" the language of the dominated. No deceptive image must be allowed a mix-up through which reasons of distinction would come to mingle with those of *amor fati*. Nothing must supply a link between the "pretension" of the challengers and the "dispossession" of the dispossessed. The evil is the community of appearances.

THE VULGAR SOCIOLOGIST AND THE DISTINGUISHED PHILOSOPHER

Here, in all likelihood, is the basis of Pierre Bourdieu's quarrel with Kantian aesthetics. The sociologist claims to offer a "vulgar" critique of this "denegating" aesthetics that is "totally ahistorical, like all philosophical thought that is worthy of the name."[57] As ahistorical, assuredly, as the "vulgar" sociologist pretending to ignore the date of the *Critique of Judgment* the better to reduce its problematic to a multisecular conflict between erudite people and those from the court. Kant, however, gives the question of "aesthetic common sense" a larger and more precisely dated theater. One year after the beginning of the French Revolution, his aesthetics presents itself as the contemporary of a century and of populations confronted with the problem of "uniting freedom (and equality) with compulsion (rather of respect and submission from a sense of duty than of fear)."[58]

The phrasing is a little contorted. Professor Kant is neither a stylist nor a warmonger but simply a thinker who does not turn away from his idea: through what means can an equality of sentiment be brought about that gives the proclaimed equality of rights the conditions of their real exercise? The great strength of the opponents of freedom is that they show it to be inapplicable on the grounds of the inequality of competences and social capacities—the gulf separating working class brutality from bourgeois civility. The very ones who say that the people are incapable of ever making a reasonable use of freedom claim that the Beautiful is a matter either of learned criteria or the pleasure of refined senses (which are, in both cases, outside the sphere of the common people). Kant refuses this absolutization of the gap between working-class "nature" and the "culture" of the élite. In the formal universality of the judgment of taste (that is to say, in the exigency of communication inherent to it), he seeks the anticipation of the perceptible equality to come, of the *humanity* that will be the joint surpassing of the culture of the dominant and the culture of Rousseauist nature.

The sociologist, who cannot be fooled, can therefore still psychoanalyze the "ahistorical" idea of a disinterested taste opposed to the pleasure of the senses, and read in it the multisecular horror of philosophic distinction for the vulgar enjoyment of working-class hedonism. In 1790 the theory of the "pleasurable" is not exactly the vision of the people. It is that of a distinguished gentleman named Edmund Burke, the same man who raises the banner against a revolution that would give carpenters and tailors the right to meddle in public affairs.[59] Kant places his bet between Burke's civility and the Rousseauist critique of luxury, an ahistorical bet in the sense that it is a new madness to think it possible to separate the community of aesthetic sentiment from the feasts of domination and competences of knowledge. The first example he uses says it all: one can judge the form of a palace and feel pleasure from it without worrying about knowing if the vanity of the great built it at the price of the sweat of the homeless.[60] An assuredly denegating position denying that the world is eternally split between persons of culture and those of nature. It denies that the only future of the idea of equality is the terror exercised in the name of a people incapable of exercising their rights. In the days following the Terror, Schiller will develop this utopian content of Kantian aesthetics: the ability to enjoy the appearance that is "the education of humanity," the fragile promise of a freedom gained beyond the opposition between working-class savagery and civilized barbarism.[61] A fiction of the possible responding to the fiction of the impossible, a utopia opening again the space bolted shut by the myth of the three metals. An "illusion of progress" in the sense in which the sociologist precisely defined *illusio*—as the possibility of playing.

"Cultural communism" hounded by the wrath of the demystifier is an illusion of that kind. Not a disincarnated reverie about art, but an ensemble of game possibilities linked to the historical mutation of the status of the artist at a time when "art," de facto, becomes more and more independent from displays of domination and rules of certification; when Mozart is striving to live without a master, Talma to strip tragedy from the varnish of the epoch's civilities and servilities, and Lenoir to preserve as works of art the confiscated treasures of former priests and aristocrats. This art that detached itself from its old functions and judges but still has not closed itself up in its autonomy then offers itself as the aim and privileged support of strategies of reappropriation; the "denegating" aesthetic gaze can now take, among the intellectuals of the proletariat, the full force of an "other" gaze [*d'un regard autre*] upon the propriety of the other that becomes an "other" gaze [*qui devient regard autre*] upon the proletarian's dispossession.

Such is the game in which working-class pathos transforms itself into an aesthetic and militant passion for reappropriation. Strangely enough, the carpenter Gauny seems to be commenting on the *Critique of Judgment* when, from the room in which he lays a parquet floor, he offers the gaze of an aesthete on the décor of his servitude: "Thinking himself at home, as long as he has not finished the room in which he nails down the boards, he likes the layout of the place; if the window opens onto a garden or over a picturesque horizon, he stops moving his hands for an instant and shifts his thoughts toward that spacious view in order to enjoy it better than the owners of the neighboring homes."[62] The acquisition of this aesthetic gaze, the paradoxical philosophy of asceticism that this dispossessed worker draws from it, this torsion of habitus that he imposes upon himself and proposes is also the claim of a human right to happiness that exceeds the rhetoric of proletarian recruiters, the battle of cottages and castles.

A denegation through which heresy comes into the sight and speech of the dispossessed. The sociologist-demystifier would like to oppose the performative efficacity of utopian or heretical discourse to the traps of allodoxia.[63] But utopian discourse is performative only in the mind of the utopian or the words of the commentator. It acts upon sensibility as a work of art, not as an injunction on action. Heresy is first and foremost augmented religion or the radicalization of aesthetic legitimacy. The stuggle for the right to speak freely is first and foremost a struggle for euphemization. It is by entering into the game of bourgeois passions (and the most "legitimate" ones) that fields of symbolic relations take shape at the limit of the classes, making possible the enunciation and utterances [l'énonciation et les énoncés] of working-class speech detached from the repetitions of amor fati. The first worker-militants began by taking themselves for poets or knights, priests or dandies.[64] An allodoxia that is the only way to heterodoxia. Borrowed passions using the only words that make reappropriation possible: borrowed words. At the price of a few malapropisms and misinterpretations: the misinterpretation of the words that aver the necessary order of things is the first word of heretical discourse. The shoemakers' insurrection is a vast misinterpretation of The Republic.

Thus cultural communism played out like the illusion that made playable the effort to give the dominated a voice. Like, that is, the operator of games of distinction through which the aesthetes and dandies of the working class gave the group a voice. What resounded in Pierre Dupont's Chant des ouvriers [Song of the Workers] was struck up in chorus in the spring of 1848—about which the poet and dandy Baudelaire produced a strange reading, yet another fictive commentary on an unknown Critique of Judgment: "What is more trivial than wealth as seen by poverty? But here, the feeling is complicated by poetic pride, by partly glimpsed pleasures of which one feels oneself worthy. . . . We too, we understand the beauty of palaces and parks. We too, we know the art of happiness."[65]

But this is where the strangeness of Baudelaire's reading resides, for these palaces, present in Kant, do not appear in the Chant des ouvriers. Baudelaire may have heard them there because they were "in the air," the air of "cultural communism." What the dandy poet calls more nicely "the infinite taste of the Republic."[66]

The ahistoricity of "distinguished" philosophy is simply its belonging to other times. The "vulgarity" of the sociologist, consequently, is only the disenchanted banality of the learned opinion of his time, which, with an amused eye, regards the witnesses of that age when philosophers believed in the future of equality and proletarians in the inspiration of poets. His polemic on "cultural communism" is in the first place the discourse of an era in which the "autonomy" of art, at the cost of its pretension, became lost in the immense chattering of the commentatory and demystificatory doxa [de la doxa commentatrice et démystificatrice].

A demystification of the "pure" artist which is in fact a radicalization of his operation. For the absolutization of art, in Flaubert the rentier, is not the "denegation" of his social status but the putting to death of "cultural communism": the putting to death of the "po-et-i-cal" aspirations of the "hysteric" Madame Bovary; the condemnation to forced labors of infinite repetition of Bouvard's and Pécuchet's autodidact desire to know. A painful murder because it is experienced in an ambiguous fraternity—because it is also the murder of the only book that was important for the pure artist, La tentation de Saint Antoine. An ambiguous fraternity through which the work of art is made capable of rolling off anywhere, even into the hands of the Bouvards and Pécuchets or the Madame Bovarys who populate interworlds from which are turned out the dreamers of the proletariat and the déclassé intelligentsia. This is when social science intervenes in sorting out what is suitable for each, demystifying the pure work of art, and giving back to the dreamy daughters of peasants and little autodidact employees a product better adapted to the ends of social critique: a reading of Flaubert or something else, telling the truth about the artist's purity; a pedagogic film on Molière or Mozart replacing the legitimacy of the work with the useful historical demystification of the craft of the actor or musician, of the Great Century or the Age of Enlightenment. For the chorus of cicadas protecting the dialogue of the philosopher and the philologist was substituted the complicity of the sociologist-king and the doxosophers in organizing the withdrawal of appearances, placing the precision of scientific language and the rigor of social critique everywhere there had been the image of division and equivocality. Thus, wrapped in games of doxa that accumulate words and in games of science that bring about the return of the repressed, the sociologist can exhibit the bar that is the alpha and omega of the articulation of the fields. Frédéric Moreau's Paris, he teaches us, stops precisely where working-class Paris begins.[67]

The bar of repression. The identity of the empire of commentary with the empire of the social. The world of the fading "work of art" is also the one where the Marxist critique of the illusions of progress has turned back into the disenchanted knowledge of the eternity of division between the possessors and the dispossessed; where the dispossessed have become the absent guardian of the universe of science, the fictive goal of illocutionary journeys to Hell through which science proves itself in stigmatizing non-science. Journeys to the land of the truth of the working-class body organized for these "deniers" who are ever only told to go and see with the assurance that they will never go, and who thus will prove eternally the necessity for science and the secret of its object.

THE EDITOR IS insisting a conclusion must be reached: it is time to say who the philosopher is and who are his poor, where the author started from and where he ended up, and what led him on a journey in which, apparently, neither the well-being of individuals nor the good of nations was dramatically at stake.

Let us then summarize. In the beginning, there was the following: philosophy defined itself in defining its other. The order of discourse delimited itself by tracing a circle that excluded from the right to think those who earned their living by the labor of their hands.

This way of putting things together supposed some cunning in its detail. By relegating artisans to the order of pure reproduction, philosophy pretended to confirm them only where they had been placed by their love for the solid realities of technical success and financial gain. And, *per contra*, it fed its own privilege with the dark bread of non-possession. But this was a double game. By elevating [*classant*] solid artisans and demoting [*déclassant*] shadow makers, philosophy rather reserved for itself this right to the luxury of appearances that command the privilege of thought. And this privilege imposed itself with all its brutality by invoking a difference in nature that confessed it was a fable. Philosophy linked its lot to a hierarchy that the lie could found only in nature.

We started from this archetypal figure of the social institution of philosophy. We arrived at the exemplary modernity of a sociology recognizing behind the games of philosophical aesthetics the law of a symbolic order based upon the exclusion of the "vulgar" enjoyments of the dispossessed, and denouncing in the freedom of philosophers the simple denegation of the social relations of domination. At first glance, these two processes possess a certain air of familiarity based on their similar good thoughts with respect to the excluded. Why then show so much repugnance toward the operation of the sociologist who tears from the philosopher the mask of his divine freedom in order to restore him to his situation as an always unfortunate candidate for power?

We'll cut to the chase. There are two reasons for this, one of which concerns the means of "demystification" and the other its ends—let us say its ethics.

On the first point, we tried to demonstrate the following: that the sociological "reversal" of Platonism is, in a way, only the confirmation, indeed the radicalization, of its interdictions. "Sociology" emerges precisely in Plato as the rationalization of the hierarchy of souls in a functional division of tasks—a provisional rationalization that philosophical irony cannot allow to have the last word. In book III of the *Republic*, Plato puts sociology back in its place to affirm the arbitrariness of the natural order commanding everyone to do his or her own business. This "own" can be recognized again as the product of the interdiction.

Sociological demystification then produces this result: it recasts the arbitrary as necessity. Where Plato reduced the serious reasons of needs and functions to the arbitrariness of the decree excluding artisans from the leisure of thought, sociology will read the philosophical illusion of universal freedom and will refute it by disclosing the difference of *ethos* that makes the artisan incapable of ever acquiring a taste for the philosopher's goods—and even of understanding the language in which their enjoyment is expounded. Nature's tale thus becomes the indisputable difference inscribed on bodies. Science points its finger at us, proves to us through photography that there are indeed bodies that have or have not been made to enjoy philosophical distinction. In disqualifying the philosopher, the sociologist simply took up for his own sake the privilege of those alone who understand the language of the initiated.

What remains is the question of what this consists of. What indeed is at stake in the merry work of this science that reduces to their common economy the true and false goods of the old hierarchies, the divisions [*partages*] between symbolic and real gold?

Others have said that what vanishes in the generalized economy that has replaced the old divisions of the discursive order is the question of value itself. And this is the stake as well of the Platonic operation. The resisting force of the "idealist," "pro-slavery," or "totalitarian" Plato is the posing in all its provocative force of the simple and vertiginous question: what is best? How can what is best be distinguished from the forest of similar-sounding expressions and closely resounding ideas: what costs more, what works better, what is more profitable? And if it proves to be that what is best is what is valuable in itself, how will this "best" (which, by definition, cannot fight) ever impose itself on the universe of social competition where the very inferiority of competitive values ensures their success every time? In the *Gorgias*, the matter can be summarized in the torsion that must be inflicted on the meaning of a word, kreïttōn, "what carries the day"—what in this circumstance must prevail through the very fact of not competing.

A vertiginous question in the strict sense. Callicles has, once and for all, established its cruelty, for the question is to know—beyond the torsion of words—whether life the right way up is not life the opposite way. And perhaps it will become even more vertiginous at the epoch when the reign of equality will announce itself to dazzled philosophers as the world at last turned upside down, *that is to say* founded upon spirit.[1] Since then, we understand that in order to preserve themselves from this, the cuisines of persuasion and medicines of habitus have had to hurl themselves headlong into gymnastics' reversals before all cows can become equally gray in the electric light of demystification.

But the vertigo is first and foremost Plato's himself. He therefore tethers his question *by force*. He has to justify this unprecedented relation—the superiority of "what does not work" over "what works," of the discourse that does not pay [qui ne fait pas recette] over the discourse that pays. To this end, he identifies rhetorical indignity with the lowness of the worker, and the discourse that pays with the "philosophy" of the people who must draw their subsistence from their hands. To establish the singularity of the philosophical "best" in the face of rhetoric's *savoir-faire* and the adjuvants of medicine, he draws the simple line that splits two loves: the love of philosophy and the love of the people. He unites within a single totality a technique (rhetoric), a character (the artisan), and a principle (democracy). In the democratic thought of Protagoras, who balances the unequal distribution of technical competences with the political community of discourse, he wants to see only the popular cuisine of rhetoric. And against Callicles, who claims the power of the skillful, he proves that the principle of this power is identical to that of artisanal mediocracy [la médiocratie artisanale]. Philosophical excellence can be defined for him only in its difference from a rhetorical *savoir-fare* assimilable to the power of the masses. Which also means that his legitimacy, unprovable in the performances of discourse, must be sustained by the fortune of a birth that is at once the royal arbitrariness of order.

The aristocratic lock-up of philosophy. But what makes its severity also makes its fragility. The political order supposed to achieve this state will ever only be the shadow of a shadow of the divine life. The best [les meilleurs] are not made first for the city's justice but for the games and music of the god. Plato's famous "totalitarianism," the distribution of orders, the immutability of laws, and the unison of hymns are certainly not the paradise of the philosopher but simply, in his sense, all that the citizen bees and ants can imitate of the heavenly music. Above them sits the order of elections and initiations, itself hanging upon the power of the tale. And the tale is always double. It speaks about distribution (attributed, *noblesse oblige*, to the fortunes of nature) but also about redistribution: the new division of souls transformed by their merits and demerits. It is not without reason that the *Phaedo* was read with so much passion in the age of Enlightenment and Public Instruction. To the democracies of the future, the palingenetic myths of Plato the aristocrat bequeath a certain idea of equality, what then will be called *the equality of chances*—the nobility of merit's encounter with the aristocracy of fortune, an event whose philosophical and political strangeness is ruined by the desire to see it merely as the "dissimulation" of inequality.

For his part, Plato has no propensity for dissimulating inequality. On the contrary, he maintains the barriers firmly. Redistribution must above all degrade false nobilities. The purpose is to refine the chorus of the cicadas, not to open it to deserving ants.[2] Between the virtue of the ones and of the others, the son of Poverty—Penia—forms a guard all the more vigilant in that he is a vagabond. It remains that if the order of discourse is protected by the childishness of the tale, one exposes it to the danger of a childhood virtue that returns more than once to ruin the artisans' *sōphrosunē*: their stubborn belief in the impossible.

Such is the virtue—the vice—that sets Rembrantsz the shoemaker on the road to Egmont with his good hopes.[3] He lives in a century of progress and the philosopher he is going to meet is of a brand-new species: someone who brings musical mystique back to the rationality of acoustics, writes in the vernacular language, and assures us that natural light is distributed to all. He is even said to communicate his science to his servants. True, on the other hand, the servants protect from some overbold artisans the peace that their master came to seek "in the midst of a great crowd of people . . . more careful of their own [propres] affairs than curious about those of others."⁴ But the "propriety" of these affairs no longer prevents words from being exchanged nor propositions from being heard. The shoemaker owes to his own perseverance the right to present himself finally for the examination that will open up to him the highest career of which a shoemaker could dream, that of astronomy. Auguste Comte, as we know, did not want any other science to initiate the proletariat into its new destinies.

This supposes an agreement concerning a new division of discourses and states, a certain idea of the rehabilitation of the artisan. The good sense that makes the shoemaker capable of elevating himself to the contemplation of the heavens must dissuade him from wanting to reform governments in a direction from which his birth had never destined him. And Auguste Comte's proletariat shall win its place in the future by abandoning the fevers of political equality to comply with its contemplative vocation and sing in chorus around the priests of science. A redistribution of prohibitions and initiations where the hope is entertained that one day the union of science and labor will overcome the rattles and humiliations of politics.

This is the idea of a certain Cartesianism as a philosophy of the Third Estate. Some theoretician of syndicalism may have sought to find it again beneath Descartes's mask.⁵ But politics always resisted this idea. So, too, have philosophy, the Muses, and the dreams of autodidact shoemakers. Whatever mechanics [la mécanique] and medicine may promise the associated workers, the question is to be found elsewhere—at the point where the ability to enjoy appearance distinguishes itself from the distribution of competences and the hierarchy of ranks.

What then remains is Glaucon's question as reformulated by Voltaire's century and, in its last decade, the guarding of appearances over which Kant and Schiller clashed. Two ways of bringing the order of discourse and of politics back to the fabrication of useful objects and the disinterested contemplation of forms. Two manners of imagining the relations between heaven and earth, the labor of artisans and the leisure of philosophers.

This is, on the one hand, the optimistic vision of an industrious world freed from corporations, superstitions, and childishness. The naturalness of ranks sees itself contested in its very principle, the naturalness of aptitudes. Well placed to perceive the paradoxes of the Platonic adaptation of functions to natures, Adam Smith

expounds the principle: "The difference between the most dis-
similar characters, between a philosopher and a common street
porter, for example, seems to arise not so much from nature, as
from habit, custom, and education."[6] At the same time, the king-
weaver's virtue must be democratized as technical capacity becomes proof of political capacity: "Can we expect that a government will be well modeled by a people who know not how to make
a spinning wheel or to employ a loom to advantage?"[7] But the
civilization of work immediately backfires on the worker. It proves
its excellence in producing "commodities" that can develop the
universal sociability of cultivated life but at the price of fixing
more firmly in their place artisans destined for the simple reproduction of their work capacity and the solitary repetition of a
machine-like gesture. The "social" then emerges as a shutting
down of the thought of leisure, the kernel of a modern discourse
about an order of discourses and states that can—and that wants
to—sustain itself only in its utility. Hegel best marks the limits of
this "modernity" when, in the *Philosophy of Right*, he has to "overcome" the sociability of political economy and conduct it toward
the rationality of the state universal by precisely what it pretended
to destroy: the police of the corporations.[8]

From which probably derives the fact that equality had to boast
more often about the sublimities of aesthetic heaven than the
benefits of labor and the critique of the *Hinterwelt*.[9] Another idea of
the rehabilitation of the workers arises perhaps in Shaftesbury's
insistence on distinguishing the aesthetic enjoyment of perspective space from every monopolizable property. This would be a
return to the Platonic theory of enthusiasm from which is drawn,
nevertheless, the unexpected consequence of a reversal of the hierarchy of leisure: "The Bridegroom-*Doge*, who in his stately Bu-
centaur floats on the Bosom of his *Thetis*, has less possession than
the poor Shepherd, who from a hanging Rock, or Point of some
high Promontory, stretch'd at his ease, forgets his feeding Flocks,
while he admires her Beauty."[10] It is in the opening of this "forgetting" that Kant can rethink the "sociability" of cultivated exchanges by setting, as an implicit principle of the very coherence
of the élites' discourse, the affirmation of an aesthetic *sensus communis* that promises the end of the gap between the savagery of the
swine and the refinements of civilized barbarism—the possible
identification between what is best and what establishes everyone's equality. Yet this new thought about aesthetic equality im-

mediately exacerbates the uneasiness of the impossible when Schiller cannot propose any other model than divine leisure and play for the aesthetic education that must redeem the fragmented society.[11] The liberal democrat Protagoras now has to reckon with Diotima, who turns people insane.

Then begin the modern figures of vertigo, the cross-plays [*jeux croisés*] between election and work, industrious demystification and heavenly egalitarianism. Revolutionary scientists [*savants*] demystify heavenly speculation and announce the reign of the producers even if this means that they encounter the discourse of the élite, who now justify their power by praising work and the productive forces for breaking down the power of the castes. Inversely, the stubborn children of the proletariat look for signs of their vocation for humanity in the heaven of the poets and philosophers. The lettered specialists of divine inspiration enjoin them to abandon these vanities likely to demote them at the risk of impersonating, in so doing, the even more powerful and hostile statue of the producer-king, the enemy of the idle. The élite of the producers do not tear themselves apart any less in trying to discover whether the best is identified with the power of the working order or the proportion of brotherly harmonies. Artists reproach the bourgeoisie for turning aesthetic excellence over to industrial leveling even if, on the other hand, they affirm themselves as the purest representatives of the work ethic. And the schools of the Republic will have a go at the squaring of the circle—at giving the children of the people the appropriate initiation in aesthetic values to establish the equality of citizen sensibilities without, in the process, separating them from the state to which they generally will have to conform, but from which the best shall be detached.

Marx finds himself at the crossroads of these paradoxes. The *Theses on Feuerbach* claim to provide the key which, in one turn, solves the enigmas of discourse and starts the revolution of the States: "social practice." Only this solution concentrates in itself all the contradictions. It is obviously fallacious to oppose practice as the foundation and instance of verification to the hypotheses of theory and reflections of speculation. In principle, practice is not opposed to theoretical speculations but to productions of technique, what Aristotle called "poietics": the free citizen's practice in the *Politics* is closer in *nature* to the philosophers' *theoria*—which it neither applies nor verifies—than it is to the artisans' technique. And the inordinately celebrated automatic shuttle that would permit dispensing with slaves only concerns, in Aristotle, the domestic organization of economy. All the equivocation of "political" economy will mark, on the contrary, the Marxian relation between enlightening practice and formative labor—as is testified to by Marx's extraordinarily ambiguous agreement with the Hegelian "labor of the negative." Hegel, he states, "comprehends objective man—true, because real man—as the outcome of man's *own* labour."[12] This "own" is what the question is all about. Already in Hegel, the insistence on the tool's "spirituality" does not prevent objectivity from entering the economic sphere through the police of the corporations. As for Marx, he cannot grant Hegel that the plow is "more honorable than are the immediate enjoyments procured by it."[13] In this, he is closer to the philosophers and economists of the Enlightenment, for whom it is not the tool that fulfills reason but its product. And it is not the State that must exceed the sociability of productions and exchanges but the contrary. Progress toward the universal becomes identified, in terms of priority, with the perfecting of transportation that allows men and ideas to circulate to the four corners of the world and that sweeps away everywhere the old grime and archaism of representations. This thinking of leisure as commerce, where the Aristotelian ideal of community governed by the Good comes to mingle with the modern vision of social commodities based on industry, in effect completes itself as a "social" theory of interpretation. Feuerbach made "the social relation of 'man to man' the basic principle of his theory."[14] He disbursed the speculations of philosophy as the properties of relations between individuals. More "radical" than he, Marx also will link "representations" of politics back to these properties, for the "social relation" proves to be the truth of what they represent—as caricatured in the zoology of Hegelian bureaucracy, and as exemplified in the last-born form that represents the *telos* of the political, democracy.

The practice that commands access to the universe of leisure thus finds in *technē* its engine and in the sociability of exchanges its end. Yet precisely between divine leisure and industrious order, Schiller clearly reactivated the distance. And he showed the effects of the divorce as the gap widened between the barbarism of civilized élites and the savagery of natural people. Marx does not like Schiller the declaimer. That Marx can evade his analysis no less is confirmed, however, by the harsh honesty of the economists: "Thus, the more society advances toward a state of splendour and power, *the less time the working class will have to give to studying and to intellectual and speculative work. . . . From another angle, the less time the working class has to exploit the domain of knowledge, the more time remains for the other class.*"[15] The powers of *technē* here confess their inability ever to promote the leisure of everyone. Communism—as equality of leisure, the participation of all in what is valuable in itself—is thrown back upon the aesthetic figure of the reintegrated man [*l'homme recomposé*].

But if the reintegrated man of Schillerian aesthetics remains the *telos* of communism, education cannot be its means. This aesthetic *telos* that must be achieved in truth is immediately contradicted by the homogenization of the *praxis* that must achieve it and of the explanatory principle of "things as they are." With the critique of the "education" that eludes the dimensions of the philosophical and political in the name of practice, it is this practice that, precisely, gets away from itself [*qui s'échappe à elle-même*]. The paths of the excellence to come then pass through the demystification of the democratic heaven, the refutation of the politics of *païdeia* and the transformation of shoemaker-thinkers into proletarians without qualities. This absence of qualities or *dispossession* of the proletarian remains the only point of contact, the only mediation between *technē* as a principle and leisure as an end. Marx's "Contribution to the Critique of Hegel's *Philosophy of Right*: Introduction" thus can be read as an ironic transposition of the Schillerian schema. In Schiller, the reason that is powerless to act directly, politically, on the sensible entrusts to the beautiful the task of educating the sensibility of a humanity to come. In Marx, on the other hand, the "sensibility" with which the people identify can be taught only through its total dehumanization. The "peculiar nature of labor" is identified with the absolute being-other of the laborer.[16] Value can arise only through generalized devaluation.

One can recognize here the matrix from which will separate the ultra-Bolshevik radicalism of philosophies of freedom and the infra-Bolshevik skepticism of sociologies of dispossession. In Marx himself, critical thought keeps tearing itself apart between its fragilely reunited extremes of sociological interpretation and aesthetic exigence.

In one respect, the cause of the excluded sees itself identified with the theoretical operation of demystification which discloses, in all excellence, that it is *nothing else than that*: a phantasmagoria of the brain in which social relations are reflected. The "onanism" of the philosophical dialogue with the divine is then asked to resign itself before the productivity of the "sexual love" that knows reality and makes it fruitful.

But the time taken by this fecund author to achieve his useful work amply attests that Marx never resolves what he expounds. He no more enjoys the "secularization" of the absolute than he does the trap in thinking that identifies the cause of the humble with the explanation of the superior by the inferior. In the prose of materialist history, he distinguishes between centuries of dwarves and centuries of giants. The literature of the "giants" represents for him the hard kernel of leisure within the social. Obviously, he does not see what happiness he could promise individuals unable to read Aeschylus, Cervantes, Shakespeare, and Dante in the original. In the face of the laws of economics, he defends the imprescriptible rights of Puck the sprite and Hans Röckle the magician. In the face of triumphant naturalism, he claims those of ancient Greek physics. And the demystification of heavenly decrees pleases him only where it takes up again Prometheus's combat—the divinity of defiance and not of the productive forces.

The critique is therefore two things in one: the reduction of the ideal figures of the best to the attributes of social subjects, and the reopening of the gap in which existence lets itself be compared to essence. It is the court pronouncing the death sentence against all forms of existence where human essence is denied, and the plane restoring this essence or any entity of that kind to "the whole of social relations." It is the suppression of the philosophy in social knowledge and its return as the distance of this knowledge from itself, ironic with regard to any consistency of the *socius*, of its modes of interpretation and management. It usually overcomes this contradiction through the parlor game called "critique of the critique"—in other words, the demystification of the demystifiers. The typical "ideologue" criticized by Marx is the strong spirit who, like Stirner or Proudhon, claims that he can cure sick spirits suffering from false ideas, replace the wastefulness of utopian reverie with the calculations of science, or mock the "religious" conception of their mission that proletarians construct. Against them, the cause of the excluded necessarily proceeds through a restoration of the nobility of the tale and of nature. But this restoration takes place at a highly determined price, one that identifies again the petty *savoir-faire* of demystification with the baseness of the artisan incapable of seeing beyond the routines and profits of his shop.

Between the plane of demystification that requires technicians freed from heavenly superstitions and the monument of the art-work that appeals to the vanishing proletarian subject, the best shy away twice from the quest of autodidact shoemakers. "It is not for tailors and cobblers," Marx ironically reminds us in comment-ing on the paradoxical infatuation of Russian aristocrats for his work.[17] We know Russia has other tricks in store for him.

What makes these tricks possible is the encounter missed by Marx between arguments for the best and arguments for the equal—that is, the thought of democratic strangeness. From the undecidability of the Marxian text then arise the two figures of the "becoming-world" of Marxism familiar to us: the Marxism of the leaders and that of the scientists. The Marxism of the leaders notes the retarding of this "social" where the political had to dissolve itself, and offers itself to substitute for it: the restoration of a royal art quick to degenerate into the reconquered power of the actor [comédien], who ascribes social identities on the basis of proffered speeches and decides that the proletariat is not where one believes it is nor revolution when one thinks it is. As for the Marxism of the scientists, it installs itself in the incompleteness of Marxist knowl-edge and applies itself to ground it in an adequate philosophy, to actualize its sociology or its economics, to complete it with a politics or an aesthetics, until this infinite work of construction turns into an interminable analysis of its own impossibility. This Marxism become its own executioner—the least harm that could happen to it, say the realists—next encounters the blunt provoca-tion of the sociologists who play the role of maverick with respect to it: Veblen, the son of a Norwegian peasant attached to artisanal values who, denouncing the parading of wastefulness in the fake Gothic splendor and painting of the heavenly choirs, reveals the ancient predator and barbaric origins of the cultivated leisure class; Max Weber, the German university scholar of the old hu-manist tradition who, borrowing from Schiller not education's already ambiguous hope but an acknowledgment of the "world's disenchantment," sketches the picture of a modernity in which technical and bureaucratic rationalization announces, in the guise of a reconciled humanity, the return to an order of castes. The thoughts of these mavericks slowly became the arguments of quotidian order to the extent that the pessimism of liberal "élites" before the "leveling" of the democratic and social age rejoined the disabused but always irascible disposition of the Marxists who retained from Marxian critique a single demystification in the name of the social: the assigning of identities and social differences to which every political, theoretical, or aesthetic emergence can be boiled down. At this conjuncture of new thoughts quickly turned old, the sociological conception of the world solidifies around one or two simple axioms: a thing cannot be valuable in itself but draws its consistency from social concourses and its worth from social distinctions.[18] Nothing new can happen that is not obtained through the arrangement of a small number of properties of a determined *socius*. Electoral sociology, mocked happily by a sociology of higher ambition, nevertheless expresses the latter's quintessence in its exact capacity to simulate democratic choice and in the involuntary irony in which the terms of its interpretations incessantly regress from an analysis of the latest technologico-social mutations to references to ancient Frankish, Celtic, or Gallic instincts.

And in this it also indicates its philosophical signification. Just as electoral sociology is the realized simulacrum of democracy, the becoming-philosophy of sociology is the mourning of the thought of equality. Denying that the subject of democracy can ever happen, sociological critique speaks of the eternal reign of the slight difference through which the brute positivity of *ethos* unites with the pure discrimination of the symbolic order. It also does its work above all in places where the reign of equality represented its possible emergence: political choice and militant engagement; public instruction and aesthetic ideal. Wherever the new had been an object of faith and become absorbed into the hope for equality, sociological critique reminds us to contemplate the reproduction of groups, the marking of distinctions, and the symbolic market of beliefs. A love perhaps deceived and a fight made in good faith, one believes it without being moved by it: sociological critique has a few reasons to think itself as being democracy made science. And it can recognize itself everywhere in the words and images of a world devoted to the democracy of demystification. By bringing the philosophers' *ariston* back to its function as a social discriminant and by inviting it to the return of the popular repressed, sociology satisfies the contradictory requirements of our liberal-corporatist order: the liberal resignation to the game of interests driving the world, and the syndicalist reduction of egalitarian hopes. The demystification of what is ideological in the name of the social becomes the ordinary fare of conforming thought where the transformation of the sovereign-people into a surveyed population, of political discourse into journalism, of instruction into pedagogy, and of aesthetics into animation of the environment all feed the transformation of democracy into its substitute, sociocracy.

The aristocratic tension of philosophy, the obstinacy of the corrupted sons of artisans in knocking on the doors of aesthetic heaven, the great distance in democratic thought between arguments for the equal and arguments for the best then become resolved in the slight distance with respect to itself of the sociological conception of the world. This demystificatory equivalence creates at the same time the interchangeability of the arguments of science observing necessity with the militant denunciation accusing the arbitrary. The double discourse fed by the sociology of school "failure" is significant above all. Sometimes it conducts generous programs that invite teaching to descend from its cultural heights to bring it nearer to popular feelings, social interactions, and idioms [parlers]; sometimes it nourishes the resentment that says difference is irreducible and the promise of instruction a lie. It is true that this resentment constitutes a knowledge in itself that can take the place of the impossible instruction. The demystification of social conditions making a lure of every democratic païdeia forms, however, the more communicable kind of knowledge. In place of the subject of public instruction—Meno's freed slave, on whom young democracy pinned its hopes a century ago—now appears a double character: the barbarian, socially incapable of understanding the foreign language of the instructor, and the smart-aleck, educated with all the necessary knowledge about the conditions that make his instruction a lure. "Equality" is then reestablished in the lucid knowledge that everyone can discover reasons for the blindness of his or her neighbor.

A double knowledge of the ignorant to which responds the double truth of science. Sometimes militant, it destroys the philosophical illusions of the best and the political illusions of the equal by imposing on us the "return of the repressed." It forces us to see undershirts sticking to bodies in working-class cafés, to recognize the unavoidable social positivities that heavenly discourse denied. Sometimes skeptical and in good company for being so, it confesses that on the territory of these unavoidable positivities, there may be, as in legendary Byzantium, only symbolic fields, places to be exchanged and beliefs put on like the jerseys of the Blues or the Greens.[19] We are ashamed by the naïveté that made us believe one day that our beliefs were a reality, and that allows us to ignore today that reality consists only in what each is willing to believe. The nihilism of the "social" that dramatically haunts Marxian discourse thus reappears as a form of professorial cunning in the manner of the fencers Euthydemus and Dionysodorus,[20] taking each time the opposing viewpoints of the student who "denies" the social and another who believes in its consistency. The privilege of the scientist is to know the equivalence between the reasons that buttress unavoidable realities and those that triumph in the leveling assurance that everything is a simulacrum. But this equivalence of dogmatism and skepticism is also the real knowledge of the sociocracy.

In this circumstance, certain questions of philosophy could recover some of their vigor. I am not thinking here of the somewhat naïve nostalgia or the slightly hypocritical aggressiveness that wishes to recall a world devoted to simulacra to its native earth of Truth. One cannot do without imitation. Aristotle, after Plato, already exhausted the reasons for it. Philosophy is more interested in knowing if it is possible to evaluate imitations, to refuse to see in them only monetary signs being exchanged at a rate fixed by the state of forces. The one who proposes to help be the best, or the equal, or the conjunction of the two, first has to imitate their figures. The question remains whether the imitation of the future is not woven more often from the hidden work of mourning. Questions of progress and decadence, of epic and comedy, that are subject to all the paradoxes and reversals: Schiller desired that we learn to imitate the freedom to come in the ruins of the Roman monuments that did not save their predecessors from servitude. A century later Nietzsche accused Wagner, the promoter of the "work of art of the future," of being in fact the comedian of his own ideal and the champion of decadence. Amid the worst horrors of a century devoted to the imitation of the "new man," Adorno thought it useful to criticize the mockeries hurled by Veblen at the fake Gothic of the *nouveaux riches*; he claimed that the ostentations of luxury still offered the promise of a sharable happiness even to their worst-off spectators, whereas banter about the painting of unproductive angels gave tacit consent to all the severities of the established order.[21] It remains important to-day to be able to judge if what our institutions, our images, and our discourses imitate is democratic hope or its mourning.

Reflections in which philosophy can find itself implicated with-out pretending to give lessons about it. The fact is that it could never affirm its traditional aristocratic requirement or its new thoughts of equality without linking its purity with the vigilant guarding of its borders. Thus did it jealously make sure to refuse the sharing [*partage*] of appearances and discourses, identifying the aspirations of autodidact thought with the corruption of mix-ture and the stigmata of bastardy, whose modern name is ideol-ogy. A refusal not atoned for by its modern impulsive flights—the day's erotic or mechanical, economic or performatic [*performa-tiques*] fascinations.

This inquiry into the strange theoretical figure of the artisan thus can end only with a question: is it possible to think at the same time the hierarchy of values and the equality of mixture? Aristotle, who was not a democrat, had been the first to ask the question. Kant, the sensible enthusiast, reformulated it for the modern age. Marx never ceased turning it around, as did, after him, the best of those who wanted to save him from Marxism. Prolonging this reflection could interest a philosophy detached equally from the melancholies of the origin and an eagerness to eclipse modernity. The stake for this is not "totally ahistorical."

THIS BOOK WAS written in France in 1983. The passage of nearly twenty years and an ocean crossing have not rendered its basic propositions either more valid or less. The pages that follow thus shall attempt simply to situate these propositions both within the evolution of my own work and the political and theoretical debates of the last thirty or so years.

My previous book, *The Nights of Labor* (published in France in 1981), allowed me to offer an interpretation—equally distant from the two poles of the then-dominant thought—of the French labor movement in the nineteenth century and of social conflict in general.[1] Against the traditions of historical materialism and political avant-gardism, it endeavored to reveal the specific nature of the intellectual revolution assumed by the emergence of working-class thought. But it opposed at the same time a counter-discourse, flourishing in that era, that valorized an idea of working-class thought rooted in craft traditions or the forms of popular culture and sociability. *The Nights of Labor* sought to show how the idea of working-class emancipation assumed, on the contrary, a strong symbolic rupture with a culture of craft or popular sociabilities— in short, with working-class "identity." Working-class emancipation was not the affirmation of values specific to the world of labor. It was a rupture in the order of things that founded these "values," a rupture in the traditional division [*partage*] assigning the privilege of thought to some and the tasks of production to others. The French workers who, in the nineteenth century, created newspapers or associations, wrote poems, or joined utopian groups, were claiming the status of fully speaking and thinking beings. At the birth of the "workers' movement," there was thus neither the "importation" of scientific thought into the world of the worker nor the affirmation of a worker culture. There was instead the transgressive will to appropriate the "night" of poets and thinkers, to appropriate the language and culture of the other, to act as if intellectual equality were indeed real and effectual.

To highlight this egalitarian intellectual revolution not only assumed a rupture with Marxist orthodoxy. It required as well a major divergence from the presuppositions that sustained the discourse of social science concerning the dominated classes, and that inspired alternative political propositions. Through the historical naïveté of resorting to working-class "cultures" and "sociabilities," through the sophisticated sociological demystification of "distinguished culture," through the development of new discourses of identity as through old discourses of class struggle—I could hear through them all the same fundamental tone, the same valorization of the "bottom" against the "top." And behind the various forms of this "progressive" valorization, I could hear the same proposition of preserving the order of things, the proposition for which Plato established the formula once and for all: let all do their own business and develop the virtue specific to their condition.

The Philosopher and His Poor thus attempted to grasp within its original theoretical core this splitting of times and occupations that assigns to the philosopher and the artisan their respective shares, and to show how most modern scientific discourses, even the progressive or revolutionary, had preserved this essential kernel. But this very formulation inscribed itself within a highly specific political and theoretical moment. What in France succeeded the exhausted leftism and the great repudiations of Marxism characteristic of the end of the 1970s was the brief euphoria of the coming to power of the Socialists. This occurrence was synonymous with an ephemeral Marxist revival and great reformist ambitions that claimed to rely upon the achievements of the social sciences for an egalitarian transformation of French society. These circumstances brought back to the fore the central program of every progressive reformism, the reduction of inequality through education. But in order to "reduce inequalities," it is first necessary to know what these are, what equality is itself, and in what way it can be efficacious within the social order. Within the conjuncture of triumphant French socialism after 1981, the dominant answer to these questions was the kind of progressive sociology embodied by two works by Pierre Bourdieu, Reproduction and Distinction. These books proposed a general interpretation of the symbolic violence that set the dominated classes in their place. According to this interpretation, such violence manifests itself through a process of imposition in which school rituals and culture games exclude the dominated by offering them an *ethos* to which they cannot adapt, and by making them bear the blame for this very failure. From this, socialist reformers readily drew up a program that aimed particularly at reducing the inequalities of school by reducing the share in it of legitimate high culture—by making school more convivial, more adapted to the sociabilities of the children of low-income classes who were then becoming more and more the children of immigration.

At issue then were two ideas of inequality, two ideas of inegalitarian symbolic violence that confronted each other. According to one, this violence resided in the imposition on the dominated class of high cultural forms and manners. According to the other, it resided on the contrary in the division that reserves for the elect the acme of thought and refinements of language while assigning to the dominated the values of an "autochthonous" culture. The political conjuncture thus gave a larger stake to the conclusions of my own research. But it also confined them in a problematic context in which two kinds of progressivism struggled with each other: on one side, the old republican pedagogy, proclaiming the universalism of the citizen and the promotion of the children of the common people through science and instruction delivered to everyone in the same way; on the other, modernist pedagogy, supported by sociological analyses of cultural reproduction and advocating a school and a cultural politics that gave high priority to adapting to the needs and manners of the disadvantaged sectors. Within the socialism then in power and its circle of intellectual counselors, these two sides strongly opposed each other—the pedagogy of the reduction of inequalities against the pedagogy of republican excellence. This political conflict doubled itself as a conflict of disciplines: to the theoretical and political ascendancy of the social sciences (which was the "pink" version of yesterday's Marxist thinking and the subdued fervor of '68) was opposed the idea of a return to the concepts of political philosophy defining the conditions of "living together" and the "common good." To the promises of social thought and social science were opposed the philosophical promises of the citizen republic.

The constraint of this context and my own difficulty in situating myself in it are noticeable in *The Philosopher and His Poor*, and more particularly in its last chapter. It seemed to me essential that I denounce the complicity between sociological demystifications of aesthetic "distinction" and the old philosophy of "everyone in his place." But this denunciation itself implied a relation of equivocal proximity to the ideological counter-movement that was to accompany the recasting of socialist ardor as liberal wisdom. As the 1980s wore on, the critique of the illusions of social science, the rehabilitation of political philosophy, and the themes of republican universalism were to blend, in France, into the great reactive current that denounced the erring ways of "'68 thought" and proclaimed a return to good philosophy, healthy democracy, and the selection of "republican" élites leading, in the end, to the simple adoration of the world government of wealth. Echoing the eulogists of the "return" was not exactly what interested me. And, after this book, my work proceeded in two essential directions that drew it away from this dominant trend. On the one hand, the critique of the presuppositions of social history and cultural sociology opened onto a vaster reflection on the writing of social science and on the idea of a poetics of knowledge, which was developed in *The Names of History*.[2] The study of the literary procedures through which social knowledge treats the speech-acts that shape history and politics has itself led to more systematic research on the connections linking the modern idea of literature with democracy and the forms of knowledge. My most recent works to appear in France—*La Parole muette*, *La Chair des mots*, *Le Partage du sensible*, and *L'Inconscient esthétique*—fall within this line of research.[3]

On the other hand, the difficulty of finding myself in a position caught between the sociological demystification of inequalities and the equivocal proclamation of the virtues of "republican universalism" forced me to take up once more the question of equality. The rapid incursion of a feeble consensus about an even more feeble democracy led to a reflection that sought to show what, if taken seriously, could be the extraordinary implications for thought itself of the word "democracy" and the egalitarian theme. The opportunity first arose through a work that appears highly anachronistic. My research led me to encounter the singular figure of Joseph Jacotot who, in the 1830s, raised the banner of intellectual emancipation and proclaimed, in the face of academicians and progressive educators, that everyone could learn on his own and without a master, and even teach someone else about which one was ignorant oneself. If I resuscitated this eccentric figure in *The Ignorant Schoolmaster*, it was not on the account of curiosities in the history of pedagogy but because of the radical manner in which Jacotot formulated the egalitarian idea.[4] Equality is not a goal that governments and societies could succeed in reaching. To pose equality as a goal is to hand it over to the pedagogues of progress, who widen endlessly the distance they promise that they will abolish. Equality is a presupposition, an initial axiom—or it is nothing. And this egalitarian axiom subtends in the last instance the inegalitarian order itself. It is in vain that the superior gives orders to his inferior if the inferior does not understand at least two things: first, the content of the order, and second, that he must obey it. But for the inferior to understand this, he must already be the equal of the superior.

What can be done within the social order with this deduction as simple in its principle as it is vertiginous in its consequences? Jacotot's pessimism led to the conclusion that the egalitarian axiom was without political effect there. Even if equality were to ground inequality in the last instance, it could be realized only individually in the intellectual emancipation that always could extend to every person the equality denied by the social order. This pessimism had an eminent merit, however, for it marked the paradoxical nature of equality—at once the ultimate principle of all social and governmental order, and that which is excluded from its "normal" functioning. It put equality out of the reach of the pedagogues of progress. It also put it out of the reach of liberal platitudes and superficial debates between those who situate equality within constitutional forms and those who situate it within the standards of society. Equality, Jacotot taught us, is neither formal nor real. It consists neither in the uniform teaching of the children of the republic, nor in the availability of bargains in supermarket displays. Equality is fundamental and absent, current and untimely [actuelle et intempestive]. From which was clarified the struggle of those proletarians who could not be the equals of the bourgeoisie whether through the education that the bourgeoisie provided them or through their own culture, but rather through the transgressive appropriation of an intellectual equality whose privilege others had reserved for themselves. But from which also was offered the possibility of rethinking democracy by exiting the conventional debate between the egalitarian indistinction of the law common to all and claims for equality grounded upon the rights or values of communities.

The situation created by the collapse of the Soviet system and the development of the consensual ideology of the Western states lent itself to this reexamination. In particular, France in 1990 presented the singular conjuncture in which the fall of the communist systems gave the bicentenary of the French Revolution the aspect of a great funeral of two centuries of egalitarian utopias. While the intellectual class retrospectively went into a rage against the illusions and crimes of the revolutionary age, the new socialist administration proposed to resolve, through the sober examination of realities and consultation between social partners, the problems that formerly occasioned the rifts of social conflict. This triumph of consensual realism over Marxist utopia nevertheless presented two paradoxes. First, it proclaimed the end of Marxism only at the cost of making triumphant its most radically determinist version, of affirming the ineluctable weight of economic constraint and of identifying exactly the task of government with that of the business agents of international capitalism. But above all, the affirmation of the end of class struggles and of "archaic" social conflicts was accompanied by the return of a much more radical archaism. The racist and xenophobic party of the National Front saw its influence growing at the same speed as the consensus. Governmental realism, supported by the *ressentiments* of the intellectual class, assured us that the conflicts and ills of the past stemmed from the fatal weight of words without bodies, of these phantoms called the people, the proletariat, equality, or class struggle. By looking at last at reality with a disenchanted eye—by identifying clearly the necessities inherent in the life of the social body, the margins of choice left to the collectivities, the partners who might join to share effort and profit among the parties of society—we were to enter finally the path of political wisdom and social peace. But the new outbursts of racism in France and ethnic warfare in Europe were contradicting this happy teleology. By showing that "realism," with its optimization calculations, was itself a utopia, they prompted a rethinking of the centrality, within the definition of democracy, of this theater of appearances that consensus sought to eliminate.

The consideration of this state of affairs at the time of the consensus led me to revive an idea that had been at the heart of *The Philosopher and His Poor*: the link between the power of equality and that of appearance. Plato's common battle against the *demos* and appearance showed this connection well (as did the place of "aesthetic communism" in workers' emancipation): appearance is not the illusion masking the reality of reality, but the supplement that divides it. That analysis allowed me to continue with the thought that democratic appearance is not identifiable with the legal forms of the legitimate State that would conceal class interests and conflicts. The "forms" of democracy are the forms of dispute. And dispute is not the opposition of interests or opinions between social parties. Democracy is neither the consultation of the various parties of society concerning their respective interests, nor the common law that imposes itself equally on everyone. The *demos* that gives it its name is neither the ideal people of sovereignty, nor the sum of the parties of society, nor even the poor and suffering sector of this society. It is properly a supplement to any "realist" account of social parties. In the natural history of the forms of domination, only this supplement can bring forth democratic exceptionality. If equality is efficacious in the social order, it is by means of the constitution of this scene of appearance in which political subjects inscribe themselves as a litigious, "fictitious" supplement in relation to every account of social parties.

From there I went on to develop in several essays and even more so in *Disagreement* a theory of politics that moved considerably away from what generally is understood by that name—that is, a theory of power and its legitimations.[5] I wanted to highlight that the forms of the political were in the first place those of a certain division of the sensible. I understand by this phrase the cutting up [*découpage*] of the perceptual world that anticipates, through its sensible evidence, the distribution of shares and social parties. It is the interplay of these forms of sensible evidence that defines the way in which people do "their own business" or not by defining the place and time of such "business," the relation between the personal [*du propre*] and the common, the private and the public, in which these are inscribed. And this redistribution itself presupposes a cutting up of what is visible and what is not, of what can be heard and what cannot, of what is noise and what is speech.

This dividing line has been the object of my constant study. It was at the heart of *The Nights of Labor*, where the assertion of worker emancipation was first of all the upheaval of this division of temporalities that anticipated the redistribution of social and political shares by making night into the laborer's time of rest—by inscribing him within the cycle of production and reproduction that separated him from the leisure of thought. It was this that was at stake in *The Philosopher and His Poor*, the Platonic allocation transforming the work's "absence of time" into the worker's very virtue. But this "absence of time" was itself only a symbolic division of times and spaces. What Plato had excluded was the slack time and empty space separating the artisan from his purely productive and reproductive destination: the space/time of meetings in the *agora* or the assembly where the power of the "people" is exerted, where the equality of anyone with anyone is affirmed. The *demos* is the collection of workers insofar as they have the time to do something other than their work and to find themselves in another place than that of its performance. It is the empty supplement accounting for social parties and organizations. The admission or refusal of this emptiness defines two antagonistic divisions of the sensible.

It is this antagonism that I wanted to systematize in *Disagreement* by splitting the current notion of the political into two concepts: police and politics [*police et politique*]. I proposed to call "police" the division of the sensible that claims to recognize only real parties to the exclusion of all empty spaces and supplements. Society consists here of groups devoted to specific modes of doing, in places where these occupations are performed, and in modes of being that correspond to these occupations and these places. I then proposed to call "politics" the mode of acting that perturbs this arrangement by instituting within its perceptual frames the contradictory theater of its "appearances." The essence of politics is then dissensus. But dissensus is not the opposition of interests or opinions. It is the production, within a determined, sensible world, of a given that is heterogeneous to it. This production defines, in a specific sense, an aesthetics of politics that has nothing to do with the aesthetization of forms of power or the manifestations of collectivity. Politics is aesthetic in that it makes visible what had been excluded from a perceptual field, and in that it makes audible what used to be inaudible. It inscribes one perceptual world within another—for example, the world in which proletarians or women may participate in a community within another in which they both are "visibly" domestic beings outside the life of the community; the world in which they both can speak within another in which they both "evidently" were capable only of moans of pain, cries of hysteria, or groans of fury. Politics is completely an affair of the antagonistic subjectivation of the division of the sensible.

The analysis of the individual and collective forms of this subjectivation, of the status of speech that gives rise to them, and of their translation into forms of learned discourse is the vital thread tying together all of my research. Not that these have followed a premeditated plan. It was due, rather, to discovered necessities and encountered contingencies that I became a historian or philosopher, a critic of sociological science or of political philosophy, a researcher in labor archives or an interpreter of literature. For me, this was not a question of opposing voices from below to discourses from above, but of reflecting on the relation of division of discourses and the division of conditions, of grasping the interplay of borders and transgressions according to which the effects of speech that seize human bodies become ordered or disturbed. Neither have I passed from politics and society to literature and aesthetics. The object itself of my research demanded that I move incessantly across the borders from which the philosopher or historian, the interpreter of texts or the scholar of social issues, claims to circumscribe his or her domain.

EDITOR'S PREFACE

1 Jonathan Rée, "The Translation of Philosophy," *New Literary History* 32 (2001): 252–53.

2 *Partage* is hardly one example among others; Rancière reflects on this word time and again in his writing, as in his recent *Le Partage du sensible: esthétique et politique* (Paris: La Fabrique, 2000). See also Jean-Luc Nancy, *Le Partage des voix* (Paris: Galilée, 1982).

MIMESIS AND THE DIVISION OF LABOR

1 See, in particular, *Le Maître ignorant. Cinq leçons sur l'émancipation intellectuelle* (Paris: Fayard, 1987) [*The Ignorant Schoolmaster: Five Lessons in Intellectual Emancipation*, trans. Kristin Ross (Stanford: Stanford University Press, 1991)]; *Les Noms de l'histoire: Essai de poétique du savoir* (Paris: Le Seuil, 1992) [*The Names of History: On the Poetics of Knowledge*, trans. Hassan Melehy (Minneapolis: University of Minnesota Press, 1994)]; *Aux bords du politique* (Paris: Osiris, 1990) [*On the Shores of Politics*, trans. Liz Heron (London and New York: Verso, 1995)]; *La Mésentente: Politique et philosophie* (Paris: Galilée, 1995) [*Disagreement: Politics and Philosophy*, trans. Julie Rose (Minneapolis: University of Minnesota Press, 1999)].

2 *Lire le Capital*, vols. 1–2 (Paris: Maspéro, 1965), featured contributions by Louis Althusser, Étienne Balibar, Pierre Machery, and Roger Establet in addition to Rancière's "Le Concept de critique et la critique de l'économie politique des *Manuscrits de 1844 au Capital*" (1:93–210). The latter appeared as "The Concept of 'Critique' and the 'Critique of Political Economy' (from the *Manuscripts of 1844 to Capital*)," trans. Ben Brewster, in Ali Rattansi, ed., *Ideology, Method and Marx: Essays from Economy and Society* (London and New York: Routledge, 1989), 74–180. The French text was reprinted as *Lire le Capital III* (Paris: Maspéro, 1973).

3 *La Leçon d'Althusser* (Paris: Gallimard, 1974). An English translation of the original critical essay appeared as "On the Theory of Ideology: Althusser's Politics," *Radical Philosophy* 7 (1974); repr. Roy Edgley and Richard Osborne, eds., *Radical Philosophy Reader* (London: Verso, 1985), 101–92 (Rancière's quoted comment appears on p. 101). For Rancière's own self-criticism, see "Mode d'emploi pour une réédition de *Lire le Capital*," *Les Temps Modernes*, November 1973; "How to Use *Lire le Capital*," trans. Tanya Asad, in Rattansi, ed., *Ideology, Method and Marx*, 181–89. All these materials were reviewed in Jeffrey Mehlman, "Teaching Reading: The Case of Marx in France," *Diacritics* 6, no. 4 (winter 1976): 10–18, which was the first sustained English-language

discussion of Rancière's work. See also Fredric Jameson's early discussion of *La Leçon d'Althusser*, "The Re-Invention of Marx," *Times Literary Supplement* (August 22, 1975), no. 3832:942–43. For Rancière's more recent thoughts about Althusser, see "Althusser, Don Quichotte, et le scène du texte," in *La Chair des mots: Politiques de l'écriture* (Paris: Galilée, 1998), 157–77; and "Althusser," in Simon Critchley and William R. Schroeder, eds., *A Companion to Continental Philosophy* (Oxford: Basil Blackwell, 1998), 530–36.

4 On Rancière's shift "from the study of Marx to the study of workers," see Donald Reid, Introduction to Jacques Rancière, *The Nights of Labor: The Workers' Dream in Nineteenth-Century France*, trans. John Drury (Philadelphia: Temple University Press, 1989), xv–xxxvii. For the history of *Révoltes logiques*, see Kristin Ross, *May '68 and Its Afterlives* (Chicago: University of Chicago Press, 2002), 124–37.

5 "Democracy Means Equality: Jacques Rancière Interviewed by *Passages*," trans. David Macey, *Radical Philosophy* 82 (March–April 1997): 29.

6 *La Parole ouvrière, 1830–1851* (Paris: 10/18, 1976).

7 "Good Times or Pleasure at the Barricades," trans. John Moore, in Adrian Rifkin and Roger Thomas, eds., *Voices of the People: The Social Life of "La Sociale" at the End of the Second Empire* (London: Routledge and Kegan Paul, 1988), 51.

8 "The Myth of the Artisan: Critical Reflections on a Category of Social History," *International Labor and Working Class History* 24 (fall 1983): 9, 10; repr. Steven Laurence Kaplan and Cynthia J. Koepp, eds., *Work in France: Representations, Meaning, Organization, and Practice* (Ithaca: Cornell University Press, 1986), 327, 329. Cf. "Ronds de fumée: Les poètes ouvriers dans la France de Louis-Philippe," *Revue des sciences humaines* 190 (1983): 33: "Worker poetry is not in the first place an echo of popular speech but an initiation into a sacred language, the forbidden and fascinating language of others" (my translation).

9 "Good Times or Pleasure at the Barricades," 50.

10 "The Myth of the Artisan," 11 [repr. Kaplan and Koepp, 330]. On iterability, see Jacques Derrida, "Signature Event Context," in *Margins of Philosophy*, trans. Alan Bass (Chicago: University of Chicago Press, 1982), 307–30.

11 *La Nuit des prolétaires: Archives du rêve ouvrier* (Paris: Fayard, 1981).

12 Rancière collected Gauny's writings in *Le Philosophe plébéien* (Paris: Maspéro–La Découverte–Presses Universitaires de Vincennes, 1983).

13 "After What," trans. Christina Davis, in Eduardo Cadava, Peter Conor, and Jean-Luc Nancy, eds., *Who Comes after the Subject?* (New York and London: Routledge, 1991), 250.

14 On equality as axiomatic, see p. 23. See also Rancière in Davide Panagia, "Dissenting Words: A Conversation with Jacques Rancière," *Diacritics* 30, no. 2 (summer 2000): 116: "it was necessary for me to extract the workers' texts from the status that social or cultural history assigned to them—a manifestation of a particular cultural condition. I looked at these texts as inventions of forms of language similar to all others. The purchase of their political valence was thus in their revindication of the efficacy of the literary, of the

egalitarian powers of language, indifferent with respect to the status of the speaker. This poetic operation on the objects of knowledge puts into play their political dimension, which elides a sociocultural reading."

15 Yves Michaud, "Les Pauvres et leur philosophe: La Philosophie de Jacques Rancière," *Critique* 601–2 (June–July 1997): 422; Herrick Chapman, Review of *The Nights of Labor, Journal of Modern History* 65, no. 3 (September 1993): 629.

16 This "method" returns in *The Ignorant Schoolmaster*, where "the distance between the author and his subject, the narrator of the story and its hero [Jacotot], keeps changing. Often it disappears altogether. An academic analysis could treat the book's pronouns and tenses, its modes of address and narrative voice or voices. It could mark the constant slippages between direct quotation and free indirect speech, *récit* and *discours*, diegesis and mimesis— all to confirm that this is not properly academic writing. A sympathetic reviewer notes somewhat desperately at one point that 'in this passage, too, Rancière finds (discovers, invents, projects?) in Jacotot one of [the book's] key arguments.' 'Finds (discovers, invents, projects?)'—what we find in *The Ignorant Schoolmaster* is that we cannot always tell when the book is speaking of Jacotot and when it speaks as Jacotot." Forbes Morlock, "The Story of the Ignorant Schoolmaster," *Oxford Literary Review* 19, nos. 1–2 (1997): 106–7.

17 Indeed, Rancière has since remarked that he "wrote *La Nuit des prolétaires* along structural lines that are closer to [Virginia Woolf's] *The Waves* than to *Les Misérables*." Solanage Guénoun and James H. Kavanagh, "Jacques Rancière: Literature, Politics, Aesthetics: Approaches to Democratic Disagreement," *Sub-Stance* 92 (2000): 16. For more on *The Waves* as a formal model for historiography, see "Dissenting Words," *Diacritics* 30, no. 2 (summer 2000): 121.

18 See especially pp. 176–79.

19 In language that links this project to his later *Disagreement*, Rancière explained recently that "the 'poor' does not designate an economically disadvantaged part of the population; it simply designates the category of peoples who do not count. Those who have no qualifications to part-take in *arkhē*, no qualification for being taken into account." "Ten Theses on Politics," trans. Rachel Bowlby and Davide Panagia, *Theory & Event* 5, no. 3 (2001), § 12.

20 Rancière published another criticism of Bourdieu, "L'Éthique de la sociologie," in the Révoltes Logiques collection: *L'Empire du sociologue* (Paris: La Découverte, 1984), 13–36.

21 For Rancière's views on Habermas, see "Dissenting Words," *Diacritics* 30, no. 2 (summer 2000): 116; on Foucault, see Guénoun and Kavanagh, "Jacques Rancière," 13, where Rancière stresses that "it's the question of equality— which for Foucault had no *theoretical* importance—that makes the difference between us."

22 See Jacques Derrida, "Plato's Pharmacy," in *Dissemination*, trans. Barbara Johnson (Chicago: University of Chicago Press, 1982), 61–171.

23 "Dissenting Words," *Diacritics* 30, no. 2 (summer 2000): 115. Rancière returns often to this scene of writing: see especially *The Names of History*, 11, 50;

and *La Chair des mots*, 125–26. The very title of *La Parole muette* (Paris: Hachette, 1998) is itself a quotation from the *Phaedrus*; see pp. 81–85.

24 *La Chair des mots*, 126.

25 *The Names of History*, 50.

26 See "Good Times or Pleasure at the Barricades," 51–58. Samuel R. Delany's history of cross-class same-sex encounters in New York City porn theaters is a striking confirmation of this phenomenon; see his *Times Square Red, Times Square Blue* (New York: New York University Press, 1999).

27 "The Myth of the Artisan," 2 [repr. Kaplan and Koepp, 319].

28 Gérard Genette, *The Aesthetic Relation*, trans. G. M. Goshgarian (Ithaca: Cornell University Press, 1999), 4–5 (my italics).

29 Martin Seel, *L'Art de diviser* (Paris: Armond Colin, 1992), 28, cited in Jean-Marie Schaeffer, *Les Célibataires de l'art: Pour une esthétique sans mythes* (Paris: Gallimard, 1996), 42; the passage is cited in Genette, *The Aesthetic Relation*, 217.

A PERSONAL ITINERARY

1 See Jacques Rancière, *The Nights of Labor: The Workers' Dream in Nineteenth-Century France*, trans. John Drury (Philadelphia: Temple University Press, 1989).

2 Pierre Bourdieu, *Distinction: A Social Critique of the Judgement of Taste*, trans. Richard Nice (Cambridge: Harvard University Press, 1984). [Bourdieu alludes to these undershirts on p. 510; the passage is cited by Rancière on p. 195 and referred to again on p. 215.—Trans.]

3 [On Gauny the floor layer, see chapter 3, note 5; and chapter 9, note 62.—Trans.]

CHAPTER 1: THE ORDER OF THE CITY

1 Aristotle, *Politics* IV 1291a.

2 Plato, *Republic* II 372a. For this passage as all other citations from Plato, I have used the bilingual text of the Éditions Les Belles Lettres. While indebted to the translators, I have revised their work more often than followed it faithfully. [Our practice has been to translate Rancière's citations from the Belle Lettres edition while consulting *Plato: The Collected Dialogues*, ed. Edith Hamilton and Huntington Cairns, Bollingen Series LXXI (Princeton: Princeton University Press, 1961), as well as *The Republic*, trans. Desmond Lee, rev. ed. (Harmondsworth: Penguin, 1987), and *The Republic*, trans. Robin Waterfield (Oxford: Oxford University Press, 1993). References to passages are indicated by Stephanus numbers.—Trans.]

3 Ibid. II 370c.

4 Xenophon, *Oeconomicus* IV 2/3, and VI 9.

5 Aristotle, *Politics* VI 1319a.

6 *Republic* III 395b.

7 Ibid. III 397a. For all the preceding material see ibid. X 595c/602b.

8 Ibid. III 406c–d.

9 Ibid. V 466e/467a.

10 Ibid. II 374c–d.

11 Plato, *Statesman* 292e.

12 Plato, *Gorgias* 512a–b.

13 Immanuel Kant, *Critique of Judgment*, trans. Werner S. Pluhar (Indianapolis: Hackett, 1987), p. 122 (§ 28).

14 Plato, *Sophist* 227a–c.

15 Ibid. 227a–b.

16 Ibid. 227c.

17 *Gorgias* 490e/491b.

18 *Republic* III 389d.

19 Ibid. III 415a.

20 Ibid. III 416e/417a.

21 Ibid. 417a–b.

22 Plato, *Laws* 846d.

23 *Republic* VIII 554a.

24 [Washington Irving retells the well-known story of the egg in his *Life and Voyages of Christopher Columbus* (New York: Thomas Y. Crowell, n.d.), 179–80: "A shallow courtier present [at a banquet], impatient of the honors paid to Columbus, and meanly jealous of him as a foreigner, abruptly asked him whether he thought that, in case he had not discovered the Indies, there were not other men in Spain who would have been capable of the enterprise? To this Columbus made no immediate reply, but, taking an egg, invited the company to make it stand on one end. Every one attempted it, but in vain; whereupon he struck it upon the table so as to break the end, and left it standing on the broken part; illustrating in this simple manner that when he had once shown the way to the New World nothing was easier than to follow it."—Trans.]

25 *Republic* IV 420e/421a.

26 Ibid. IV 421a.

27 Plato, *Hippias Minor* 368b–d.

28 Aristotle, *Politics* I 1260a.

29 When Marx replies to Proudhon that the suppression of the traffic in money for the sake of commodity exchange does not get us out of the circle of political economy, he is being very precisely Aristotelian—even if Marx uses the argument to prove the case of communism, where Aristotle pleads for the "domestic" limitation of the economic sphere.

30 *Republic* IV 430a.

31 Ibid., 443c.

32 Plato, *Charmides* 165a. On the possible misreadings of "Know Thyself," particularly in the *Charmides*, see Pierre Aubenque, *La Prudence chez Aristote* (Paris: Presses Universitaires de France, 1963), 166.

33 *Charmides* 173b–c, and 172d.

34 *Republic* V 454c–e.

35 Ibid., 434a.

CHAPTER 2: THE ORDER OF DISCOURSE

1 *Republic* VI 495d–e.
2 *Symposium* 215b.
3 *Republic* VI 496a.
4 *Republic* VII 535c/536d.
5 Ibid. VI 492a/493a.
6 *Meno* 82a/86c.
7 Ibid. 97d–e.
8 *Phaedrus* 274 e/275b.
9 Ibid. 275e.
10 Ibid. 258a.
11 Ibid. 273e.
12 Antisthenes regarded love as a "vice of nature," according to Clement of Alexandria. Fr. G. A. Mullachius, *Fragmenta philosophorum graecorum* (Paris, 1867), 280.
13 *Phaedrus* 256e.
14 *Laws* VII 817b.
15 *Phaedrus* 245a.
16 *Protagoras* 339a/347a.
17 *Phaedrus* 248d–e.
18 *Sophist* 223b.
19 *Laws* III 700c. Remember that the pedagogues in question are not teachers but slaves taking care of children. The topicality of the education issue invites us to recall this difference between free *paideia* and slavish pedagogy.
20 Ibid. 700e/701a.
21 *Ion* 535e.
22 Literally "as if one had rented their ears." *Republic* V 475d.
23 *Laws* II 659b–c.
24 *Phaedrus* 259a.
25 *Laws* VII 808a.
26 *Phaedo* 82a–b.
27 On music as proper to man, see *Laws* II 653e/654a. On the games men should play in keeping with their nature as puppets of the divinity, see *Laws* VII 803c/804b.
28 *Laws* II 665c.
29 *Gorgias* 481d.
30 *Symposium* 221e.

CHAPTER 3: THE SHOEMAKER AND THE KNIGHT

1 Traditionally, the motto hung above the entrance to Plato's Academy.
2 Hoffmann's "Meister Martin der Küfner und seine Gesellen" ["Master Martin the Cooper and His Associates," one of the interpolated stories from *Die Serapionsbrüder* (1819–21).–Trans.] is said to have given Wagner the idea for

Die Meistersinger, although the only similarities are the historical framework and the theme of the artist-artisan relationship.

3   Hippolyte Tampucci, Préface, *Poésies* (Paris: Paulin, 1833).

4   Anthime Corbon, *De l'enseignement professionnel* (Paris: Baillière, 1855).

5   Louis Gabriel Gauny to A. Barrault, 26 June 1854 (Fonds Gauny, Saint-Denis Municipal Library). [For more on Gauny, see Jacques Rancière, ed., *Louis Gabriel Gauny: Le philosophe plébéien* (Paris: Maspéro–La Découverte–Presses Universitaires de Vincennes, 1983).—Trans.]

6   Jean-Jacques Rousseau, *Émile, or On Education*, trans. Allan Bloom (New York: Basic Books, 1979), 197.

7   Lerminier, "De la littérature des ouvriers," *Revue des Deux Mondes*, November 1841, 972.

8   *L'Artiste*, April 1845.

9   Charles Nodier, "De l'utilité morale de l'instruction pour le peuple," *Rêveries* (1835; repr. Paris: Plasma, 1979), 182–83.

10 Richard Wagner, *Opera and Drama*, trans. W. Ashton Ellis (1893; repr. Lincoln: University of Nebraska Press, 1995), 56–57, 95–99.

11 Friedrich Nietzsche, Postscript to *The Case of Wagner*, in *Basic Writings of Nietzsche*, ed. Walter Kaufmann (New York: Modern Library, 1968), 639.

12 Friedrich Nietzsche, "Skirmishes of an Untimely Man," § 40, *Twilight of the Idols*, in *The Portable Nietzsche*, ed. Walter Kaufmann (New York: Viking, 1968), 545.

13 Georg Friedrich Daumer, *Die Religion den neuen Weltalters* (Hamburg, 1850). [Daumer is perhaps best known today for his *Kasper Hauser* (1832), the subject of Werner Herzog's film (1975).—Trans.]

14 Karl Marx and Frederick Engels, "Reviews from the *Neue Rheinische Zeitung*," *Collected Works* (New York: International Publishers, 1978), 10:246 (all further references will be cited as *CW*). On this text and on Marx's literary references more generally, readers may consult S. S. Prawer, *Karl Marx and World Literature* (Oxford: Oxford University Press, 1978), 171–72.

15 *Rapports des délégations ouvrières à l'Exposition de 1867*, Enquête sur le dixième groupe, I, 5.

16 Karl Marx, *Capital*, vol. 1, ed. Frederick Engels, trans. Samuel Moore and Edward Aveling (New York: International Publishers, 1967), 488.

17 Engels to Bernstein, 1 March 1883, *CW* 46:448.

18 Eleanor Marx Aveling, "Karl Marx," *Reminiscences of Marx and Engels* (Moscow: Foreign Languages Publishing House, n.d.), 250–52.

19 *Capital* 1:408.

CHAPTER 4: THE PRODUCTION OF THE PROLETARIAT

1   Karl Marx and Frederick Engels, *The German Ideology*, *Collected Works* (New York: International Publishers, 1976), 5:41–42 (all further references will be cited *CW*).

2   Ibid. 5:31, 35–37, 43–45. Apart from the exception noted in parentheses, the German word used by Marx and Engels is *Produktion*.

3   Ibid. 263.

4   *The Holy Family, or Critique of Critical Criticism*, CW 4:19–20.

5   *German Ideology*, CW 5:39, 37.

6   Ibid. 43.

7   *The Poverty of Philosophy*, CW 6:186.

8   *Economic and Philosophic Manuscripts of 1844*, CW 3:302.

9   Marx, *Capital*, vol.1, ed. Frederick Engels, trans. Samuel Moore and Edward
    Aveling (1867; repr. New York: International Publishers, 1967), 361.

10 [Literally a "non-place," *non-lieu* suggests as well the "no place" of utopia. In
    juridical contexts a *non-lieu* is the dismissal of a case.—Trans.]

11 *Manifesto of the Communist Party*, CW 6:494.

12 *The German Ideology*, CW 5:39.

13 *Difference between the Democritean and Epicurean Philosophy of Nature*, CW 1:84.
    [Massilia, now Marseilles, was the site of a battle with the German Cimbri
    tribes in 101 B.C.—Trans.]

14 *The German Ideology*, CW 5:50.

15 G. W. F. Hegel, *Aesthetics*, trans. T. M. Knox (Oxford: Clarendon, 1975), 843.

16 The story is told by Heine, *De l'Allemagne* (Paris: Presses d'aujourd'hui, 1979),
    284–85.

17 *The German Ideology*, CW 5:53.

18 *The Holy Family*, CW 4:37.

19 Ibid. 36–37.

20 *The Poverty of Philosophy*, CW 6:190.

21 Marx to Engels, 6 May 1854, CW 39:449.

22 [The editors of the *Collected Works* describe the *Straubinger* as "travelling jour-
    neymen in Germany. Marx and Engels used this term for German artisans,
    including some participants in the working-class movement of that time,
    who were still largely swayed by guild prejudices and cherished the petty-
    bourgeois illusion that it was possible to return from capitalist large-scale
    industry to petty handicraft production" (38:579).—Trans.]

23 *Economic and Philosophic Manuscripts of 1844*, CW 3:313.

24 [See Rancière, "The Journey of Icarus," in *The Nights of Labor: The Workers'
    Dream in Nineteenth-Century France*, trans. John Drury (Philadelphia: Temple
    University Press, 1989), 349–416.—Trans.]

25 Bert Andréas, ed., *Documents constitutifs de la ligue des communistes, 1847* (Paris:
    Aubier Montaigne, 1972), 159.

26 Engels to Marx, mid-November to December 1846, CW 38:94.

27 Ibid. 93.

28 Ibid. 92.

29 Marx to Engels, 18 May 1859, CW 40:440.

30 Engels to Marx, 13 February 1851, CW 38:290. [Engels alludes here to 2
    Samuel 15:18: "And all his servants passed by him; and all the Cherethites,
    and all the Pelethites, and all the six hundred Gittites who had followed him
    from Gath, passed on before the king."—Trans.]

31 Marx to Engels, 25 August 1851, CW 38:440.

32 Engels to Lassalle, 18 May 1859, CW 40:444.

33 Marx to Engels, 8 October 1858, *CW* 40:346.

34 Marx, "Speech at the Anniversary of the *People's Paper*" (14 April 1856), *CW* 14:656.

CHAPTER 5: THE REVOLUTION CONJURED AWAY

1 Karl Marx and Frederick Engels, *The Manifesto of the Communist Party, Collected Works* (New York: International Publishers, 1976), 6:495 (all further references will be cited *CW*).

2 Goethe, letter to Schiller, cited in Ludwig Feuerbach, *Manifestes philosophiques: Textes choisis (1839–45)*, trans. Louis Althusser (Paris: Presses Universitaires de France, 1973), 15.

3 *Manifesto of the Communist Party*, *CW* 6:494, 502.

4 Ibid. 6:494–95, 487.

5 *The Eighteenth Brumaire of Louis Bonaparte*, *CW* 11:143.

6 *Class Struggles in France*, *CW* 10:56.

7 *The Eighteenth Brumaire of Louis Bonaparte*, *CW* 11:143.

8 [*L'Arroseur arrosé* is a well-known short film (1895) by the Lumière brothers.—Trans.]

9 See Pierre Caspard, "Un aspect de la lutte des classes en France en 1848: Le recrutement de la Garde nationale mobile," *Revue historique* 2 (1974): 81–106.

10 See Marx's review of Chenu's *Les Conspirateurs*, *CW* 10:311–25.

11 Heine, *De la France* (Paris: Aubier-Montaigne, 1930), 104. See also S. S. Prawer, *Karl Marx and World Literature* (Oxford: Oxford University Press, 1976), 201–2. On Marx's relationship with Heine, see Paul-Laurent Assoun, *Marx et la répétition historique* (Paris: Presses Universitaires de France, 1978).

12 *The Eighteenth Brumaire of Louis Bonaparte*, *CW* 11:146.

13 *Class Struggles in France*, *CW* 10:50–51.

14 Ibid. 115.

15 *The Eighteenth Brumaire of Louis Bonaparte*, *CW* 11:139.

16 Ibid. 173.

17 *The Civil War in France* (second draft), *CW* 22:536.

18 Ibid. 269.

19 [The passage contrasts the arid region of Les Cévennes (which was Protestant and politically progressive) with the agriculturally fertile Morbihan (which was Catholic and reactionary).—Trans.]

20 *The Eighteenth Brumaire of Louis Bonaparte*, *CW* 11:192–93.

21 *The Civil War in France*, *CW* 22:314.

22 *The Eighteenth Brumaire of Louis Bonaparte*, *CW* 11:149.

23 Ibid. 150.

24 Engels to Marx, 13 April 1866, *CW* 42:266.

25 *The Eighteenth Brumaire of Louis Bonaparte*, *CW* 11:176. Compare the similar portrait of Jules Favre in *The Civil War in France*, where he is depicted as a man forced to make history so as to avoid bankruptcy court (*CW* 22:313). Compare, too, this remark in a letter from Marx to Engels (29 January 1858): "A large number of French bourgeois, with commercial ruin staring them in the

face, are anxiously awaiting the day of reckoning. They now find themselves in much the same STATE as Boustrapa [Louis Napoleon] *before* the coup d'état" (*CW* 40:256).

26 *The Eighteenth Brumaire of Louis Bonaparte*, *CW* 11:149.

27 *Class Struggles in France*, *CW* 10:117.

28 Marx to Engels, 18 May 1859, *CW* 40:440.

29 "Speech at the Anniversary of the *People's Paper*" (14 April 1856), *CW* 14:655. [The English edition mistranslates *die Siege der Wissenchaften* as "the victories of art."—Trans.]

30 "English," 9 February 1862, *CW* 19:163.

31 Marx to Johann Philipp Becker, 26 February 1862, *CW* 41:342.

CHAPTER 6: THE RISK OF ART

1 Karl Marx, *The Eighteenth Brumaire of Louis Bonaparte*, *Collected Works* (New York: International Publishers, 1979), 11:106 (all further references will be cited *CW*).

2 Marx to Engels, 25 February 1859, *CW* 40:393.

3 Marx to Weydemeyer, 25 March 1852, *CW* 39:70.

4 Engels to Marx, 23 September 1851, *CW* 38:461.

5 Engels to Marx, 14 April 1856, *CW* 40:34.

6 Engels to Marx, 24 August 1852, *CW* 39:165.

7 Engels to Marx, 23 September 1851, *CW* 38:461.

8 Engels to Marx, 7 October 1858, *CW* 40:344.

9 "If the great industrial and commercial crisis England has passed through went over without the culminating financial crash at London, this *exceptional* phenomenon was only due to—French money." Marx to Danielson, 19 February 1881, *CW* 46:62.

10 Engels to Kautsky, 12 September 1882, *CW* 46:322.

11 Engels to Kautsky, 8 November 1884, *CW* 47:214. Engels's letter to Bebel dated 11 December 1884 contains a very similar analysis (47:232–34).

12 Marx to Lassalle, 22 February 1858, *CW* 40:271.

13 Engels to Marx, 11 June 1866, *CW* 42:285–86.

14 Marx to Engels, 7 July 1866, *CW* 42:290.

15 Ibid. 289–90.

16 Engels to Marx, 9 July 1866, *CW* 42:294.

17 Marx to Engels, 14 February 1858, *CW* 40:266.

18 Engels to Marx, 18 February 1858, *CW* 40:268.

19 Engels to Marx, 2 October 1866, *CW* 42:320.

20 Marx to Engels, 3 October 1866, *CW* 42:322.

21 Marx to Freiligrath, 29 February 1860, *CW* 41:82.

22 Marx to Kugelmann, 9 October 1866, *CW* 42:326.

23 Engels to Marx, 13 February 1851, *CW* 38:290.

24 Ibid.

25 Marx to Engels, 11 December 1858, *CW* 40:360. [The French translation of the latter phrase is "Tout est bourgeois."—Trans.]

26 Marx to Lassalle, 22 February 1858, *CW* 40:271. [The Latin tag "I detest and repudiate the common people" is from Horace, *Odes* III, I, 1.—Trans.]

27 Jean-Paul Sartre, *L'Idiot de la Famille: Gustave Flaubert de 1821 à 1857* (Paris: Gallimard, 1988–), vol. 3.

28 Marx, *Capital*, ed. Frederick Engels, trans. Samuel Moore and Edward Aveling (1867; repr. New York: International Publishers, 1967), 1:253.

29 Marx to Engels, 10 February 1866, *CW* 42:223.

30 *Capital*, 1:48.

31 Jenny Marx to Kugelmann, 3 April 1871, *Lettres à Kugelmann*, ed. Gilbert Badia (Paris: Éditions sociales, 1971), 187.

32 Marx to Siegfrid Meyer, 30 April 1867, *CW* 42:366.

33 Marx to Engels, 31 July 1865, *CW* 42:173.

34 Marx to Danielson, 10 April 1879, *CW* 45:355.

35 Marx to Engels, 25 February 1867, *CW* 42:347–48.

36 Cf. Engels to Bebel, 30 August 1883, *CW* 47:53: "You ask why I of all people should not have been told how far the thing had got. It is quite simple. Had I known, I should have pestered him night and day until it was all finished and published." In the letter from 31 July 1865 already cited, Marx wrote that the three volumes were complete, except for three chapters! (*CW* 42:173).

37 See Engels to Bracke, 11 October 1875, *CW* 45:95: "If they don't understand these things, they should either leave them alone or else copy them word for word from those who are generally admitted to know what they are talking about."

38 Marx, "Economic Manuscript of 1861–63 (Relative Surplus Value)," *CW* 34:136. See also pp. 237 and 448, where the allusion to Milton recurs.

39 *The Civil War in France* (First Draft), *CW* 22:490. See also S. S. Prawer, *Karl Marx and World Literature* (New York: Oxford University Press, 1976), 365.

40 [Rancière uses the standard French translation *arrière-monde* for *Hinterwelt*. There is, however, no standard English equivalent, which is variously rendered "afterworld" (Kaufmann) or "backworld" (Common).—Trans.]

41 Engels, *The Dialectics of Nature*, *CW* 25:319.

42 Marx, *A Contribution to the Critique of Hegel's Philosophy of Right: Introduction*, *CW* 3:178.

43 Engels, "Introduction to Karl Marx's *The Class Struggles in France* (1895)," *CW* 27:524.

CHAPTER 7: THE MARXIST HORIZON

1 [Marx highlights in *Capital*, vol. 1, a poem by "Antipatros, a Greek poet of the time of Cicero, [who] hailed the invention of the water-wheel for grinding corn, an invention that is the elementary form of all machinery, as the giver of freedom to female slaves, and the bringer back of the golden age." *Capital*, ed. Frederick Engels, trans. Samuel Moore and Edward Aveling (1867; repr. New York: International Publishers, 1967), 408. Sir Richard Arkwright (1732–92) was an English industrialist and inventor who pioneered the factory system for the mass production of textiles; Marx refers to him frequently

and often disparagingly in *Capital*, vol. I (e.g. 424). See also chapter 3, p. 69.—Trans.]

2   From Sartre to the "desiring machines" of Deleuze there has been in French philosophy an evident fascination with materialism and the machine. Sartre writes of the freedom "of a thing among things" in an article from the 1930s reprinted in *Situations I* (Paris: Gallimard, 1947), "Une idée nouvelle d'Edmond Husserl: L'Intentionnalité." In it he praises Husserl for having turned consciousness into a "thing among things" as opposed to the idealist conception of the assimilating and digesting consciousness. The phrase "it works" is the start of Gilles Deleuze's and Félix Guattari's *Anti-Oedipus*, trans. Robert Hurley, Mark Seem, and Helen R. Lane (New York: Viking, 1977). The reversal of the Platonic phrase about the body as the tomb or prison of the soul comes from Michel Foucault's *Discipline and Punish*, trans. Alan Sheridan (New York: Pantheon, 1977).

3   [The allusion is to Sartre's novel *La Nausée* (1938).—Trans.]

4   Thus Roland Barthes opposes in an exemplary way the "pneumatic" interpretation of Fischer-Dieskau and the "electronic" interpretation of Panzéra: "The breath is the *pneuma*, the soul swelling or breaking, and any exclusive art of the breath is likely to be a secretly mystical art (a mysticism reduced to the demands of the long-playing record). The lung, a stupid organ (the lungs of cats!), swells but does not become erect: it is in the throat, site where the phonic metal hardens and assumes its contour, it is in the facial mask that signifying breaks out, producing not the soul but enjoyment." *The Responsibility of Forms*, trans. Richard Howard (New York: Hill and Wang, 1985), 271. On the "music of the soul," see also Sartre, especially *The Words*, trans. Bernard Frechtman (New York: George Braziller, 1964).

5   Barthes, *The Responsibility of Forms*, 265–66.

6   See Nicolas Malebranche, *The Search after Truth*, trans. and ed. Thomas M. Lennon and Paul J. Olscamp (Cambridge: Cambridge University Press, 1997), book I, chapter 19, 82–84.

7   See V. I. Lenin, *Materialism and Empirio-Criticism: Critical Notes Concerning a Reactionary Philosophy* (New York: International Publishers, 1927), which reproaches empirio-criticism for repeating Berkeley's idealism. This is, in a larger sense, the continuing problem of Marxism after Marx: how can materialist thought recover the "active side" of a dialectic always monopolized by idealism?

8   [On *Hinterwelt*, see chapter 6, note 40.—Trans.]

9   The note of humor concerning this "generosity" may obscure the point that these social knowledges present themselves as the critique of philosophical illusions. At the same time, however, they interiorize, as givens or rules of method, notions or principles that are merely commandments, philosophical prohibitions whose origins efface themselves.

10 [On the cherry tree see chapter 6, p. 77.—Trans.]

11 Plato, *Euthydemus* 275d–277c.

12 See Engels, *Dialectics of Nature, Collected Works* (New York: International Publishers, 1987), 25:313–587 passim.

13 Sartre, "The Artist and His Conscience," *Situations*, trans. Benita Eisler (New York: George Braziller, 1965), 218–19.

CHAPTER 8: THE PHILOSOPHER'S WALL

1 Jean-Paul Sartre, "Response to Albert Camus," *Situations*, trans. Benita Eisler (New York: George Braziller, 1965), 77.

2 Ibid., 76.

3 Sartre, *The Communists and Peace, with a Reply to Claude Lefort*, trans. Martha H. Fletcher, John R. Kleinschmidt, and Philip R. Berk (New York: George Braziller, 1968), 9.

4 Ibid., 212.

5 Ibid., 192.

6 Ibid., 28.

7 [Here and throughout this chapter Rancière plays on the double sense of *avoir raison*, figuratively "to be right" and literally "to have reason."—Trans.]

8 See Sartre's "Cartesian Freedom," *Literary and Philosophical Essays*, trans. Annette Michelson (New York: Criterion, 1955), 169–84.

9 Maurice Merleau-Ponty, *Adventures of the Dialectic*, trans. Joseph Bien (Evanston, Ill.: Northwestern University Press, 1973), 105.

10 Ibid., 168.

11 Ibid., 139.

12 Sartre, *Critique of Dialectical Reason*, vol. 1, *Theory of Practical Ensembles*, ed. Jonathan Rée, trans. Alan Sheridan-Smith (London: Verso, 1976), 178.

13 [The town of Bouville is the setting of Sartre's novel *La Nausée* (1938).—Trans.]

14 Sartre, "Departure and Return," *Literary and Philosophical Essays*, 146. Sartre is commenting here on a book by Brice Parain. But doesn't he also have in mind the astonishingly similar formulations of Goethe's *Wilhelm Meisters Wanderjahre* (*Wilhelm Meister's Travels* [1821–29])?

15 Sartre, *Critique of Dialectical Reason*, 100.

16 Ibid., 102–3.

17 Ibid., 233.

18 I simply repeat here the interpretation that Sartre offers for anarcho-syndicalism, which he obviously obtained from Michel Collinet's *L'Ouvrier français: Esprit du syndicalisme* (Paris: Éditions ouvrières, 1951).

19 Sartre, *Critique of Dialectical Reason*, 325.

20 Ibid., 309.

21 Ibid., 269.

22 Ibid., 310, 312.

23 Ibid., 341.

24 Ibid., 360.

25 Ibid., 441.

26 Ibid., 662.

27 Ibid., 662.

28 See Sartre, *The Ghost of Stalin*, trans. Martha H. Fletcher with John R. Klein-schmidt (New York: George Braziller, 1965).

29 Sartre, *Critique of Dialectical Reason*, 478.

30 [The Hungarian Prime Minister Erno Gero unwittingly precipitated the Revolution of 1956 by ordering police in Budapest to fire upon a peaceful demonstration.—Trans.]

31 Philippe Gavi, Jean-Paul Sartre, and Pierre Victor, *On a raison de se révolter: Discussions* (Paris: Gallimard, 1974), 100.

32 [Sartre served as executive chairman of the Vietnam War Crimes Tribunal established by Bertrand Russell in 1967. After the deaths in 1970 of sixteen coal miners in an explosion at Hénin-Liétard, Sartre presided in Lens over a "people's tribunal" that found the state responsible for the murder of the miners.—Trans.]

33 *On a raison de se révolter*, 168–71.

34 On this point see the very suggestive article by Michel Sicard, "Le dernier rendez-vous," in the issue of *Obliques*, nos. 24–25 (1981), which he edited, and which was devoted to the theme of "Sartre and the Arts."

35 Sartre, "The Prisoner of Venice," *Situations*, 41f.

36 Ibid., 33.

37 Ibid., 33.

38 See Sartre, "Saint Marc et son double," in the issue of *Obliques* cited above, 171–202.

39 Ibid., 191.

40 Sartre, "The Prisoner of Venice," 46.

41 Sartre, "Saint Marc et son double," 196.

42 "Reading the old [*Good Soldier*] *Schweik* on the train, I am again overwhelmed by [Jaroslav Hašek's] grand panorama and by the genuinely unconstructive attitude of the people, which, being itself the only constructive element, cannot take a constructive attitude to anything else. . . . his indestructibility makes him the inexhaustible object of maltreatment and at the same time the fertile ground for liberation." Bertolt Brecht, *Journals*, trans. Hugh Rorrison, ed. John Willet (London: Methuen, 1993), 278–79.

43 See Sartre and Michel Sicard, "Penser l'art: Entretien," in the issue of *Obliques* cited above, 20.

44 Sartre, "Departure and Return," 125–68.

45 Sartre, "The Unprivileged Painter: Lapoujade," *Essays in Aesthetics*, trans. Wade Baskin (New York: Philosophical Library, 1963), 74.

46 Ibid., 72.

47 Sartre, "Masson," *Situations IV* (Paris: Gallimard, 1964), 397.

48 Sartre, "Alexandre Calder, Mobiles Stabiles Constellations," cited by Michel Sicard, "Esthétiques de Sartre," in the issue of *Obliques* cited above, 147–48.

49 [Croisset, near Rouen, was the home of Gustave Flaubert.—Trans.]

CHAPTER 9: THE SOCIOLOGIST KING

1 Sartre, "The Artist and His Conscience," *Situations*, trans. Benita Eisler (New York: George Braziller, 1965), 211.

2 Ibid., 210–11.

3 G. W. Leibniz, *Monadology* (§ 28), in *Philosophical Texts*, trans. Richard Franks and R. S. Woolhouse (Oxford: Oxford University Press, 1998), 271–72.

4 [At Rancière's suggestion we depart here from Richard Nice's translation, which renders Bourdieu's *classant et classé* as the more status-neutral "classifying and classified." See, e.g., *Distinction: A Social Critique of the Judgement of Taste* (Cambridge: Harvard University Press, 1984), 481.—Trans.]

5 [Barthélémy-Prosper Enfantin and St. Amand Bazard succeeded Claude-Henri de Rouvroy St. Simon as the *pères suprêmes* of the Saint-Simonian movement.—Trans.]

6 Bourdieu, *Distinction*, 177.

7 Ibid., 516.

8 Bourdieu, *Sociology in Question*, trans. Richard Nice (London: Sage, 1993), 32. [The English translation of this passage omits the key phrase "*selon la logique du chaudron énoncée par Freud*" (according to the 'kettle logic' set out by Freud), to which Rancière alludes in the title of this section. Freud defines kettle logic as "the defense put forward by the man who was charged by one of his neighbors with having given him back a borrowed kettle in a damaged condition. The defendant asserted first, that he had given it back undamaged; secondly, that the kettle had a hole in it when he borrowed it; and thirdly, that he had never borrowed the kettle from his neighbor at all." *The Interpretation of Dreams*, in the *Standard Edition of the Complete Psychological Works of Sigmund Freud*, ed. and trans. James Strachey (London: Hogarth, 1953), 4:119–20. See also *Jokes and Their Relation to the Unconscious*, SE 13:62 and 206.—Trans.]

9 Ibid. 10, 134.

10 Bourdieu and Jean-Claude Passeron, *Reproduction in Education, Society and Culture*, trans. Richard Nice (London: Sage, 1977), 162.

11 Bourdieu and Passeron, *The Inheritors*, trans. Richard Nice (Chicago: University of Chicago Press, 1979), 22.

12 Ibid., 45.

13 Ibid., 73.

14 [Rancière puns here on the word *emploi*, meaning both "use" and "job," in the phrase *emploi du temps* ("timetable" or "schedule").—Trans.]

15 Bourdieu, *Sociology in Question*, 120.

16 "The podium, the chair, the microphone, the distance, the pupils' habitus," *Sociology in Question*, 64 (my emphases).

17 Bourdieu and Passeron, *The Inheritors*, 23.

18 Bourdieu and Passeron, *Reproduction In Education*, 54.

19 [A reference to the following lines from "Le pélican" by Robert Desnos, published in his posthumous *Chantefables et chantefleurs* (Paris: Grund, 1952): "Le pélican de Jonathan, / Au matin, pond un œuf tout blanc / Et il en sort un pélican / Lui ressemblant étonnamment. // Et ce deuxième pélican / Pond, à son tour, un œuf tout blanc / D'où sort, inévitablement / Un autre qui en fait autant. (Jonathan's pelican / Lays a very white egg in the morning / And from it a pelican comes out / That it surprisingly resembles. // And this second pelican / Lays in its turn a very white egg / From which comes out, inevitably / Another that does as much.)"—Trans.]

20 Bourdieu and Passeron, *Reproduction in Education*, 13–14.

21 Ibid., 38.

22 Ibid., 25.

23 Bourdieu, *In Other Words: Essays towards a Reflexive Sociology*, trans. Matthew Adamson (Stanford: Stanford University Press, 1990), 180.

24 Bourdieu, *The Logic of Practice*, trans. Richard Nice (Stanford: Stanford University Press, 1990), 135.

25 Bourdieu, *In Other Words*, 180.

26 Bourdieu, *Sociology in Question*, 24.

27 Ibid., 23.

28 Ibid.

29 Bourdieu, *The Logic of Practice*, 66.

30 Ibid., notably chapter 6, "The Work of Time," 98–111.

31 Ibid., 60.

32 Bourdieu, *Language and Symbolic Power*, ed. and with an introd. by John B. Thompson, trans. Gino Raymond and Matthew Adamson (Cambridge: Harvard University Press, 1991), 127.

33 Bourdieu, *Distinction*, 19; and *Sociology in Question*, 104.

34 Bourdieu, *The Logic of Practice*, 57.

35 Bourdieu, *Distinction*, 47.

36 Ibid., 174.

37 Ibid., 44–45.

38 Bourdieu with Luc Boltanski, Robert Castel, Jean-Claude Chamboredon, and Dominique Schnapper, *Photography: A Middle-Brow Art*, trans. Shaun Whiteside (Stanford: Stanford University Press, 1990), 58.

39 Bourdieu, *Distinction*, 34–35.

40 Bourdieu, *Sociology in Question*, 115.

41 Bourdieu, *Distinction*, 232–41.

42 Bourdieu, "The Production of Belief: Contribution to an Economy of Symbolic Goods," trans. Richard Nice, *Media, Culture and Society* 2 (July 1980): 261–93.

43 Bourdieu, "The Invention of the Artist's Life," trans. Erec R. Koch, *Yale French Studies* 73 (1987): 75–103.

44 Bourdieu, *Distinction*, 214.

45 [An allegory furnished by players of the game of rugby.—Trans.]

46 Bourdieu, *Distinction*, 251.

47 Ibid., 55.

48 Ibid., 354–71.

49 Ibid., 369.

50 Bourdieu, *Language and Symbolic Power*, 126.

51 Bourdieu, *Distinction*, 510.

52 Bourdieu, *Sociology in Question*, 41–48.

53 Bourdieu, *Distinction*, 180.

54 Ibid., 338.

55 Ibid., 432. [Maurice Thorez was secretary general of the French Communist Party from 1930 until his death in 1964.—Trans.]

56 Ibid., 433–34.

57 Ibid., 493.

58 Immanuel Kant, *Critique of Judgment*, § 60 (appendix, "Of the Method of Taste"), trans. J. H. Bernard (New York: Hafner, 1972), 201.

59 Edmund Burke, *Reflections on the Revolution in France*, ed. Conor Cruise O'Brien (Harmondsworth: Penguin, 1968), 138.

60 Kant, *Critique of Judgment*, § 2, 38–39.

61 Friedrich Schiller, *On the Aesthetic Education of Man*, ed. and trans. Elizabeth M. Wilkinson and L. A. Willoughby (Oxford: Clarendon, 1967), esp. letters 5–10.

62 "Le travail à la tâche," in Gabriel Gauny, *Le philosophe plébéien* (Paris: Maspéro–La Découverte–Presses Universitaires de Vincennes, 1983), 45–46.

63 Bourdieu, *Language and Symbolic Power*, 127–36.

64 Cf. Jacques Rancière, *The Nights of Labor: The Workers' Dream in Nineteenth-Century France*, trans. John Drury (Philadelphia: Temple University Press, 1989).

65 Charles Baudelaire, "Reflections on Some of My Contemporaries," in *Baudelaire as a Literary Critic*, trans. Lois Boe Hyslop and Francis E. Hyslop (University Park: Pennsylvania State University Press, 1964), 270.

66 Baudelaire, "Pierre Dupont," in ibid., 59.

67 Bourdieu, "The Invention of the Artist's Life," 75–103. [Frédéric Moreau is the protagonist of Flaubert's *l'Éducation sentimentale*.—Trans.]

For Those Who Want More

1 G. W. F. Hegel, *The Philosophy of History*, trans. J. Sibree (New York: Dover, 1956), 447.

2 [A reference to La Fontaine's famous poem "La Cigale et la fourmi" (The Grasshopper and the Ant).—Trans.]

3 [On Rembrantsz see pp. xxii–xxiii.—Trans.]

4 René Descartes, *Discourse on Method*, trans. John Veitch (Buffalo: Prometheus, 1989), 29.

5 Maxim Leroy, *Descartes, le philosophe au masque* (Paris: Rieder, 1929), and *Descartes social* (Paris: Vrin, 1931).

6 Adam Smith, *An Inquiry into the Nature and Causes of the Wealth of Nations*, ed. Edwin Cannan (Chicago: University of Chicago Press, 1976), 19–20. One may recall in this connection that the "coarseness" which in Plato is antithetical to philosophical nature becomes identified with the Greek for what is "specific to the porter" (*phortikon*). Cf. in particular *Phaedrus* 256a.

7 David Hume, "Of Refinement in the Arts," in *Political Essays*, ed. and with an introd. by Charles W. Hendel (New York: Liberal Arts, 1953), 125. This may remind us also of the article on "Art" from the *Encyclopédie*: "In what system of Physics or Mathematics can we notice more intelligence, sagacity, or consequence than in the machines for spinning gold thread and making stockings, and in the trades of the trimmers, gauze makers, drapers and silk workers?"

8   Hegel, *Philosophy of Right*, trans. T. M. Knox (Oxford: Oxford University Press, 1952), §§ 197, 208, 231, 256.

9   [On Nietzsche's *Hinterwelt* see chapter 6, note 40.—Trans.]

10 Shaftesbury, *The Moralists: A Philosophical Rhapsody* (London: Printed for John Wyat at the Rose in St. Paul's, 1709), 208.

11 Friedrich Schiller, *On The Aesthetic Education of Man*, ed. and trans. Elizabeth M. Wilkinson and L. A. Willoughby (Oxford: Clarendon, 1967).

12 Marx, *Economic and Philosophic Manuscripts of 1844*, *Collected Works* (New York: International Publishers, 1975), 3:333 (all further references will be cited as *CW*).

13 Hegel, *Science of Logic*, trans. A. V. Miller (London: George Allen and Unwin, 1969), 747. See on this passage Jürgen Habermas's commentary, *Theory and Practice*, trans. John Viertel (Boston: Beacon, 1973).

14 Marx, *Economic and Philosophic Manuscripts of 1848*, *CW* 3:328.

15 Germain Garnier, notes on his French translation of Adam Smith, *The Wealth of Nations*, cited by Marx, *Economic Manuscript of 1861–1863*, *CW* 30:301 (Marx's emphases).

16 I leave aside theological interpretations of this schema. G. M. Martin Cottier, *L'Athéisme du jeune Marx, ses origines hégéliennes* (Paris: Vrin, 1959), recognized in this connection (via Luther and Hegel) the *kénose* of Saint Paul. One will excuse here a rather natural sentimental preference for Habermas's interpretation (see note 13) that returns, through Schelling, to the *alter deus* of the shoemaker Jakob Boehme.

17 "The Russian aristocracy are educated, in their youth, at German universities and in Paris. They always yearn for the most extreme [theories] the West has to offer. It is pure *gourmandise*, like that practiced by part of the French aristocracy during the 18th century. *Ce n'est pas pour les tailleurs et les bottiers* [it is not for tailors and cobblers], as Voltaire said at the time about his own Enlightenment. It does not hinder the very same Russians from becoming scoundrels as soon as they enter government service." Marx to Kugelmann, 12 October 1869, *CW* 43:130–31.

18 On such distinctions and gatherings, see Jean-Claude Milner, *Les Noms indistincts* (Paris: Le Seuil, 1983).

19 Pierre Bourdieu, "A Lecture on the Lecture," in *In Other Words: Essays towards a Reflexive Sociology*, trans. Matthew Adamson (Stanford: Stanford University Press, 1990), 194.

20 [Socrates's eristic counterparts in Plato's *Euthydemus*.—Trans.]

21 T. W. Adorno, "Veblen's Attack on Culture," *Studies in Philosophy and Social Science* 9, no. 3 (1941): 389–413.

AFTERWORD (2002)

1   Jacques Rancière, *The Nights of Labor: The Workers' Dream in Nineteenth-Century France*, trans. John Drury (Philadelphia: Temple University Press, 1989).

2   *The Names of History: On the Poetics of Knowledge*, trans. Hassan Melehy (Minneapolis: University of Minnesota Press, 1994).

3　*La Parole muette: Essai sur les contradictions de la littérature* (Paris: Hachette, 1998); *La Chair des mots: Politiques de l'écriture* (Paris: Galilée, 1998); *Le Partage du sensible. Esthétique et politique* (Paris: La Fabrique, 2000); and *L'Inconscient esthétique* (Paris: Galilée, 2001).

4　*The Ignorant Schoolmaster: Five Lessons in Intellectual Emancipation*, trans. and with an introd. by Kristin Ross (Stanford: Stanford University Press, 1991).

5　See Jacques Rancière, "Politics, Identification, and Subjectivization," in John Rajchman, ed., *The Identity in Question* (New York and London: Routledge, 1995), 63–70; *Disagreement: Politics and Philosophy*, trans. Julia Rose (Minneapolis: University of Minnesota Press, 1999); and "Ten Theses on Politics," trans. Rachel Bowlby and Davide Panagia, *Theory and Event* 5, no. 3 (2001).

JACQUES RANCIÈRE is an emeritus professor of philosophy at the University of Paris-VIII (St. Denis).

ANDREW PARKER is a professor of English at Amherst College.

CORINNE OSTER received her Ph.D. in comparative literature at the University of Massachusetts, Amherst.

JOHN DRURY is a freelance translator.

Library of Congress Cataloging-in-Publication Data
Rancière, Jacques.
[Philosophe et ses pauvres. English]
The philosopher and his poor / by Jacques Rancière;
edited and with an introduction by Andrew Parker ; translated
by John Drury, Corinne Oster, and Andrew Parker.
p. cm.   Includes bibliographical references.
ISBN 0-8223-3261-2 (cloth : alk. paper)
ISBN 0-8223-3274-4 (pbk. : alk. paper)
1. Communism and philosophy. 2. Platonists.
3. Philosophy, Marxist. I. Parker, Andrew, II. Title.
HX533.R3613 2004   335.4'11—dc22
2003019215

being a spectator supposively means that he/she
is removed from the possibility of knowing and act
new concept of the emancipated spectator (youth
values directly incorpopased in the living Practices. .
what we need to purone is